CRAZY, CRAZY HOLLYWOOD
WHAT REALLY HAPPENS BEHIND THE SCENES

by **STEVE SIPORIN**

CRAZY, CRAZY HOLLYWOOD
©2012 STEVE SIPORIN

ALL RIGHTS RESERVED.

No part of this book may be reproduced in any form or by any means, electronic, mechanical, digital, photocopying, or recording, except for in the inclusion of a review, without permission in writing from the publisher.

Published in the USA by:

BEARMANOR MEDIA
P.O. BOX 71426
ALBANY, GEORGIA 31708
www.BearManorMedia.com

ISBN-10: 1-59393-277-4 (alk. paper)
ISBN-13: 978-1-59393-277-0 (alk. paper)

Printed in the United States of America.

BACK COVER PHOTO BY STUDIO PEARL.

BOOK DESIGN AND LAYOUT BY VALERIE THOMPSON

FOR
MARIE ARY-ALMOJUELA
AND
DAVID LOSTEGAARD
WITH DEEP APPRECIATION

CONTENTS

BEGINNINGS 1

HOLLYWOOD 7

MOVIE DIRECTORS: Gods or Mere Mortal Men 21
    Michael Gordon and Directing Furniture 22
    A Grand Old Man Lights the Way 31
    Vincente Minnelli and The Ferris Wheel 33
    Cecil B. DeMille had His Secrets 39

RETAKES: Movie Lingo for a Second Chance 45
    Woody Allen and His Tweed Jacket 46
    Fred Zinneman, A Man with No Retakes 51

SOUND: When Movies Became Talkies 57
    Playback and The Boy Genius 62
    Looping 76
    Kim Stanley 77
    Zsa Zsa Gabor 80
    Dubbing 82

ACTORS, ACTORS EVERYWHERE 87
    Barbara Hershey and The Stunt Man 93
    Kirk Douglas Goes for a Ride 97
    Robert Montgomery and His Rage 102
    Paul Newman and The Lady reporters 105
    There's Many a Slip Between the Script
        and the Screen 113

Orson Welles and The Magic Rabbit 117
Barbara Eden and The Harper Valley P.T.A. 125
Jon Voight's Lucky Break 129
Faye Dunaway Certainly Did It Her Way 131
Louis B. Mayer and Mama's Chicken Soup 135

ACTING TAKES MORE THAN TALENT AND AMBITION 139

TO BECOME A PRODUCER 145

THEN ALONG CAME MY "DAVIDS" 155

WHAT HAVE I MISSED? TV, OF COURSE! 165
The Debbie Reynolds Show 165
The Wild Wild West 169
Mannix and Womanix 171
Gunsmoke 172
The Partridge Family 173
Movin' On 176
A Sensitive, Passionate Man 177
Guyana Tragedy: The Story of Jim Jones 182

FROM THE FRYING PAN INTO THE VIDEO FIRE 189

CRAZY, CRAZY VIDEOS 207

LOOKING BACK 215

DVD OFFER 231

INDEX 233

OSCAR WINNERS 239

BEGINNINGS

Had anyone told me that one day I would be standing on this particular street, facing a 19th century Victorian house on Lot 3 of the Metro-Goldwyn-Mayer studios in Culver City, California, I would have thought they were nuts. But here I was, on that street, looking at a house built not for a real family to live in, but for a pretend family to act in as though it were real. It was just a movie set. Make believe!

As I stood there it wasn't quite *déjà vu*, but I knew I had seen the house before. Not as it was now, devoid of life, but bustling with kids and excitement in a glorious, Technicolor movie. I would have seen it at a Saturday afternoon movie matinee at the Allerton Theatre two short blocks from where I lived with my parents in New York City's East Bronx. It would have been sometime in the early 1940s when America's "greatest generation" of men were off fighting World War II. My memory zigged, zagged and I remembered! *Meet Me in St. Louis!* The movie was *Meet Me in St. Louis*, a musical starring MGM's fabled singing star, Judy Garland. The year was 1944 and I was eleven.

As I looked at the street there were no street signs giving it a name, just street poles waiting for signs to be installed that would name the street for the next movie to be filmed there. I remembered that in the movie Judy sang a song called "The Boy Next Door." If I had had a Smartphone with me that day I would have Googled the lyrics. No need to. I hummed a few bars and the words came back to me. Judy sang that she lived "at 5165 Kensington Avenue and he lived at 5163." For me, that street would forever be Kensington Avenue!

My childhood Saturday afternoons were spent bedazzled by the movie magic that flickered on the not-so-silvered screen of my neighborhood movie palace, the Allerton Theatre. Hoping to lure avid patrons to the movies more than once a week, it was common practice in those days for neighborhood theaters to change their movie bill twice a week, on Wednesdays and Sundays. With its cartoons, newsreels, action-adventure serials and a double bill of two wonderful Hollywood feature films, Saturday matinees at the Allerton Theatre were absolutely heaven for me! The four hours went by in a flash! Had the theater manager not cleared the theater I might have stayed in my seat as it all unreeled again. If I was extremely lucky, the very next day, Sunday, I might see the new bill if my parents decided to make the Sunday matinee a family outing and take me and my younger sister along.

Each Saturday after lunch, like clockwork, my mom would slip me a copper-filled wartime dime and I'd race the two blocks from my home to the theater. It seems whenever I arrived at the Allerton there already were kids my age lined up waiting for the box office to open, clutching their admission dimes and candy counter pennies. Television, though invented, was on hold in deference to wartime priorities. TV viewing wouldn't become available to the American people until after Hitler and Hirohito yelled "Uncle" and World War II was over.

After one Saturday matinee I remember racing home to tell my mom some very exciting news. The movie being shown the following Saturday was on a reserved-seat basis. I had to buy my ticket in advance. And, gasp! because it was a very special movie, the admission price was going to cost, gasp! two cents more than usual! A whole twelve cents! The movie? *Gone with the Wind* in its very, very first reissue.

As I stood on that street on Lot 3 with the rays of California's warm sun giving life to the empty street, I had no inkling that one day I would be back there filming a scene for an MGM movie called *The Impossible Years* with the street dressed for the 1960s and not 1904 as in *Meet Me in St. Louis*. Or that one night I would be assigned by MGM to work as an additional assistant director for crowd control on a film called *Soylent Green* starring Charlton Heston. The street overflowing with extras in need of control was the same

New York street on MGM's Lot 2 where Gene Kelly's dancing feet had splashed rain-filled puddles as he sang and danced to "Singin' in the Rain" in the 1952 movie of the same name. Nor did I know that in a few short years I would be having the time of my life working with many of Hollywood's celebrated stars, Paul Newman, Orson Welles, David Niven, Faye Dunaway, Glenn Ford, Jack Lemmon, Jon Voight, Barbara Eden and James Arness among them.

The Hollywood publicity machine is famous for cranking out tons of stories promoting their stars, their films, anything new and exciting to let the world know what's happening in front of the camera and behind the scenes. There is one story about how "playback" was invented that has been told over and over again that is not how it actually happened. Yes, it did occur during the filming of the movie film historians consider the first true movie musical ever produced in Hollywood, namely *The Broadway Melody*. The year was 1928. The studio was MGM. But it wasn't the clever idea of the head of MGM's sound department as the story is usually told. It was his brother-in-law's idea, the man who gave him his job, the man who was MGM's head of production at the time, the man who his peers labeled "The Boy Wonder."

The true story was told to me by a man who was there in 1928 at the very moment when the idea for "playback" tumbled from the lips of "The Boy Wonder." To make "playback" work the art of "lip-synching" came into being! The first step in "playback" was to pre-record a star singing the song. Then the record of that song would be given to the star to take home and practice singing the song to the record. Later, when they filmed the musical number, the record would be played back through speakers placed strategically around the set and the star would mouth the words that she or he had practiced. To make it appear as though the song's lyrics were coming out of the singer's mouth at that very moment of filming, every star, featured player or chorus singer, would pretend they were actually singing the song. That became known as "lip-synching." If the star didn't have the vocal chops to carry off the song, but was billed as a singer/dancer, then she or he would match their lip movements to the prerecorded song being played back, recorded by a studio vocalist. The movie-viewing audience was not let in on this arrangement. They believed they were actually hearing that star, that performer singing that song. For years it was Hollywood's dirty secret that many of moviedom's favorite singing stars couldn't carry a tune to save themselves and were singing to someone else's pre-recorded voice. In 1969 over a bowl of Mama Mayer's Chicken Soup in the MGM commissary the true story of "playback and lip-synching" was revealed to me. The man sitting at the lunch table with me was a long-time employee of MGM. As an art director on *The Broadway Melody* he was in the screening room in 1928 when the necessity for playback arose!

In February 1965, when I was in my early thirties, I tired of the cold winters on the East Coast so I moved westward to sunny Los Angeles. No job waiting for me, just youthful enthusiasm and unbounded faith in myself. Los Angeles meant Hollywood, home to the film factories and fantasy machines that had turned out the movies I loved as a kid and continued to love as an adult. I was touring Lot 3 as well as Lots 1 and 2 because my cousin George, a dentist in the San Fernando Valley, had a patient named Lin Parsons, Jr., who had a high-powered position at MGM. From our conversations, Cousin George knew that I wanted to work in Hollywood films and more important, had the credentials to do so. I had worked in live television in New York City as an associate director for ABC's flagship station, WABC-TV. That meant I was already a member of the illustrious Directors Guild of America. To work in Hollywood films as an assistant director one needed to first be a member of the DGA.

And because I was, Cousin George used his connection to arrange for me to meet his patient who just happened to be MGM's production manager! Lucky me! It was in the summer of 1965. After a pleasant chat, where I stated my background, qualifications and my ambitions, Lin Parsons let me know there were no openings for me at that time. Instead, he suggested I might enjoy a tour of the studio while I was there. Immediately I said, "Yes," thrilled to be able to see where many of the movies I loved were created. It would be one year later before I would get a call from Lin's office to work at MGM.

My career as an assistant director extended over eighteen years from 1965 through 1982. As I worked in the movie industry, it became very apparent to me that the dream machine, as fascinating as it was to be part of, was a very crazy business. The craziness of Hollywood created new doors that opened up for me a world I never dreamed I'd be a part of. It wasn't the traditional form of showbiz that the movie studios and Americans had enjoyed for years. It was a new form of technology that would become so lucrative for the movie studios that they would embrace it whole-heartedly. And so did I! To my mind, the new direction I found myself moving in was just as crazy as where I had been and could only have been ignited in me by crazy, magical Hollywood.

As a kid, my mom did give me those extra two cents to see a special presentation of *Gone With the Wind*. I sat glued to my seat that Saturday matinee at the Allerton Theatre, hypnotized as I watched Vivien Leigh and Clark Gable race in their horse-drawn buggy through the burning streets of the City of Atlanta. The massive roaring flames that engulfed Atlanta and its rail yard fascinated me. I didn't become a pyromaniac. But once I left the movie business, flame-filled images would play a large part in my life. And burn. And burn. And burn.

And as you read on, you'll realize that this book is not a conventional biographical book. Why? Simply because in crazy, crazy Hollywood I didn't lead a conventional life!

HOLLYWOOD

When I arrived in Los Angeles in the spring of 1965, I didn't have a job. The closest I came to the movie world was when I took a part-time job at the Century City Parking Garage in Beverly Hills collecting parking fees as the cars exited and Debbie Reynolds paid hers as she drove out. In those days the new TV shows produced during pilot season were intended only for the three major broadcast networks, ABC, CBS and NBC. This was before cable TV expanded the venues for new programs and new niche interests, such as a food channel or a sports channel, etc.

Filming of pilots in 1965 occurred in the last two months of the year. With production companies gearing up to shoot new pilots and still shooting the regular shows of the season, there were just not enough accredited second assistant directors in the Directors Guild to work on all the shows. I got a call from the DGA. There was a pilot that needed a Second. But first, to acquaint myself with the second assistant's duties, the DGA would arrange for me to observe a Second in action on the 20th Century-Fox TV series *Peyton Place*. No pay. Would that interest me? Would a woodchuck chuck wood? My answer was a big "Yes!"

After two weeks of dogging the footsteps of the Second, soaking up his duties, realizing there was no similarity between this job and my previous experience in broadcast TV as an associate director, the DGA assigned me, this time with pay, to a situation-comedy called *My Brother the Angel*. Starring in the show were Tommy and Dick Smothers, real-life brothers who had a successful comedy act with the recurring theme of Tommy complaining to his brother Dick that "Mom liked you best!" In the TV series, Tommy had died and was a bumbling apprentice angel. He returns to earth to help his brother Dick, a rising business executive, but his help always misfires. It's brother Dick who must straighten things out. That assignment lasted only four weeks until the end of pilot season. Once again I was unemployed, but now I could place my name on the DGA's Assistant Directors' Availability List. Now it was official. I was qualified to be hired as a second assistant.

The DGA labels the job in television as "associate director." You are the director's right-hand man, sitting next to him in the control room when working on a program like *The Big News*, as I did at WABC-TV in New York City. But when you're working the eight-hour shift in the Master Control Room signing the TV station on-or-off-the-air, switching from the local to national shows, inserting commercials during the breaks, coordinating the technicians, cueing the announcer on duty, you are technically directing. There's no one with the title "Director" present—just you, the associate director.

In the movie world the Directors Guild defines the people who support the director not as "associate" but as "assistant directors." There are two on every movie: the first assistant, who is usually chosen by the director, and the second assistant, who is selected by the first. The second reports back to the first, but his duties are to assist both the first and the director, to be their behind-the-scene's eyes, ears and legs.

In July of 1966, after working for Screen Gems on a new, not-yet-aired sitcom called *The Monkees*, inspired by the huge musical success of those four lads from Liverpool, the Beatles, Columbia Pictures assigned me to my first feature film; it was *Luv*, a comedy based on a successful Broadway play. Columbia's studios were then located in Hollywood at Sunset Boulevard and Gower Avenue, convenient for me, just a ten-minute drive from where I lived in the hills beneath the famed Hollywood sign.

In the 1920s the area where Columbia Pictures studios stood was known as Poverty Row because of all the small, struggling production companies that were clustered there. Most of them never became successful and just vanished from the scene. The area was also known as Gower Gulch because many of those small production companies specialized in westerns, those cowboy and Indian shoot-'em-ups that recalled earlier times in our nation's history.

Luv starred Jack Lemmon, Peter Falk and Elaine May of the Nichols and May comedy team. The first two weeks of shooting were to be in New York on one of the bridges that crossed the East River. I was so excited. Imagine! I'd be returning to the Big Apple where I had been born and had previously worked. But now I was on the crew of a major Hollywood film, starting an exciting new career. Sad to say, it wasn't to be. It was probably a better idea from the producer's financial point of view to hire a New York-based second assistant then to take me along, a newly-ordained Second. Not only would the N.Y. second know the ins-and-outs of working the streets of Manhattan, it would be less expensive for Columbia if I remained in Hollywood. I'd still be paid my weekly rate, but the studio wouldn't have to pay my airfare, higher location DGA rates, and per diem fees for meals, or pay my hotel room charges. All that money was saved by hiring a New York-based second assistant working out of the New York DGA office, living at home. Here was my first encounter with the business part of showbiz!

On the day the cast was flying to New York I had my first assignment. I was to drive out to Malibu in a car driven by a studio driver to collect a statuesque, buxom blonde actress named Nina Wayne who was Peter Falk's love interest in the film. We were to take her to the Los Angeles International Airport for her flight back east. Nina was living with her boyfriend, John Barrymore, Jr., scion of the famous stage and screen Barrymore acting family. In a few years John, Jr., would father Drew Barrymore, who became a sensation as a child actor in Steven Spielberg's movie *ET*. Perhaps because of the Barrymore blood flowing through her body, rich with the DNA of several generations of theatrical talent, Drew escaped the jinx that prematurely ended the careers of many of the child actors who preceded her. Her career flourished as she grew into young womanhood.

Nina's house sat directly on the Pacific Coast highway. Its backyard was the sandy beach that led to the Pacific Ocean surf. I rang the door bell. No answer. Rang again. Still no answer. Knocked loudly on the door. No answer. Went around to the side of the house and banged on a window. No one was home. Was I at the wrong house? Had I goofed big time on my first assignment?

The driver took me to the nearest pay phone (there were no cell phones in those days) and I called the studio. Not to worry. Nina forgot she was being picked up and had a friend drive her to the airport. She was at the airport with the others waiting to fly out. I breathed a sigh of relief. Although her flight took off that day, her career never did. I always thought the dumb blonde she played in the movie was not too much of a stretch for her.

Walter Matthau was to have been cast in *Luv* teaming for the second time with Jack Lemmon. The two actors had had great success working together for the first time in *The Fortune Cookie* (1966). More important, they liked each other and enjoyed acting together. But Matthau had just suffered a heart attack. Although he was recovering nicely, Columbia was unable to get the necessary insurance on him. Instead of Matthau, Peter Falk was cast to play the part of Lemmon's old friend and Elaine May's husband. For Elaine it was her second picture on a three-picture deal with Columbia. Unfortunately, Elaine would not be a great success as a film actress, but would prove more successful later on as a movie director and script writer.

I admired Elaine's brilliant improvisational skills and comedic technique. I had seen her in action at the top of her form. Back in my New York days at WABC-TV, Channel 7, I had worked on a local late night talk program, *The Les Crane Show*. It was a live show and Elaine was an in-studio guest one night. In one segment phone calls were taken from people calling in to talk with the celebrity guest. A man did just that and spoke to Elaine. Before he knew it (if he ever realized it), he was in a Nichols and May sketch. He was the patient to Elaine's psychoanalyst. She turned their conversation on the telephone into a session on her couch to the amusement of all of us in the studio and control room.

One chilly morning we were to film a scene from *Luv* that was set in a junkyard. Rather than go off the studio lot, the art director and set decorators had rigged the studio's cluttered electrical shop to look like a junkyard. Elaine shuddered and told me she was cold. I offered her my not-very-expensive cardigan sweater which she gladly wore. At the end of the day she didn't return the sweater. I never got it back. When the film wrapped, I mentioned the purloined sweater to the unit manager. He took $10 out of his pocket, gave it to me and said he would charge it to the film.

Months after the film was completed and I was still on the Columbia lot working on *Bewitched*, the successful TV situation

Knowing that I wanted some evidence that I actually worked on *Luv*, the set photographer motioned me to get into the picture as he clicked away. The director was talking with his cast. Starting clockwise from Jack Lemmon looking down at his script; next to him, Alan DeWitt, Jack's dialogue coach; then your author wearing the sweater I loaned to Elaine May and never got back; and finally, the director, Englishman Clive Donner, listening to Elaine May. AUTHOR'S COLLECTION

comedy starring Elizabeth Montgomery, I learned that Elaine was in the looping stage to correct some dialogue. I always admired Elaine so I went up there just to say "hello." She greeted me. With a twinkle in her eye she looked at the warm jacket I was wearing and said she really liked it. To this day I don't know if she was just giving me a compliment or was aiming to borrow it or if she remembered the sweater I had loaned her, but I got out of there fast, with the jacket on.

When the movie completed filming, as a remembrance of the film, I asked Elaine to autograph an amusing photograph of her and Jack Lemmon in a Ferris wheel gondola. The photo caught Jack's lips amazingly squared as he strained to say "I love you" at Elaine's urging. Instead of signing on the front of the photo, Elaine turned the photo on its back side and printed her name not in a flourish but in tiny letters and drew a cartoon of a woman with a

ABOVE: Elaine May is urging a reluctant, square-lipped Jack Lemmon to say he loves her in the movie *Luv!*

ON THE RIGHT: Elaine signed her very unique autograph on the back of the photograph rather than on the front.
AUTHOR COLLECTION

flourish of breasts. It was charming. Certainly unusual! I was puzzled why she hadn't signed on the front as I expected. Had I offended her by asking for her autograph? I had planned to ask Jack Lemmon to also autograph the photo but I didn't fearing another unexpected reaction.

While I was still working on the Columbia lot after *Luv* was completed, I snuck on to Stage 14 where they were filming a big musical production number for *Funny Girl* (1968) directed by William Wyler. Girls! Girls! Girls! Voluptuous Ziegfeld chorus girls in their flimsy, very sheer, gorgeous costumes performing on a lavish movie set with glittering staircases that in my eye surely led straight to musical heaven! Wow! In the midst of all that pulchritude was Barbra Streisand acting and singing in her first film, reprising her Broadway triumph as Ziegfeld star Fanny Brice. She was stage center in that spectacular musical number, a pillow stuffed under her dress so she would appear pregnant. Barbra as Fanny was defying the great Broadway showman Florenz Ziegfeld by singing the song "His Love Makes Me Beautiful" her way, with pregnancy as an unexpected comedy twist. Maybe it wasn't an MGM musical, but it was the Hollywood of my childhood afternoons in the Allerton Theatre!

In August of 1967, Teddy's, the answering service I used, before telephones self-answered, told me I had a message from Lin Parsons at MGM. Was I available to work as a second assistant on a western called *Day of the Evil Gun?* It was produced by the King Brothers for MGM. The director was Jerry Thorpe, whose father Richard Thorpe had been directing movies in Hollywood since the early 1930s. I would soon learn that for many men and women with whom I worked, the movie business was their family business. It wasn't theirs by inheritance, but by choice. And why not! It was an exciting business that encouraged your creativity and you worked with talented and interesting people. Best of all, the pay was excellent.

The stars of *Day of the Evil Gun* (1968) were Glenn Ford and Arthur Kennedy, both actors that I admired and remembered having seen in wonderful films in my childhood. The gentleman in charge of Glenn's wardrobe whispered something confidential to me. Glenn would report for costume fittings before each of his movies and the new costumes chosen would be hanging in his dressing room from the first day of shooting. But if they were for a western movie he never wore them. He only wore a favorite cowboy hat and a lived-in jacket that he had worn previously in his other westerns that he kept at-the-ready in his closet at home. I thought that was just an actor being superstitious, that to insure the success of the current western film he was shooting he had to wear the same costume, the same clothes he had worn in his previous successful western. However, that may not have been the case! Hank Moonjean, a very prominent and well-respected MGM assistant director and later producer of many Burt Reynolds films worked with Glenn Ford in several MGM films including *The Teahouse of the August Moon* (1956) costarring Marlon Brando and *It Started with a Kiss* (1959) costarring Debbie Reynolds. Moonjean wrote a very entertaining and informative memoir of his career entitled, *Bring in the Peacocks*. I thought the word "Peacocks" was Moonjean's code word for "actors." It wasn't. There's actually a great story about filming white peacocks in the movie *Kismet* (1955). You'll have to read that for yourself.

Moonjean also writes in his book how frugal Glenn Ford was. When Moonjean and other guests were invited to Ford's home for a sit-down dinner, Glenn served each guest one hot dog and one hot dog bun. No seconds! Though Glenn was earning big bucks for his movie roles and was well-dressed, something in his life made him a penny-pincher. At the end of each film, including *Day of the Evil Gun*, he would take home all of his wardrobe, the unworn new clothes as well as his favorite oldies! What a deal!

There is a story in Moonjean's book, *Bring in the Peacocks* about the great dramatic actress, multiple Oscar winner and Warner Bros. star Bette Davis that I'd like to share with you. Moonjean was the assistant director assigned to the MGM film *The Catered Affair* (1956). Bette Davis starred in the movie as Agnes Hurley, a frowsy, disillusioned Bronx housewife married to a cab driver played by Ernest Borgnine. When their daughter, played by Debbie Reynolds, announces she's going to get married, Agnes insists on a fancy wedding, a catered affair with all the trimmings which will cost way more than they can afford. It's the wedding Agnes never had that she wants for her daughter.

One day on the set, Bette asked Moonjean if he was of Armenian ancestry. He said he was. Bette was delighted. She told him that she and her current husband, Gary Merrill, loved Armenian food. With a twinkle in her eye, she asked to be invited to his home for an Armenian dinner. Moonjean didn't give her request another thought. But a week later Bette once again asked about the dinner. This time he responded " How about next Saturday." That was fine with Bette.

Glenn Ford wearing his preferred, favorite cowboy duds. *Photofest*

Moonjean went to his mother's house and asked her to prepare a wonderful, traditional Armenian meal for an actress with whom he was working. His mom spent an entire week cooking and preparing. Came Saturday evening Bette and Gary Merrill arrived. So did Moonjean's two brothers and their wives eager to meet Bette and Gary. They all enjoyed a wonderful meal with many, many delicious courses. After dinner Moonjean's mom, an Armenian immigrant who didn't speak English very well, approached Bette and said, "You. Come with me. We wash dishes."

There was an embarrassed hush in the room. Moonjean and his family were aghast! They tried to dissuade their mom, saying they would help with the dishes later. But his mom would have none of that. She said to everyone, "I work all week cooking for this lady. She come help me wash dishes."

Bette Davis, moviedom's grande dame, stood up and without another word, went with his mom into the kitchen. They shut the door behind them. Everyone wondered what the two of them could possibly talk about since Moonjean's mom spoke so little English.

An hour passed and the two dishwashers came out of the kitchen smiling. Soon after, Bette and Gary left, thanking Moonjean and his mom for a wonderful dinner and evening. The next day a beautiful orchid plant arrived as a thank you gift from Bette tor Moonjean's mother! Bette was a classy lady!

Keeping wardrobe for themselves after a movie was finished, as Glenn Ford did after *Day of the Evil Gun*, was an on-going custom in those days, especially for actresses who coveted the beautiful, one-of-a-kind outfits that were designed just for them to wear in their films. The studio looked the other way to that practice not wanting to incur the anger of their stars. It all stopped when the IRS discovered what the actors and actresses were doing and told them if they took wardrobe home for personal use, they would have to declare it as income and pay federal taxes on the clothes. I don't know if that stopped Glenn Ford.

What was most exciting for me about *Day of the Evil Gun* was that the company traveled to Mexico to shoot the outdoor scenes. There I was working in a foreign country for the first time and receiving a bigger paycheck because of the higher location wages and per diems as opposed to the studio rates paid in Hollywood. Many a crew member sought out location assignments on a regular basis. By living frugally on the location and squirreling away the extra money they were earning, they could set aside cash to buy a home, pay off a mortgage or fund a child's college education.

Our first shooting location was in and around Torreon, Mexico. Once we were there another of Glenn Ford's unusual habits became apparent to me. First thing in the morning, he often created a scene about something inconsequential, raising his voice, stomping about. Keeping talent happy was high on my list of duties. I'd rush to Glenn's side showing concern. Was there something I could do? I was anxious to calm him down. One morning Bob Crutchfield, who was a publicist assigned to the film, took me aside. Ignore the morning scene, he whispered. It was just Glenn's way of energizing himself, gearing up his acting chops for the day's work. As quickly as his anger arose, just as quickly it would disappear. From then on when Glenn arrived on set I tried to stay out of his way.

At the end of every movie there is a tradition to throw what's called "a wrap party" for the crew and cast to commemorate the end of filming and the time they worked together. That was true for *Day of the Evil Gun*. The company had moved from Torreon to Durango, Mexico. A large empty store in town was chosen as the site for the party. To gain admission you had to show a ticket provided by the producer. I later learned because the party site was in the heart of downtown, the ticket was the suggestion of the jefe, the chief of the Mexican crew. Indeed, standing outside on the street, looking in, was a wide-eyed crowd of Mexican locals, several trying to con their way in. Very visible through the store's windows the crowd could see several buffet tables offering the best in food and drink. A Mexican orchestra was hired for everyone's enjoyment. We were having a wonderful time. Halfway thru the party, a very angry member of our Mexican crew came up to me. He asked me who invited those people, pointing to three locals who were gorging themselves at the buffet tables, each building a mound of food on the plate that they were holding, enough to feed a family of four! I told him I didn't know who they were.

His eyes blazing he said "We Mexicans are a proud people. We take care of our own. It is a great embarrassment to us tonight, you allowing such a shameful thing to happen. We know there are poor and hungry people in our town. We take care of our own," he repeated.

Bob Crutchfield overheard my conversation with the angry crew member. Perhaps thinking the star could do no wrong, he told me that it was Glenn Ford who when he had entered the party had handed out extra tickets in his possession to the locals who were now gorging themselves. Fortunately, we didn't have to shoot the next day. If we had, there might have been a very angry Mexican crew present, perhaps refusing to work. I'm sure Glenn's intentions were honorable but when you're in a foreign country the customs and sensitivities are often quite different from those back home and should be observed by one and all, including the high priced talent. Perhaps the reason the Mexican jefe suggested to the producer that tickets be issued to all invitees was that he feared there would be party crashers!

One important lesson I took away after working with Glenn Ford was that I had to separate an actor's off-screen personal, often-erratic behavior from the heartfelt admiration I had for his on-screen talent. And Glenn Ford was an excellent actor.

When a film was nearing completion, if the studio or shooting company wanted the services of the film's assistant director on their very next movie, they had to inform you within ten days before the film wrapped. If they didn't then you were free to start calling your contacts, letting them know you would soon be available. In addition, you could list yourself on the DGA Availability Roster indicating the date you were available to start a new job.

MGM didn't have another film lined up for me when shooting wrapped on *Day of the Evil Gun*. I did return to MGM at the beginning of 1968 to work on a heist film called *The Split* (1968). In that film a group of professional criminal's band together for a daring heist in broad daylight. The job? To steal the cash receipts of that day's professional football game at the Los Angeles Coliseum.

It had an all-star cast. Football great Jim Brown, singer Diahann Carroll playing his love interest, Gene Hackman, Jack Klugman, Ernest Borgnine, Broadway's Julie Harris, and, in his first film on American soil, Canadian-born Donald Sutherland. The director was from England, Gordon Flemyng. The producers were Robert Chartoff and Irwin Winkler who had had great success the previous year with *Point Blank* (1967) starring Lee Marvin and Angie Dickinson. Like *Point Blank*, *The Split* was based on a mystery-adventure novel written by Donald E. Westlake under the pseudonym of "Richard Starke."

One day I was in a studio car with Diahann Carroll and her hair dresser driving from the Los Angeles planetarium to another location. Diahann told a story on herself. She loved jewelry and would always commemorate a special occasion in her life or a special performance by buying a piece of jewelry. And, unfortunately, just as often as she bought a piece of jewelry, she lost one. At one point in her life she was engaged to actor Sidney Poitier. He'd given her a diamond-encrusted wristwatch as a token of his love. But that love did not last and they broke off their relationship. Try as hard as she could, Diahann confided, the one piece of jewelry she could never lose was the watch sweet Sidney had given her.

We were filming a scene at San Pedro, the harbor of Los Angeles. In the scene, a satchel containing money had accidentally dropped down between the sides of two huge cargo ships that were anchored in the harbor. No actors were involved in the shot. The director,

Flemyng, described the effect he wanted. The camera was to follow the satchel down as it falls. The director of photography was Burnett Guffey. He was no slouch. He had won an Oscar in 1954 for Best Cinematography—Black and White for the Fred Zinnemann-directed film *From Here to Eternity*. Frank Sinatra fans remember the film because it was "Ol' Blue Eyes'" Oscar-winning, non-singing, dramatic role that reenergized his career after he had hit a very low ebb both as actor and singer. Probably more moviegoers remember the film for the steamy love scene between Burt Lancaster and Deborah Kerr lying on a sandy Hawaiian beach, oblivious to the ocean waves crashing over their bodies.

Guffey listened to Flemyng's idea for filming the satchel's fall. The best way to film it, Guffey said, was with a zoom lens. I stood next to the first assistant. We were both listening to their exchange. It was nearing the end of the day. We were concerned about not going into overtime or losing light. We knew that Guffey's suggestion to use a zoom lens would be a quick solution and not lengthen our day. But it wasn't for us to say.

No, barked Flemyng! As he saw the shot, he said, it would be more exciting if the camera actually followed the satchel down. Guffey explained that he could do that, but a special rig would have to be built to hold and lower the camera. Extra precaution would have to be taken so that the rig wouldn't break causing the camera to be damaged or fall into the harbor waters below. Very carefully choosing his words, Guffey tried to explain that it would be faster and safer if he used a zoom lens, with the camera stationary, being held by the camera operator and the zoom lens doing all the work.

Again, Flemyng said no! He insisted on his way. The first assistant turned pale. Movie crews always aim to please the director. Give him what he wants. Guffey looked over to the first assistant who nodded his okay. Reluctantly, Guffey ordered his camera crew to rig the camera to conform to Flemyng's concept of the shot. Perhaps Guffey's only other choice was for him to have walked off the film, but he'd been around too long and had seen directors come and go.

Knowing the work day and their light was fast fleeting away, Guffey and his crew worked quickly. Finally, they were ready. The shot was accomplished to the camera operator's approval on the third take. Our work for the day was finished. No overtime!

The next day the producers looked at the dailies from the previous day at the San Pedro harbor. They saw the shot of the satchel falling between the two cargo ships. All the producers loved it. Perfect! To a man, they all thought it was filmed with a zoom lens. So much for Gordon Flemyng's idea.

Several weeks later, when filming had been completed, the actors and crew were saying their goodbyes at the wrap party for *The Split*. No one there would have imagined that in our midst was a future TV and movie star. Donald Sutherland's wife accompanied him to the party. In her arms she held their two seven-month-old twins, a boy and a girl. The boy would grow up to be Kiefer Sutherland, star of the television action series *24* and feature films *The Lost Boys* (1987) and *Young Guns* (1988). Who knew then!

MOVIE DIRECTORS
Gods Or Mere Mortal Men

Some say that on his set the director of a movie is "God." His is the "final word" all await and by which all filming decisions are made. God-like or not, visualizing a film's script and bringing it to the silver screen, is all in the mind's eye of the director. It's his job, his vision. The unwritten rule on any set is to give the director what he wants or at least let him choose. For example, an actor needs a cigarette case for a scene. A wise property master will select three cases and show them to the director for him to select the one to be used. Quite often, if what he's been shown is not to the director's liking, with new input from the director, the property master will seek out other selections to show the director. A major part of any director's daily job is solving problems and making choices.

Many an actor who insists on doing it "his way" forgets that after his performance is done, what's been captured on film is now in the hands of the director and his film editor. If an actor delivers an interpretation that is new, that the director hadn't envisioned, that the director feels works for the film, no problem. That remains in the film. But if the director is unhappy with the actor's performance, feels the actor wasn't cooperating with him or at least on his same wave length, then—snip! snip!—the actor's scenes are shortened or even cut from the film.

If, however, the actor's dialogue or action can't be cut or abridged because what he says contains story points needed to advance or clarify the plot, the resulting edit may be an actor's worst nightmare. With his editing tool, the director can rearrange the actor's performance, play the actor's best scenes over his back or over another actor's close-up. That's why wise actors as well as his creative team and crew members know it's in their best interests to cooperate with the director. But since we are all mere mortals, there are often misunderstandings on the set.

MICHAEL GORDON
and Directing Furniture

Webster defines the word "coincidence" as "an event or two or more events at one time, happening apparently by mere chance."

That was the case one morning in the fall of 1968. I was still an eager second assistant director, now working on my fourth feature film, a film at MGM called *The Impossible Years* (1968). It was based on the Broadway stage success written by Bob Fisher and Arthur Marx, the son of comedian Groucho Marx. For Arthur MGM was a homecoming since his father and uncles, the Marx Brothers, had filmed several of their great comedies on MGM stages in the 1930s.

The Impossible Years, starring David Niven as the college professor father of two teenage daughters, was about the problems any father encounters during those "impossible years" when daughters become teenagers and begin dating boys. Although I had worked with such famous movie stars as Jack Lemmon and Glenn Ford, David Niven had more history behind him. He was a major actor from the pre-World War II Hollywood. In the 1930s he had been under contract to Samuel Goldwyn, had made films that I saw as a child, had acted with other greats like Ronald Colman, Merle Oberon, Laurence Olivier and Cary Grant. When I addressed him as "Mr. Niven," he said, "Please, call me David."

Often at the end of film, the leading players will give the assistant directors a "thank you" gift. One day near the end of the shoot David Niven came up to me and asked if I were a drinking man. I said I preferred wine over hard liquor. At the end of the filming, a large package was delivered to my front door from an exclusive liquor store in Brentwood. It was a case of twelve bottles of excellent white wine. Very generous and thoughtful.

The first assistant director on *The Impossible Years* was Artie Jacobson. Artie was an old timer in the business. He began working in films in 1928 at Paramount Pictures Long Island studios in New

York City. He eventually moved to California to better his career, which was now nearing 40 years long. As his "thank you" gift from David Niven he received a large coffee table book about the early days of motion pictures. To Artie's delight, he found a picture in the book of his wife. When Artie met her, she was a chorus girl at Paramount in Hollywood. In the picture she and another pretty lady were standing arm-in-arm on either side of a young Bing Crosby in an early Paramount musical. David Niven probably had no idea that Artie's wife was pictured in the book or even that she was a Paramount chorus girl. With a tear in his eye, Artie said to me it was the best "thank you" gift he ever received!

Later that year, Paul Newman, who was known to love a cold bottle of beer, gave me as a "thank you" gift a beautiful pewter beer mug. It was inscribed with his initials, "PLN" (the "L" standing for his middle name of Leonard), the name of the film, *Butch Cassidy and the Sundance Kid*, and the date "1968." A few years earlier, when *Luv* wrapped, as his "thank you" gift Jack Lemmon had given me a bottle of Jack Daniels. No inscription. Just the brand label!

Playing David Niven's oldest daughter in *The Impossible Years* was a gorgeous 17-year-old actress on loan from 20th Century-Fox appearing in her first major role, a young actress named Christina Ferrare. Her movie career never took off, but she went on to become one of the nation's top fashion models, a local and cable TV talk show hostess and the steadfast second wife of automobile wiz John DeLorean. Bravely, Christina endured the publicity glare of his legal battles when he was arrested for cocaine trafficking. He was never convicted. Several years later they were divorced. While filming *The Impossible Years*, Christina was still a high-school student nearing graduation. California law required that for three hours a day she be schooled in her dressing room every day she worked. Her studio teacher was the same woman who had been Shirley Temple's teacher 30 years before.

Directing the film was Michael Gordon. Mr. Gordon was a short, erudite gentleman, who had directed a string of successful plays on Broadway. His greatest success in films was directing *Pillow Talk* (1959), Universal's comedy with Doris Day and Rock Hudson, considered very racy for its day. Producing *The Impossible Years* was Laurence Weintraub, a veteran MGM producer who had been associated with many of the glorious MGM films of the thirties and forties.

On this particular morning, before I left my home for the studio, I happened to read an article on Hollywood directors in an esoteric film buff's magazine called *Films in Review*. The main thrust of the article was that in Hollywood there were certain directors whom the writer of the article called "furniture directors." You could identify those directors, the writer sneered, because the furniture in their films was always so important and plush. One of the directors cited by the writer was Michael Gordon, the very director I would be working for on *The Impossible Years*.

What a coincidence, I thought. Even more of a coincidence was that on that very morning the key personnel were going to walk down to Stage 15 on the MGM lot with Michael Gordon to inspect the main set that was ready for principal photography which was to begin in three days.

Stage 15 at MGM is a very big stage, in fact the second largest movie studio stage in the world at over 42,000 square feet. At one end still stood a grand staircase that had been built for the royal palace in Grace Kelly's last MGM movie *The Swan*, before she became a real princess marrying Monaco's Prince Rainier. The staircase was ornate and very large. Because it would be very expensive to tear down, it was wiser to let it stand; ready to be repainted, redressed and generally spruced up if needed for use in another MGM film.

For *The Impossible Years*, Stage 15 housed the interior set for the home in which David Niven and his movie family lived and where most of the movie would be shot. The set included the interiors of the ground floor of a rather large house, with a living room, dining room, library study, hallways, kitchen, and banistered staircase leading up to the second floor where the bedrooms were supposedly located. Actually, the bedroom sets were on the same Stage 15 floor as the main rooms, which made them easily accessible for filming. Because the locale for the movie was Southern California, the indoor set on Stage 15 included a landscaped backyard with a large, water-filled swimming pool to accommodate the splish-splash teenage pool party in the script.

I was still fairly new to big-time moviemaking. I stood on the periphery of the group as the others inspected the interior sets on

Stage 15. The house was big. The furnishings elegant, just what one might expect in a lush MGM movie. There was a grand piano and crystal chandeliers. The color scheme of the rooms and furniture was pale green and a silvery gray. Beautiful, I thought to myself.

But "furniture director" Michael Gordon didn't think so. A dispute seemed in the works. Gordon's argument was the back story of the character Niven played. A back story is the previous history of a character that isn't spelled out in the script; it is what the actor or the director creates to give substance to the character. In this script we know Niven is a college professor with a wife and two daughters but not much more. Gordon's back story for the Niven character was that he and his family had recently purchased and moved into this big house which was costing them a pretty penny. His salary wasn't enormous and he really didn't have the funds to completely furnish a new house. Gordon said the family would have brought along with them from their previous home some of their older, lived-in furnishings. Besides, the way the set was decorated and furnished didn't seem to be the same as the sketches the art director had shown Gordon and that he had signed off on in pre-production.

Gordon turned to me. "Steve," he said, "you'll find those sketches on my desk in my office. Please get them."

I raced back to MGM's Thalberg Building, to Mr. Gordon's office on the second floor, picked up the sketches from his desk and returned lickety-split to Stage 15. On the way back I took an unauthorized peek at the color sketches. The first thing I noticed was that the basic colors of the furniture, rugs and wallpaper were in earth tones, browns, rusts, beiges, not the elegant greens and silvery grays that now dressed Stage 15.

Michael Gordon won the argument. When there's a problem, crews work quickly. The very next day the entire set was repainted and refurnished in the earth tones of the sketches. The grand piano remained (a space filler, I think), but the crystal chandeliers were gone.

The writer of the article I had read in *Films in Review* that morning had hit it on the nose, at least with the Michael Gordon I witnessed that morning. He had "directed" the furniture to coincide with his vision of the film. There's no question that the director's vision, what he sees in his mind's eye and his ability to translate that vision to film can make or break a film. Had Gordon not made his furniture preferences perfectly clear to the art director in a previous discussion? Or had the art director decided he knew best and overrode the color scheme Gordon approved? In the end, the film's director is the auteur, responsible for all the details on the film. His vision must be fulfilled, for his interpretation sets the tone for the film. Whether it's actors, camera moves, or furniture, his word is the final word. And Michael Gordon knew that!

Aside from the many successful Broadway shows and Hollywood films that he directed, Michael Gordon left the film industry another legacy: His grandson is actor Joseph Gordon-Levitt, the son of one of Gordon's two daughters. Young Joseph made his mark first in television in the zany situation comedy *3rd Rock from the Sun* that was a hit on network TV for five years beginning in 1996. Among his growing list of feature films are *(500) Days of Summer* (2009), co-starring Zooey Deschanel, the daughter of Caleb Deschanel, an acclaimed director of photography; *Inception* (2010), starring Leonardo DiCaprio; and *50/50* (2011), where his character suffered a rare cancer.

Appearing in *The Impossible Years* as a doctor was Ozzie Nelson, who first became famous in the 1930s as an entertainer and bandleader of the Ozzie Nelson Orchestra. Ozzie married Harriet Hilliard, a vocalist and actress, and soon they were a family with two sons, David, the eldest, and Ricky, the wisecracking youngster. First on radio then on ABC television, Ozzie created a very successful family comedy called *The Adventures of Ozzie & Harriet*. Eventually, all four Nelsons appeared as themselves portraying what many felt was the ideal 1950s family. Ricky grew up on the show from a wisenheimer kid to a handsome teenager. Like his parents, he was a gifted singer. Ozzie carefully nurtured and showcased young Ricky's singing career in the weekly series and Ricky Nelson became every screaming teenage girl's heartthrob singer. By the time Ozzie was cast by Michael Gordon in *The Impossible Years* his TV show *The Adventures of Ozzie & Harriet* was long gone from prime time, but still re-running in syndication, still in the public's collective memory. That included mine.

Film buff that I was I played it cool. I didn't go gaga when I worked with or encountered a famous face. There I was walking through a narrow hallway in the basement of MGM's Thalberg building, my shoulder within touching distance of Elvis Presley's shoulder as we passed by each other. Elvis and his posse were coming from the screening room I was heading towards. I was cool. There was the man himself! But I walked on by. One day I saw this little lady in a funky bathrobe being unobtrusive, observing the *McCloud* TV show that we were shooting on a Universal stage, not looking like the iconic star she was. It was Joan Crawford taking a break from a TV movie that was the pilot for *Rod Serling's Night Gallery TV* series. Miss Crawford's segment was called "Eyes" in which she played the richest woman in the world who is going blind. With her wealth she buys the eyes of another woman. Unfortunately her purchase has some unexpected consequences befitting a Rod Serling script. Her director was a young Steven Spielberg, directing his very first film in Hollywood. Seeing MGM's great star, Mildred Pierce herself, the Queen of Pepsi-Cola, the iconic Joan Crawford! No big deal! I was still cool!

But when I had to phone Ozzie Nelson at home to give him his shooting call for the next day I lost it, big time. Harriet Nelson answered the phone. The sound of her oh-so-familiar voice sent me back in time. I could barely speak I was so star struck! As quickly as I could I gave her Ozzie's call and hung up. How glad I am now that Harriet and I weren't using today's smart phones, capable of showing the people on either end of the call. I was beet-red blushing! Far from cool!

An important responsibility for any second assistant director is making sure an actor or actress reports on time for their early morning make-up call. If they are late for make-up, chances are they will be late to the set and hold up the company from starting to film on time. A no-no for the money men in the Thalberg Building. Actors generally need less time for their makeup and wardrobe than the female of the species. So if the shooting call was 8 a.m. unless there was an intricate wardrobe or make-up for him, an actor's call would be 7:30 a.m., reporting directly to the set or stage where the filming was scheduled. His make-up person would be there waiting for him. An actress with both make-up and hair to be done needed at least an hour and a half to get ready. Since the crew didn't open the set until 7 a.m., an actress for an 8 a.m. call would be asked to first report to the studio's make-up department rather than the set. All this is spelled out on each day's call sheet that every actor and every crew member has received.

Such was the case for lovely Lola Albright who appeared as David Niven's on-screen wife in *The Impossible Years*. When she was in the first take of the day her call was 6 a.m. Lola was a trouper. At the start of filming she told me that as long as she had her coffee or a breakfast waiting for her when she arrived; I needn't be there to check up on her. Since it took me a half hour to drive to M.G.M. from my home beneath the Hollywood sign, I would phone the make-up department promptly at 6:15 a.m. Lola never failed me. She was always there. Happily I'd drive off to be on the set for the crew's 7 a.m. call.

Hanging on the walls of MGM's make-up department were life masks of many of MGM's stars. Usually the masks were made so that the make-up department could create special prostheses like scars, wrinkles, false noses to transform the actor's or actress' face as called for in the plot of the movie. Or perhaps the face needed to be aged from the star's real youthful look to that of a middle aged or old person.

William J. "Bill" Tuttle was the head of MGM's make-up department when I worked there. He was considered the pioneering make-up artist in Hollywood having a career that began in the 1930's and lasted for four and a half decades. In 1965 he was awarded an Honorary Oscar for his make-up transforming Tony Randall into seven different characters for MGM's film *7 Faces of Dr. Lao* (1964). It wasn't until 1982 that the Academy Awards created an Oscar category for make-up artists, the first winner being Rick Baker for *An American Werewolf in London* (1981).

Often Bill Tuttle was simply called upon to make MGM's beautiful women and handsome men look like themselves, only more so. Or to devise special make-up that wouldn't be ruined by water for a star like Esther Williams whose specialty was under water. Or to turn an actor like Kirk Douglas into the famous Dutch artist Vincent Van Gogh for MGM's biographical movie *Lust For Life* (1965).

Bill's specialty was making those life masks. His top secrets were the ingredients he used to make the masks. Basically what he did

Makeup Master, William J. "Bill" Tuttle in his workroom with some monster and character masks he created for MGM films as well as a casting of a pair of glamorous legs. Hanging on the wall are several of the over 100 Life Masks he made. Can you recognize and name the actors and actresses whose masks are displayed? Turn the page for answers.
USC Hugh M. Heffner Moving Image Archives.

was first make a mold of the artist's face, applying a Vaseline-like base to make sure the goop didn't stick to the star's face when the mold was removed. If the mold was perfect, he would then fill it with a plaster-like substance and Voila! There was a replica of that actor's or actress' face, eyes shut.

Among the masks hanging on the wall I recognized the faces of Elizabeth Taylor, Lana Turner and Ava Gardner, all legendary beauties in their prime. There was also a mask for beautiful Eleanor Parker who we usually don't think of as an MGM star. She began her film career at Warner Bros. in 1941 when she was only 18 years old. During the 1940's her career blossomed at Warners, a highlight being in 1944 when Warner's remade Bette Davis's classic film *Of Human Bondage* with Eleanor in Bette's role. Many in the industry thought Warner Bros. was giving then troublesome Bette a warning that there was another dramatic actress as talented as she on their payroll. In 1950 Eleanor was nominated for an Oscar for her role in Warner Bros. *Caged* playing a young newlywed sent into a corrupt prison system that changes her into a hardened convict. In the 1950's Eleanor left Warners and began free-lancing and it was then that she did a string of films for MGM including *Interrupted Melody* (1955), a biography of polio inflicted opera star Marjorie Lawrence. For that role Eleanor received another Oscar nomination.

I asked Bill Tuttle which of the many ladies who had masks on the wall had the most beautiful face. He smiled at me and said it wasn't a question of beauty. That was in the eye of the beholder. But if I had asked him which of those actresses with masks on the wall had a perfect face, he would have to say Eleanor Parker! I was taken by surprise! Not Elizabeth or Lana or Ava? No, Bill replied. Eleanor's features were a rarity. They were evenly proportioned and symmetrical. If you held a mirror to one half of her face it would create a reflection that looked exactly like her full face without the mirrored reflection. Claudette Colbert is said to have favored her left profile and would try to have that side of her face photographed whenever possible. With Eleanor Parker, Bill said, her face could be photographed from any angle. It was just perfect and flawless.

When the MGM studios were sold in 1972 and all the long time employees were released from their contracts, Bill Tuttle took his collection of masks with him. Over the years he had been teaching his craft to film students at the University of Southern California (USC) in Los Angeles. When he died in 1999 he willed over one hundred life masks to USC's School of Cinematic Arts where they are stored in vaults in the Hugh M. Heffner Moving Images Archives, named in honor of the founder of *Playboy Magazine.* Selected masks

---

Life Masks Identities: Top Row (L to R) Maria Schell, Joan Crawford, Stewart Granger, Lloyd Nolan, Fred Astaire, Anne Francis. Beneath Anne Francis are (R to L) Martha Raye, Jimmy Durante, Red Buttons, and Marisa Pavan (twin sister of Pier Angeli). Tuttle is holding a completed character mask for Lee J. Cobb in *The Brothers Karamazov* (1958). The white wigged head below him is for a Morlock in *The Time Machine* (1960). The two character masks standing side by side are both for actor Hurd Hatfield in *The Picture of Dorian Gray* (1945), the film adaptation of Oscar Wilde's novella of the same name in which a portrait of Dorian Gray is hidden away, ageing and reflecting his evil and decadent life style while in real life he remains young and handsome. At the end of the film these masks were used in a series of shots to reveal as he lay dying how he reverted to his true identity. We see through the magic of the masks the metamorphosis of his handsome, forever youthful face as it becomes the ravaged face of a very old depraved man as we have seen in the portrait hidden away. And the glamorous legs? Cyd Charisse!

are occasionally put on display when they relate to a particular exhibit about the motion picture industry. They can be seen by the public just by making an appointment with the H. M. Heffner Moving Images Archives at USC. Though stored in the archives they remain a wonderful record in plaster of a very beautiful and perfect time in Hollywood!

A GRAND OLD MAN
Lights the Way

When principal photography is completed, as I've written before, a custom on most major films is to have a "wrap party" to celebrate the conclusion of the film. It's a chance for the entire cast and crew and often their spouses or significant others to party and feel good about the work they've accomplished together. Usually, the producer will pay for the party. Sometimes, these wrap parties are held in hotels or restaurants. More often than not, they are held on the studio lot, often on the same stage where the film was shot. What with the wonderful landscaped backyard and the water-filled swimming pool on Stage 15, it was a natural setting for the wrap party for *The Impossible Years*.

William Daniels was the cinematographer or director of photography on *The Impossible Years*. Daniels was a grand old man at MGM. He was Greta Garbo's favorite cinematographer and filmed 21 of her MGM films, from the first silent, *Torrent*, in 1926 through the Lubitch comedy *Ninotchka* in 1939. In 1948 he won his Oscar for Best Cinematography for *The Naked City*, a semi-documentary film shot in a gritty, naturalistic style on the grimey streets of New York City. For Daniels it was quite a departure from the lush, controlled sets at MGM that he was accustomed to photographing. The Oscar was truly a testament to his talent and genius. He would go on to photograph such classics as *Cat on a Hot Tin Roof* (1958), with Paul Newman and Elizabeth Taylor, and the all-star *How the West Was Won* (1962). For both, he was nominated for the Best Cinematography Oscar. I worked with him not only on *The Impossible Years* in 1968 but the following year, 1969, on *The Maltese Bippy* which starred comedians Dan Rowan and Dick Martin of television's

In the background, the working pool built on MGM's Stage 15 for *The Impossible Years* where the wrap party was held. Inside the house, bikini-clad Christina Ferrare, her poppa David Niven, and one of her boyfriends, red-headed Michael McGreevy, listen attentively to another of Christina's beaus, bearded hippie, Jeff Cooper. LARRY EDMUNDS

Laugh-In fame. "Bippy" was a meaningless catch word made popular by Dan and Dick on *Laugh-In*. Using it in the movie's title was a ploy to attract the *Laugh-In* audience. It failed. The movie was still-born. It opened and closed in a week.

In 1968, returning to MGM's Stage 15 to film *The Impossible Years*, was a like a homecoming for cinematographer Daniels. It was the last day of shooting and the wrap party was that evening, as soon as shooting was finished. Since the beautiful backyard set with a pool was chosen as the site of the party and because it was on an MGM stage, lighting the party fell under Daniels jurisdiction.

The lighting gaffer on the show was a gentle, portly little man named Morrie. He had been Daniels head electrician for several years on several movies and enjoyed working with the "Old Master," as Morrie called him. Daniels instructed Morrie and his crew to find time to light the pool area for the party. In case Daniels needed him, Morrie told me what he would be doing.

An hour later, the area was lit for the party. Morrie and his crew of men had done a dramatic job, spotlighting an area for the dance floor and the many tables and floral arrangements that had been set up around the pool for the party. There was a definite party-enhancing, dramatic light pattern playing on the area. But when we all gathered there for the party, I sensed the lighting was not the same as I had seen it before. I asked Morrie why the change. Morrie told me that when he and his crew had finished lighting the area, it was second nature for him to ask Daniels to check it out.

Daniels frowned. The set was too dark. *The Impossible Years* was a comedy. Throughout his career when filming a comedy, he used lots of light to create an upbeat, happy visual look. As far as Daniels was concerned, the same applied to the wrap party for comedy. No dramatic dark shadows! Daniels had Morrie redo the lighting. Brighter, livelier and upbeat.

Oh, yes! The wrap party was a happy success in its new look—brighter, livelier and upbeat.

VINCENTE MINNELLI
and The Ferris Wheel

While I was still wearing army fatigues in South Korea in the summer of 1968, MGM was producing a major Technicolor motion picture called *Some Came Running* starring Frank Sinatra, Dean Martin and Shirley MacLaine. The film was based on the bestselling novel by James Jones about disillusionment in a small Midwestern town after World War II as the fighting men returned to civilian life. Five years before, in 1953, Sinatra's career had taken a decided upturn when he won the Best Supporting Oscar for portraying Maggio in *From Here to Eternity* based on the novel that made James Jones a literary sensation. Perhaps Sinatra thought lightning would strike again when he signed on to act in another bestselling James Jones novel. It didn't. More a character study than a narrative story, it is best remembered for Shirley MacLaine's dramatic performance as an unlucky small-town floozy stuck on boyfriend Frank Sinatra. Assigned to direct the film was Vincente Minnelli, one of MGM's top directors. My friend and future working partner Tom McCrory was Minnelli's second assistant director.

Tom McCrory and I met in 1973 when we worked on the TV show *The Partridge Family* for Screen Gems, the television producing arm of Columbia Pictures. Tom and I hit it off. I practically read his mind. Whenever he was onto a new assignment he would call me and see if I might be available to be his Second. Tom told me of his experience with Minnelli and the Ferris wheel. This story and some others Tom experienced working with Minnelli so unnerved Tom that when *Some Came Running* wrapped he set up a special bank account he privately referred to as his "F – – k Minnelli Fund!" It was only to be dipped into when he was impelled to walk away from a job because he could no longer work with a director. Fortunately, he never had cause to use the fund. But then he never chose to work with Minnelli again.

As a serious lover of movies, I knew of Vincente Minnelli's career achievements and his filmography. Minnelli was admired for his exceptional artistic taste and his eye for beauty. As a young man, before he came to Hollywood, he had been the art director and set designer for the lavish stage shows that accompanied the films shown at Radio City Music Hall, the famed movie theater in New York City, noted to this day for the high-kicking chorus-line dancers, the Rockettes.

As a designer and a director, I suspect Minnelli possessed a trait called "structural visualization." Since 1922, the Johnson O'Connor Foundation, through their aptitude testing and research, have found that gifted movie and stage directors, as well as architects and designers, are known to possess "structural visualization." These creative people, in their mind's eye, before they even put down on paper or stage what they are creating, instinctively know not only how it should look, but also if for them it will be artistically correct. And once they have their "vision" they seldom deviate from it. There's no record that Minnelli took the Johnson O'Connor test for "structural vision," but to my eye viewing the perfection in his films, I wholeheartedly believe he possessed that trait.

The brass at MGM, having seen his achievements directing many successful Broadway shows, thought Minnelli had the potential to be a movie director. After a period of observing movie production, Minnelli was given his first directing assignment on the 1943 all-black musical *Cabin in the Sky*, starring Lena Horne, Ethel Waters and Eddie "Rochester" Anderson. Eddie was better known as Rochester, Jack Benny's comedic manservant on Jack Benny's radio shows heard each Sunday at seven p.m. over the airwaves in those days. Minnelli went on to direct such classic MGM musicals as *Meet Me in St. Louis* and *The Pirate*, both starring MGM's most gifted musical star, Judy Garland. It was during the filming of *Meet Me in St. Louis* that Minnelli and his leading lady Judy Garland fell in love and married. Not the least of Minnelli's life achievements was that when he was married to Garland, he fathered singer-actress-entertainer Liza Minnelli, who was awarded an Oscar in 1973 as Best Actress for the musical drama *Cabaret*. In 1958 her father had won his own Best Director Oscar for the Lerner and Lowe original film musical *Gigi* starring Belgian-born Audrey Hepburn and Frenchmen Louis Jourdan and Maurice Chevalier.

Because *Some Came Running* was about small-town life, in the months of planning prior to the shooting, the producer, director and art director had flown from Culver City to the Midwest to seek out a suitable small town for the exterior shots. Not only would the town have to have the right look, but it would have to accommodate the logistics of a movie crew and their shooting schedule. The town that Minnelli chose was Madison, Indiana, located on the shores of the Ohio River in Jefferson County.

Filming in Madison was to begin in just a few days. Minnelli and his MGM crew were already in town. To be thoroughly prepared and to avoid any unexpected last-minute complications, the unit manager scheduled a tour of all the selected shooting sites. The purpose of any location scouting is to familiarize the key crew members with what the director plans at each site and what is expected of each department and their crew members at each location. Location scouting was then, and still is, a necessary and normal operating procedure on any film. Among the crew members with Minnelli was his second assistant director, my friend Tom McCrory.

At each location, Minnelli detailed how and what he planned to shoot there, the camera angles, the special effects that might be needed. The key personnel listened attentively, trying to determine what special challenges might arise for their departments. Will they need extra set-up time? Additional equipment? Additional personnel?

Frank Sinatra in his army uniform listens as director Vincente Minnelli gives him some ideas about the scene being filmed in *Some Came Running*. *Photofest*

Is the natural light better on this location for a morning or an afternoon shoot?

If anyone foresees a problem by pinpointing it during this pre-shoot scouting tour, the potential problem can be discussed, and, hopefully, resolved. Sometimes the director is forced to rethink what he plans to do, especially if a crew member discovers a problem on the location that had not been foreseen until then. Quite often, despite the problem, the director sticks by his guns. Usually that motivates the crew to draw upon their combined experience to overcome the unforeseen obstacle. This is when Hollywood crews really show their mettle and why they are respected worldwide.

On this morning, Vincente Minnelli and the crew were scouting a camera angle near the town's county courthouse. The end of the movie called for a chase through a small-town carnival. A working carnival that traveled throughout the Midwest had been hired to portray itself. It came complete with sideshows and amusement rides that included a Ferris Wheel. Minnelli explained he would be filming a tie-in shot that showed the county courthouse and its relationship to the carnival and the Ferris Wheel in the field beyond. Waiting in front of the courthouse were the owners of the carnival. They were on hand so that Minnelli could spot where he wanted the Ferris wheel erected. Once Minnelli selected the site for the Ferris wheel, the carnival's roustabouts would set it up. Setting it up meant actually constructing it piece by piece just as it was done whenever the carnival came to a new location. It would take the carnival men eight to ten hours to physically erect this particular Ferris Wheel. When the Wheel was up, more time was needed for the film's electricians to rig it with movie lights per the art director.

To help Minnelli spot the exact site for the Ferris Wheel, the carnival owners had one of their roustabouts standing with a white flag in the field beyond. Minnelli walked to a spot across from the county courthouse where he thought he would place the camera. He lifted his viewfinder to his eye and framed his picture. With a twist of the mechanism, Minnelli's viewfinder could simulate the size of various camera lenses so that he could approximate the size of the shot he had in mind.

Minnelli eyed the scene through his viewfinder. Everyone watched him, including the carnival owners, new to the intricacies of moviemaking and thrilled to be involved. Minnelli adjusted his viewfinder and took a few steps back. In the field beyond, the roustabout with the white flag stood still not moving from his original spot. Minnelli dropped his viewfinder, turned to the unit manager and gave the okay. Exactly where the roustabout with the white flag was standing would be the exact center of the Ferris Wheel.

With the okay given, the carnival men went to work immediately. Piece by piece they erected the Ferris Wheel from the ground up. First the struts, then the crossbeams and supports, then the completed sections were joined and raised. Finally, the gondolas were hung in position. By the time the Wheel was standing in all its glory, it was evening. A night crew of movie electricians began rigging the wheel with miles of cable and movie lights under the direction of the electric gaffer and his second in command, known in the industry as his best boy. The next afternoon, with the Ferris Wheel completed and ready for review, the unit manager brought Minnelli and key crew members back to the location in front of the county courthouse.

Once again, Minnelli stood on the same spot in front of the courthouse. With his right hand he lifted his viewfinder to his eye and viewed the scene. Then, with his left hand ever so slightly, he began making a "move-it-over" motion. It seems that as he viewed the scene today, the Ferris Wheel wasn't in the right place. He wanted it moved more to the right.

The carnival people exploded. In order to move the Ferris Wheel it meant they had to dismantle it completely and rebuild it from the ground up. And that couldn't be done until the crew of electricians removed the extra movie lighting that they had rigged on the Wheel. No way, said the carnival owners, why not move the position of the camera? Minnelli held firm, explaining that until the Wheel had been erected he hadn't realized that he couldn't frame it and the county courthouse as he visualized it. To get the shot, the Ferris Wheel had to be moved. Minnelli had spoken. Had the "structural visualization" I believe Minnelli possessed finally kicked in? We'll never know.

And so the Ferris Wheel was moved amidst much grumbling with an extra fee, Tom McCrory told me, slipped to the carnival owners by the unit manager. Perhaps only God can make a tree, but a movie director can move mountains...err, Ferris Wheels.

CECIL B. DEMILLE
Had His Secrets

Cecil B. DeMille was considering Anne Baxter for an important role in his planned remake of *The Ten Commandments* (1956). The legendary director had first filmed the biblical story in 1923 as a silent epic. The new version was to be his masterpiece, in breathtaking Technicolor, with a star-studded cast and thousands of extras, to say nothing of spectacular visual effects such as the parting of the Red Sea as Moses and the Israelites fled Egypt.

As in any family, in DeMille's there were some secrets. DeMille and his wife Constance had four children. Cecilia, the eldest, was their natural-born daughter, but the other three, Katherine, John and Richard, were adopted. Richard found out he was adopted when he was eight-years-old from a playmate. Something always troubled young Richard. If he was adopted, why did he look so much like the portrait of Cecil's father, Henry deMille, which hung in Cecil's study?

When Richard was in his thirties he was finally told that his real father was Cecil's older brother, William deMille, and his mother was a writer with the celestial name of Lorna Moon. That name clicked with me. Where had I seen it or heard it? I had just attended the 45th Cinecon Film Festival at the Egyptian Theatre on Hollywood Boulevard in the heart of Hollywood. Among the many old and historic films screened at the four-day festival was a silent movie called *Her Cardboard Lover* (1928). That's where I had read the name Lorna Moon. It was in the opening frames of the film. Lorna Moon! What an unusual name, I thought. Was it real? Or was it a wonderful theatrical name conjured up for the movies? The name stuck in my mind.

This Lorna Moon was credited for writing the witty title cards interspersed in the silent movie that told the film's story and spoke for the silent stars. The film starred newspaper publisher William Randolph Hearst's paramour Marion Davies. I would later read that the silent film was based on a stage play that starred Tallulah Bankhead in theaters in London and New York in the 1920s.

Richard only found out that the man he thought was his uncle was in reality his biological father when William de Mille lay on his death bed. Or that Agnes de Mille, whom he thought was his first cousin, was his half-sister, seventeen years older than himself. In the very talented de Mille family, Agnes was the famous choreographer who had revolutionized theatrical dance on the legitimate stage when she choreographed a dream ballet in the Broadway musical *Oklahoma!* Their father William was also a playwright and a silent movie director. He wasn't as famous as his kid brother Cecil, but his films received greater critical acclaim.

William was a womanizer, as was Cecil. Though Cecil's wife knew he played around, she was pleased with her life and discretely closed her eyes to his dalliances. Many of his paramours worked with him at the studio. Mrs. de Mille and "the women" were very cordial to one another. William de Mille had had an affair with Lorna Moon, a beauty who was a newspaper woman, a novelist and a screenwriter. She was considered very bohemian in her lifestyle even for the Jazz Age 1920s. When she gave birth to William's baby in 1922, she gladly gave him up to be adopted by Cecil and his wife, so that he could be raised as a true de Mille, with all its privileges and prestige. She was indeed the Lorna Moon who had written the titles for *Her Cardboard Lover.* All this would be confirmed in a book I bought marked down to seven dollars at the famous Strand Bookstore on the corner of Broadway and East Twelfth Street in Manhattan. Richard had written the book, *My Secret Mother, Lorna Moon*, published in 1998 in an attempt to discover his true identity, his maternal ancestry and what made his mother tick. I've used Richard's book as my source for his family's stories.

The anecdote about Anne Baxter was told to me by my friend Dee Somers who worked at Warner Bros., rising from secretary to Director of Studio Services. When I phoned her as I was writing this book to confirm the anecdote's authenticity, she couldn't remember who had told it to her. All the people involved are long gone. As a film-maker, Cecil B. DeMille knew the value of a good story. This is good story, whether true or not. It's the kind of anecdote that's passed on at the studios from one movie worker to another.

Anne Baxter was a seasoned and respected actress in Hollywood. In 1947 she had received an Academy Award statuette for Best

Cecil B. DeMille stands alongside a camera used to film his final movie, *The Ten Commandments* (1956). With him in costume for the film is actor H. B. Warner in his last credited role as Amminadab. Warner is regarded as the definitive Jesus Christ for his role in DeMille's silent biblical epic *King of Kings* (1927). Photofest

Supporting Actress for her performance as the opium-addicted Sophie in *The Razor's Edge* (1946), 20th Century-Fox's filming of Somerset Maugham's classic novel. A granddaughter of architecture's grand old man, master builder Frank Lloyd Wright, Anne was eager to work with DeMille, cinema's grand old man, before he retired or died. Because DeMille was already in his seventies, chances were that *The Ten Commandments* might be his last film.

The day before she was to meet with DeMille in his office to discuss working on the film, Anne talked to her friend Irene Sharaff, one of Hollywood's foremost costume designers. Irene had worked with DeMille many times. Anne asked the designer for advice. What could Anne do that might help her get the part in de Mille's picture?

"Get a pedicure," Irene advised.

Anne was surprised. She looked down at her feet and exclaimed, "What's wrong with my feet?"

Anne Baxter as Queen Nefertiti wearing the royal sandals that showcased her pedicured, dainty tootsies in *The Ten Commandments*. Photofest

"Nothing," her friend laughed. "Just get a pedicure."

So Anne had her petite tootsies given the full treatment. Each foot was buffed, oiled and powdered; each toe nail trimmed, shaped and polished to a glow.

The next day, dressed beautifully, Anne went to DeMille's office on the Paramount lot for her appointment. Cecil greeted her warmly. He sat behind his huge desk and with great enthusiasm told her about his exciting plans for filming *The Ten Commandments*. Charlton Heston was already cast as the adult Moses. Yul Brynner was to play Ramses, Egypt's Pharoh. And DeMille was considering Anne for the part of Nefertiti, the Queen of Egypt. As he spoke, DeMille emphasized to Anne that because the film was set in biblical times, Anne would have to wear sandals if she were cast in the part. Would she mind showing him her feet now?

Not at all, Anne replied.

Anne slipped off her modern-day high-heeled shoes and extended her bare feet for viewing. DeMille got down on the floor on his hands and knees, and with great care, he examined Anne's dainty, finely pedicured bare feet. Was DeMille's interest in Anne's pretty feet just part of any good director's concern with every detail of his production? Or did Irene Sharaff know another of DeMille's personal secrets? Did she know he had a foot fetish? Did Anne's pretty feet get her the part? Who can be sure!

Most people think that "de Mille" is a French name. Not so. It's Dutch, originally spelled "de Meld." Before families adopted patronymic surnames, "de Meld" simply told people that Cecil's ancestors came from the tribe of the Melds. Over the centuries, the name underwent many changes ending up "de Mille." But Cecil had another thought about his name. Although in private life he signed his checks and used the spelling "de Mille," on the big screen he thought "DeMille" with a capital "D" and the words joined together would be better understood and remembered by the movie-going public, according to Richard de Mille's book.

RETAKES
Movie Lingo for a Second Chance

Filmmaking is one of the biggest crapshoots around. When the assistant director calls for silence on the set and says "Roll Camera," the gamble begins. With the camera rolling, the assistant cameraman marks the film with the "clap" of the clapboard, synchronizing audio and visual portions of the film for the purpose of later editing. The information on the clapboard also identifies the "take" from all the others that came before and that will follow. Next, the director calls "Action" and whatever is rehearsed happens. Actors move, talk, the horses come over the horizon. Whatever! There is no guarantee that what is captured on the celluloid running behind the lens on that "take" will be okay.

The saying is "No one sets out to make a bad movie." Despite many months of careful preparation, despite the best intentions and best efforts put forth by all the talented men and women behind and in front of the camera, there are films that just don't make it! It could be one lonely take that's to blame or an entire sequence. The reasons for a less-than-perfect take are as diverse as the egos involved and the day-to-day working conditions. Perhaps the director had too light a touch and didn't control all the elements he should have. Perhaps an actor's performance is off target, too shrill or not shrill enough. Perhaps the movie is confusing because a story point was inadvertently dropped or not developed sufficiently. Perhaps the problem is technical; the film is too dark and murky because the scene was under lit by the cinematographer. Perhaps the film was scratched as it rolled through the camera because the camera assistant inadvertently loaded it incorrectly.

No matter what the reasons are that a film in first assemblage doesn't seem to play right, moviemakers have a second chance to correct the errors and make the film work. That chance is called "a retake." As long as the set for the scene is still available or something like it can be improvised, as long as there's money in the budget and the needed actors are still available, the director or the producer can decide to retake or reshoot the scene or scenes that don't seem to work. And keep their fingers crossed!

WOODY ALLEN
and His Tweed Jacket

A few days after Christmas in 1971, I was called to work as an assistant director for one day of retakes for a feature film called *Play It Again, Sam* (1972). It was a Paramount film, directed by Herb Ross, starring Woody Allen and Diane Keaton. Woody had originally written *Play It Again, Sam* for the Broadway stage and had starred in the Broadway production, enjoying a popular success. His inspiration for the play had been the classic Warner Bros. film *Casablanca* (1942), which won the 1943 Academy Award as Best Picture and starred Humphrey Bogart and Ingrid Bergman. Woody's title, *Play It Again, Sam*, came from Ingrid Bergman's often-parodied line in the original film.

When Paramount bought his play for the movies, Woody was signed to write the screen adaptation and to play the leading role as he had done on Broadway. The role he had written for himself was the typical Woody Allen character his public loved to watch: An ineffectual little man who for all his posturing never seems to get the girl he wants. The character is a movie buff with a particular fondness for the romantic, tough guy style of Humphrey Bogart in *Casablanca* (1942).

In his fantasies, Woody wishes that he could be as successful with women as his idol Bogart. And who better to tutor him in Bogart's style and technique than Bogie himself. To that end, whenever Woody needs some advice about the women in his life, the ghost of Humphrey Bogart appears, played in a dead-on impersonation by actor Jerry Lacy, complete with a Bogart-like trench coat and

RETAKES: MOVIE LINGO FOR A SECOND CHANCE | 47

Woody Allen in a pensive mood in front of a poster of his character's favorite movie, *Casablanca*, the classic film Woody used as inspiration for *Play It Again, Sam*. Photofest

slouch hat. Bogie's ghost can only be seen and heard by Woody, not by any of the other characters in the story.

Among the retakes to be shot on the day I was called in to work was a take-off of the final scene in *Casablanca* on the tarmac of an airport. In the 1942 film, directed by Michael Curtiz, Bogart as "Rick" has just said goodbye to his true love "Ilsa" played by Ingrid Bergman. He watches hard-eyed as she boards the plane that will fly her and her husband "Victor," played by Paul Henreid, out of the movie *Casablanca's* World War II intrigue and into the safety of the free world at a time when real intrigue festered in the real city of Casablanca in Western Africa's Morocco.

Heroic Bogart stands alone in the misty airport as the airplane takes off. As the plane rises to the safety of the air, Conrad Veidt, as the villainous German officer, arrives. Realizing that Ilsa and her husband have flown away he attempts to make a phone call to have the plane turned back. When Veidt pulls a gun so does Rick, whose bullet kills Veidt. With Veidt dead, Claude Rains, as the corrupt French officer, utters the classic line, "Round-up the usual suspects," because he doesn't want Rick to be arrested. As the movie ends, Bogie and Rains, now buddies in crime, walk off together into the airport mist, friendly enemies.

In the movie *Play It Again*, Sam, the last scene also occurs at a misty airport. Woody has just said farewell to the woman he loves, Diane Keaton, who is flying off to her true love. Like Bogie in *Casablanca*, Woody, standing alone on the tarmac, knows that he has made the right choice, allowing the woman he loves to go to the man she loves. At that moment, the ghost of Humphrey Bogart appears beside Woody. The film cuts from a single shot of Woody to a "two-shot" of Woody and Bogie's ghost. Then, just like Bogart and Rains in *Casablanca*, Woody and the ghost walk off together into the airport mist as "The End" credit comes up. It was from the single cut of Woody to the "two-shot" of Woody and Bogie's ghost that the retake was needed to accommodate a dialogue change between Woody and the ghost.

The night before we were to shoot the retake, Paramount's costume department discovered that the tweed sports coat Woody had worn in the scene was three thousand miles away in Woody's New York City bedroom closet. On most films, actor's wardrobe is provided by the production. If the film is modern dress, the costume designer goes shopping for new clothes appropriate for the character. If the wardrobe is for an historical time other than the present or has special requirements, it is rented or made-to-order. Usually, when principal photography is completed, all the clothes purchased or made specifically for the film are stored in the studio's wardrobe department either to be used in a future film or to be available for a retake in the film where it was originally worn. On occasion, especially in a modern-dress film, actors often supply their costumes from their personal wardrobe. That's what Woody had done.

The tweed sports coat Woody had chosen to wear in the final scene had a distinctive weave with an unusual combination of colors. The wardrobe master said there was little possibility of finding a duplicate jacket in Hollywood in time to double for the missing sports coat three thousand miles away.

No problem, the producer said. The company wasn't filming the airport retake until after darkness that evening. With the three-hour time difference between east and west coasts, there was still enough time to fly Woody's sports coat from New York to Hollywood on a commercial jet liner.

So, at 7 a.m. Pacific Time, the producer telephoned Woody's assistant in New York and explained the situation. Arrangements were made. The tweed coat was scheduled to be shipped air freight on a non-stop flight that would arrive at the Los Angeles International Airport no later than 5 p.m. Pacific Time. The production office would have a studio car and driver waiting at the airport to pick up the jacket, then drive it across town to the Burbank Airport where the company would be shooting the retake. The jacket should be in the hands of the wardrobe man no later than 6:30 p.m. That was at least a half hour before we were planning to film the retake.

At 4 p.m. the film crew was arriving at the Burbank Airport, unloading equipment and setting up for the retake on an unused airstrip off to the side of the airport. The set up for the scene wasn't very complicated and would be accomplished quickly, according to Owen Roizman, the cinematographer.

But at 5 p.m. the sports coat was not arriving at the Los Angeles Airport as anticipated. There had been a mix-up and the jacket had not been shipped on the expected jet. It was to arrive on a later plane due at LAX shortly after 7 p.m. our time. If this situation had occurred when we were in the midst of principal photography with many scenes left to shoot, the director, Herb Ross, would have found some other scene in the schedule to shoot while we were waiting. But all that was left was this one retake with Woody wearing that darn tweed jacket!

So the company began improvising. Instead of taking the customary on-location half-hour dinner break, the company was given a leisurely full hour to dine. After dinner, a light drizzle began. It was perfect for the scene, but meant that the cinematographer had to readjust the lighting he had already set up. Great! More legitimate work to fill the waiting time. He ran the scene several more times with the stand-ins. Finally, there just wasn't anymore vamping that could be done. The cinematographer said he was ready. That meant only one thing. Bring in the actors.

As the second assistant director, I went to Woody's dressing room trailer, parked some 200 feet away, to tell Woody we were ready for him on the set. Visiting Woody was his second wife, actress Louise Lasser, known for her TV series *Mary Hartman, Mary Hartman*, a late-night comedic take-off on daytime soap operas.

Woody asked for the tweed sports jacket that still hadn't arrived. When the director is ready for an actor on the set, it's my responsibility as the assistant director to bring that actor to the set. No excuses! Thinking quickly, I said, "Woody, Herb wants to rehearse the scene, run the dialogue a few times, check the camera moves, even without the jacket!"

Woody understood. He shrugged his shoulders and obligingly came along. As we walked the 200 feet from his trailer to the set, to my alarm, a small Piper Cub airplane came taxing towards us. This wasn't supposed to happen. The air traffic controllers had been directing all air and ground traffic away from our work area to avoid the possibility of an accident. Still, the Piper Cub headed straight for Woody and me, its lights shining on us. We walked faster.

The Piper Cub came to a screeching halt five yards away from us. A small door on the passenger side opened. A man I'd never seen before hopped out and ran towards us. He was carrying something on his arm. It was Woody's tweed sports coat. The man reached us and held out the jacket for Woody as though he were a valet dressing his master. Woody slipped his arms into the sleeves, adjusted the fit, walked onto the set, dressed in the correct wardrobe, ready to shoot the retake.

The scene was rehearsed one time. Filmed! All departments signaled thumbs up! Smiling, the director Herb Ross called a wrap!

Amazing! At the precise moment in time that the jacket was finally needed, the precise moment when the company was finally ready to film the retake, it all came together! Woody's tweed jacket arrived! Not a moment too soon! Not a moment too late! Hollywood magic at work!

Many would think that the cost of hiring the Piper Cub to fly the needed jacket from LAX, the Los Angeles airport, to the Burbank airport where we were filming was an extravagant waste of money and typical of Hollywood excesses. But it was far cheaper for the studio to pay for the small plane than having to reschedule the shoot for another day and having to pay the entire crew and actors yet another day's salary.

Many years later in 2003, the Burbank Airport was officially renamed the Bob Hope Airport, in honor of the comedian and movie star, a long-time resident of nearby Toluca Lake. Hope had died at the age of 100 earlier that year. He had stored his personal airplane for many years at the Burbank airfield. The official ceremonies renaming the airport occurred December 17, 2003, the 100th anniversary of the Wright Brothers first flight.

FRED ZINNEMANN
A Man Without Retakes

Sometimes when a retake might be needed the possibility just isn't there. As in the case of director Fred Zinnemann's film version of the play A Man for All Seasons (1966). A costume picture set in the time of England's King Henry the Eighth, *A Man for All Seasons* was the major award winner and critical success of 1966. Adapted by Robert Bolt from his stage play, the film won six Oscars, including Best Picture, Best Director for Fred Zinnemann, Best Adapted Screenplay for Robert Bolt and Best Actor for Paul Scofield.

Zinnemann is not a director that we often celebrate today, although in his four decades as a director he personally won two Oscars, guided 19 actors into nominations for Best Acting, of which six did win, including Gary Cooper for *High Noon* (1952) and Donna Reed and Frank Sinatra for From *Here to Eternity* (1953).

In *A Man for All Seasons*, King Henry the Eighth, played by Robert Shaw, wants to divorce his aging wife, Kathryn of Aragon, who cannot bear him a son. With a divorce, he planned to marry Ann Boleyn. Sir Thomas More, the Lord Chancellor of England, played by Scofield, will not endorse the King's intentions. A devout

A happy Fred Zinnemann on location. LARRY EDMUNDS

Roman Catholic, Sir Thomas knew divorce was not permitted by his religion. Since Henry the Eighth was also a Roman Catholic, Sir Thomas felt Henry must abide by the church's rules. When Henry's appeal to the Pope in Rome is refused and the Pope will not grant the divorce, Henry formed his own church, the Church of England, and gave himself his divorce. A King's prerogative, I guess.

In the movie, at a meeting of an inquiry committee which was more of a trial than just an inquiry, Sir Thomas refuses to sign the Act of Succession. For his refusal he is imprisoned for a year in the Tower of London and then in 1535 beheaded.

Among the raves for the movie many critics referred to Zinnemann's filming of the last major confrontation at the inquiry committee between Sir Thomas and King Henry's court when Sir Thomas will not acquiesce to the King's demands and remains steadfast to the tenets of his religion. The majority of the scene was played in a long shot on Paul Scofield's back. And though we didn't see Scofield's face, the emotion and the power of his performance still shone through.

Zinnemann, who had also won the recognition of his peers by winning the 1967 Directors Guild of America Best Director award for the film, was in attendance for a special screening of the film for the Guild's membership at the Directors Guild Theatre on Sunset Blvd. in Los Angeles in 1967. After the movie was screened, Fred Zinnemann rose from his seat to a burst of appreciative applause from those in the theater. I was among those in the audience applauding him and pleased to be there to hear him speak and answer questions. Someone in the audience complimented Zinnemann on how masterful and daring he had been in filming that final scene on Scofield's back and not using facial close-ups.

Zinnemann smiled and shook his head. He said he would like to set the record straight. It should be no surprise to everyone in the audience that he had indeed filmed the necessary close-ups and other frontal shots of Scofield. It was in his second nature as a seasoned director to do so. But something unexpected had occurred. The film for those shots had been sent to the film laboratory for development, but had been lost somewhere on the way. No one knew where the film was. And he wasn't told of the loss until several days later. By then the set for the trial scene had been torn down.

Paul Scofield's back to the camera as he's interrogated by the King's court. *Photofest*

Zinnemann was not only the film's director but also its producer. He was well aware that the film did not have a big budget and there wouldn't be any more money forthcoming from the studio, Columbia, to rebuild the set or reshoot the sequence. So there were no retakes possible. Had there been the funds, Zinnemann said, he would certainly have scheduled retakes. Instead, Zinnemann made do with what he had.

The film, missing those close-ups and frontal shots, still went on to sweep not only the Academy Awards (1967), but the Golden Globes (1967), and the British Academy Awards (1968), a tribute to the genius of Fred Zinnemann. And as I have mentioned before, for many moviemakers it's a family business. It was so in the Zinnemann family. His son, Tim, became a member of the Directors Guild, working as a highly regarded first assistant director, unit manager, and director.

SOUND
When Movies Became Talkies

"Wait a minute! Wait a minute! You ain't heard nothin' yet! When the audience at the Warner Theatre in New York City on October 6, 1927 heard Al Jolson speak those now famous words and then unloosen his golden tonsils singing the song "Toot, Toot, Tootsie" at the premiere of *The Jazz Singer*, Warner Bros. first part-talking, part singing film, it was electrifying! Jolson said a mouthful. The days of silent films were soon over. Jolson's voice had been recorded on a system called Vitaphone that the Warner brothers owned. It was recorded "live" at the very moment that Jolson spoke and sang on the Warner studio stage back in Hollywood. When *The Jazz Singer* was shown in theaters, it was the projectionist's responsibility to coordinate playing Jolson's voice on a gramophone record supplied by Warner Bros. in tandem with a special film strip of Jolson singing. That was before sound technicians figured out how to add the soundtrack to the actual film that ran through the movie theater projector. Till that innovation was common practice, God help the projectionist if he failed to get the voice on the gramophone record in perfect synchronization with the lip movement of the singer or actor on the screen.

With sound the studio executives had new problems. Some of their biggest silent stars were laughed off the screen because they had a voice quality that didn't match their image. Others had heavy foreign accents that made them unintelligible.

Some of the great silent stars were given time to develop their speaking voices. It wasn't until four years after *The Jazz Singer* that MGM in 1930 would proclaim "Garbo Talks!" in the publicity for MGM's great silent star in her first speaking role in the film version of Eugene O'Neil's *Anna Christie* (1930). Garbo's husky tone with a slight Swedish accent worked perfectly for the role of Anna and her persona. Garbo's fans were thrilled and Garbo was a success in the "talkies."

Independent film producer Samuel Goldwyn had made several audience-pleasing silent films by teaming his two contract players, Hungarian-born Vilma Banky and Englishman Ronald Colman. Though Miss Banky studied hard to rid her voice of its accent, she was not successful. Her career in American films was over. She went back to Europe where her career flourished for awhile. On the other hand, Colman's well-modulated, beautifully pitched voice matched his handsome face and audiences loved him. He would go on to become a major screen presence in American films through the 1950s, appearing in such classics as Frank Capra's *Lost Horizon* (1937), *Random Harvest* (1942) with Greer Garson and winning his Best Actor Oscar for *A Double Life* (1947).

With voice quality and diction now an important part of an actor's on-screen appeal, new stars that had proven themselves in the theater and on the Broadway stage, who had stage voices with good diction, were imported to Hollywood and given minimum contracts with time to prove themselves. Many would become major stars, like Barbara Stanwyck, Bette Davis, Humphrey Bogart, Edward G. Robinson and James Cagney. The lovely would-be starlets who flocked to Hollywood would now have to speak pretty as well as look pretty.

The new technology of sound called for new ideas in producing films. Musicals were the first big innovation. Out in Culver City, Metro-Goldwyn-Mayer put all of its resources into producing a full-scale musical considered the first true movie musical. It was called *The Broadway Melody* and went on to win the 1928/1929 Academy Award as the Best Picture of the Year and to break box office records.

The Academy Awards and The Academy of Motion Picture Arts and Sciences (AMPAS) were the brain child of MGM's Louis B. Mayer. He met with other movie executives in May of 1927 and they agreed with him to establish AMPAS believing the organization might serve to mediate industry problems. Their main objective was public relations believing that the academy would enhance the image of films. Mayer also believed the Academy should present awards to the creative people in the industry. By honoring their achievements, Mayer thought everyone who made pictures, from the above-line stars to the below-line technicians would be motivated to create better films. And better films would appeal to bigger audiences and translate into bigger and better box office. Mayer was a man who wanted quick action! He pushed to have the consideration time for the awards begin as soon as possible. And so they set the first award eligibility period to begin a mere three months from their May meeting, namely August 1, of 1927 and end July 31, 1928. And that pattern of eligibility bridging two years (1927/1928, 1928/1929, etc.) would continue for several more years until they realized it was awkward. That and other kinks in their rules and regulations were examined and revised making the awards a smoother operation. Mayer had MGM's head art director Cedric Gibbons design the gold statuette that is still presented to the winners. Bette Davis claimed she named the statuette "Oscar" because the derriere of the golden guy reminded her of her first husband's derriere.

Today films are eligible for Oscar consideration if they are exhibited for at least one week in Los Angeles in one calendar year, from January 1st to December 31st. *The Broadway Melody* was filmed in 1928 and released February 1, 1929 which made it eligible for the 1928/1929 awards. Catch-up time for the awards was five years later at the Sixth Annual Academy Awards presentation on March 16, 1934, at the Ambassador Hotel in Los Angeles. Films released from August 1, 1932, through December 31, 1933, a full 17 months, were considered eligible for the various awards. *Cavalcade*, not a very popular movie with the Hollywood crowd, won Best Picture in 1934.

The first time films released in the same year were considered for the Academy Awards were those released in the calendar year 1934. They were awarded February 27, 1935, at the Biltmore Hotel in downtown Los Angeles. To everyone's amazement, Columbia Pictures won a clean sweep of the top five awards: Best Picture: *It Happened One Night* (1934); Best Director: Frank Capra; Best Writing, Adaptation: Robert Riskin; Best Actor: Clark Gable, who had been loaned to Columbia by MGM's Louis B. Mayer as a punishment for some offense; and Best Actress Claudette Colbert, who wasn't the first choice for the movie and only accepted the role when Capra agreed to double her salary. Claudette wasn't even planning to attend the award ceremonies. She was about to leave town for a vacation when Columbia learned she might be winning the Oscar. They caught her before she boarded her train at the Union Station in downtown Los Angeles and rushed her to the nearby Biltmore Hotel still wearing her traveling suit to accept the statuette. Although the studio had received Oscar nominations prior to this picture, its "grand slam" success virtually single-handedly lifted Columbia out of the ranks of poverty row.

The Broadway Melody broke all box-office records across the nation when it was released and was followed by many other "all singing, all dancing" movies produced at MGM and the other Hollywood studios. It wasn't its backstage story that attracted moviegoers. The plot was simple: Two sisters who have a singing-dancing vaudeville act are trying for their big break on Broadway. Both are in love with the same song-and-dance man. Silent star Bessie Love made a successful transition to the sound era playing one of the sisters as did beauteous Anita Page who played the other sister. For the male lead MGM had high hopes for tenor Charles King. Already a big star in vaudeville and Broadway musicals, King was cast as the song-and-dance man, the girl's love. But he never caught on with the film going public and eventually returned to Broadway.

What was big box office in *The Broadway Melody* were the extravagant musical production numbers, especially the sequence called "The Wedding of the Painted Doll." It was during the filming of this number that a problem arose that inspired a new technique. It would prove most helpful from then on in the filming of musical numbers. It was a technical innovation that allowed directors to easily expand their coverage of the musical numbers they filmed. Years later, recording and rock stars would adopt the same technique when they appeared on television. Pop stars found the technique advantageous as they sang their hearts out while touring the world in concerts that filled vast stadiums with hordes of fans. The innovative technique was simply called "playback" and it begat what many called, who found it difficult to do, playback's evil sister "lip-synching!"

In 1938 Merrill Pye dated MGM's spectacular dancing star Eleanor Powell. *Photofest*

During my time at MGM, I was fortunate to become friends with the man who in 1928 was an art director on *The Broadway Melody*. Specifically, he designed only the sets and backdrops for the musical production numbers performed on the theatrical stage of the movie's Broadway theater, and that included the set for "The

Wedding of the Painted Doll." And he was in the MGM screening room when he heard the concept that would be called "playback" first discussed. His credit at the end of *The Broadway Melody* reads: "Musical Presentations ... Merrill Pye."

PLAYBACK
and The Boy Wonder

Financier Kirk Kerkorian's purchase of the Metro-Goldwyn-Studios in 1969 from Canadian investor Edgar Bronfman wasn't because he wanted to own a studio that produced movies. His interest was in the real estate the studio stood on and in the history and glory associated with the MGM brand. His aim was to sell off all of MGM and raise money to build a hotel in Las Vegas that reflected the great movies produced in Culver City. He planned to call the hotel the MGM Grand. Immediately, he sold Lot 3. Gone was that Victorian house where Judy Garland peeked out a window and sang about "The Boy Next Door" in *Meet Me in St. Louis*. Also gone was Lot 2 where Gene Kelly had danced to "Singin' in the Rain," sold to builders planning a condominium housing project. Movie lovers the world over flocked to MGM when Kerkorian's hirelings held an 18-day auction in 1970 of MGM's movie memorabilia, props, costumes, scripts, posters, anything of value. Everything that was red hot and could bring in cold cash in Culver City was on the auction block. Then, Ted Turner, the cable mogul, purchased what was left of the MGM studios from Kirkorian. He held on to his purchase for only 74 days, and then sold it back to Kirkorian. Crafty Turner didn't sell everything back. He kept MGM's vast library of films and TV shows dating back to 1924. That was his sole reason for purchasing MGM in the first place. Now that Turner owned them outright, they would become the backbone and the initial main source of programming for Ted's Turner's cable channels, first TNT and then TCM, Turner Classic Movies. The glorious movies that Thalberg and Louis B. Mayer and their successors had produced over the years at MGM were now destined to be seen by an even larger audience then when they were first released in movie theaters. Via Turner's movie channels they would be broadcast day after day, year after year, playing and replaying for an eager cable audience, many who were seeing these movies for the first time, thanks to Turner's clever purchase.

In all these money dealings the moguls and financiers each got what they wanted. Only the people who worked at MGM lost out. The actors and actresses that had called MGM home for years, the talented craftsmen that had created the movie magic had to seek employment elsewhere. If Kirkorian hadn't virtually gutted MGM, Merrill Pye might have continued working there and celebrated 50 years as an art director at Metro. Instead, he left MGM and began to freelance.

The first work credited to Merrill at MGM was "settings" on Greta Garbo's first silent film for MGM, *Torrent* (1926). During his long career he worked on many of the classic films we associate with MGM. When Alfred Hitchcock came to Metro to film *North by Northwest* (1959), starring Cary Grant, Merrill was one of the people on the team of art directors that were Oscar-nominated for Best Art Direction.

I first met Merrill at MGM when I was working on *The Debbie Reynolds Show*, a situation comedy, in the spring of 1969. Whenever I could, I would join him for lunch in the commissary because I was eager to hear his stories about the early days at MGM. Later, in August, 1973, when I was second assistant director to my friend Tom McCrory, the first assistant on *The Partridge Family* filming at the then-Warner-Columbia Ranch in Burbank, I resumed my friendship with Merrill. He was filling in on *The Partridge Family* for a vacationing art director. In a set that was supposed to be a very elegant executive office Merrill had his staff dress the floor with a very large Aubusson carpet. I was struck by how huge it was. Merrill told me there were only two carpets in the world this large in this particular design, a flat weave tapestry which bore the name Aubusson, named for the town in France where this style of carpet making originated in the 18th century. One of the two carpets still in existence was housed in a museum in France. The other was this one from the Warner Bros. Property Department. At the beginning of World War II wealthy people in Europe in need of money to escape from the advancing Nazi war machine gladly sold their personal treasures for a pittance of what they were worth. The first

Mrs. Jack Warner went to Europe and purchased this Aubusson carpet along with other treasures for her home in the Beverly Hills. When she later redecorated and decided she no longer needed the huge Aubusson, she had a ready cash buyer in the Warner Bros. property department, courtesy of her husband Jack.

Merrill wasn't the primary art director on *The Broadway Melody*. That title went to the famous Cedric Gibbons. Gibbons delegated to Merrill the job of designing the stage sets and backdrops for the musical numbers performed on the stage of the Broadway theater in the film. When Merrill first told me the story of how playback came to be, I spoke with many of the sound technicians I worked with at MGM and at Warner Bros. trying to get corroboration for Merrill's tale. One technician said the word that went around was that Douglas Shearer, the head of MGM's sound department in 1928, had the idea for playback, but no one knew for sure. I didn't find anything on the subject when I first researched early sound films, but as I sat down to write this book an answer to my question was right under my nose.

That is the nose of my good friend Marty Kearns, a film buff extraordinaire, former president of Cinecon, a national film society that holds annual film screening conventions in Los Angeles. Give Marty the name of a movie and then challenge him to name the movie stars appearing in that film, chances are he'll name them. When I mentioned to Marty I was trying to verify what Merrill had told me about playback, he pulled a book off his library shelf that I had not read. It was titled *A Song in the Dark*, subtitled *The Birth of the Musical Film*, written by Marty's friend Richard Barrios, published by Oxford University Press in 1995. As the subtitle suggests, the book goes into the history of when silent films gave way to talking pictures and the movie musical was born, a brand-new American art form. Barrios devotes an entire chapter to MGM's *The Broadway Melody*. In it he writes the following: "Technical innovation entered when Thalberg [author's note: Production manager at MGM at the time] decided to retake the Technicolor "Wedding of the Painted Doll" sequence, and sound technician Douglas Shearer suggested they could reuse the recording made the first time, thus giving birth to playback recording."

I don't doubt what Douglas Shearer was involved in playback at MGM. After all, he was the head of the sound department. What makes me doubt the veracity of that statement is how brief it is. To me it sounds like what remains of a longer conversation after having been passed on from person to person to person. It seems to have lost something in transition. When author Richard Barrios was doing his extensive research for his excellent book, I believe that no one involved with the first use of playback was still alive. Barrios didn't have the opportunity to speak directly with someone who actually worked on *The Broadway Melody*. But I did. Merrill Pye. In 1969 when I lunched with Merrill Pye, here's what he told me.

Harry Beaumont was the director of *The Broadway Melody*. To recreate on film how a big Broadway musical number was staged was a new challenge for him as well as others directing their first musical films. Beaumont came up with what he thought was a sensational idea. He believed that when audiences across America viewed "The Wedding of the Painted Doll" production number on their neighborhood movie screen they should feel they were sitting in the best orchestra seats in a Broadway theater and had the best view of the performance on the stage. Beaumont had his director of photography, John Arnold, set up the camera in what they approximated was center orchestra of a Broadway theater, back far enough to frame the full width and height of a theatrical stage's proscenium arch. The shot would include a few rows of patrons, the conductor waving his baton, the musicians playing their instruments in the orchestra pit as well as the full stage with the chorus girls and the stars strutting their stuff. Today we'd call that a long shot...a very long, wide shot! To make the number even more spectacular, it would eventually be filmed in a limited Technicolor process, still in its infancy, and a novelty to moviegoers accustomed to black-and-white silent films. Unfortunately, the color print of the number has been lost or is yet to be rediscovered in someone's attic.

When Beaumont finished shooting the lavish musical number, he screened it for MGM's head of production, Irving Thalberg. Because Thalberg was so successful in the movie business at a very young age he was nicknamed "The Boy Wonder." He was only 21 years old when he was appointed executive in charge of production

Thalberg and his wife Norma Shearer in the early 1930s. She was a star in MGM's silent films who made a successful transition to the talkies. She won the Best Actress Oscar in 1930 for MGM's *The Divorcee* and is remembered for playing the lead in MGM's *The Women* (1939). *Movie Collectibles*

at Universal Pictures and only 24 when Louis B. Mayer enticed him to be head of production at the newly formed MGM. Throughout his short career (he died age 37) Thalberg oversaw every aspect of the films he produced. He had the extraordinary ability to select the right script, choose the right actors, gather the best production staff and turn out a string of quality pictures that were also very profitable. He was one of the first to set up sneak previews to test his films with a real audience. Along the way he fell in love with and married MGM star Norma Shearer.

Because Merrill Pye was responsible for designing the stage scenery for the "Painted Doll" number, he was also at the screening for Thalberg eager to hear Thalberg's reaction to his art work. Merrill told me Beaumont was beaming as the musical number unreeled on the viewing room screen, one long continuous wide, wide shot from the opening downbeat to the very last curtain fall.

Thalberg liked it. He asked to view the other dailies that had the coverage of the sequence, the medium and close-up shots of the leading players as well as the dancers and singers, the additional footage that the film editor would use to build and pace the sequence. Beaumont explained he hadn't filmed anything else. Just the one, long shot! He explained his concept to recreate on film what a live audience would see if they were seated in the best, center orchestra seats of a Broadway theater.

Thalberg didn't buy the idea of just one shot. He wanted the sequence punched up, film-style, with close-ups and medium shots. Thalberg ordered Beaumont to go back and shoot them. Beaumont said that wasn't possible because the orchestra was in the pit of the theater, actually playing live for the singers and dancers as they performed on stage. He explained he was unable to move past the orchestra to get his camera in closer for the shots Thalberg asked for. Merrill Pye told me that Harry Beaumont was so positive that the number was dynamite as he filmed it, that he offered to buy the sequence "as is" from MGM and release it himself as a musical short, musical shorts being very popular at that time.

Thalberg didn't even consider Beaumont's offer. He was thinking. He asked Beaumont to correct him if he was wrong. Hadn't all the music and singing for the number already been recorded? Beaumont said it was. Thalberg had just heard it. It was right up there on the screen in the dailies they had just viewed.

In that case, Thalberg said, have the sound department make a duplicate copy of the musical track. In those days it would have been transferred to a 12-inch gramophone record. Thalberg told Beaumont to dismiss the live orchestra. Then the orchestra pit would be empty and not hinder Beaumont moving his camera in closer, even up on the stage. Instead of a live orchestra playing the music for the close-ups and medium shots, the sound technicians would "play back" the gramophone records over loudspeakers positioned strategically on the set. As the music blared out from the loudspeakers, each performer would hear his or her own singing voice. Keeping time with the "play back" they would mouth the words to the songs, even sing along aloud if they wished, making it appear that they were actually singing the songs for the first time. The two words "play back" were condensed to "playback" in movie lingo. The action of the singers mouthing with their lips the words to the pre-recorded songs became known as "lip-synching" referencing that the mouth movement of the singer must be synchronized exactly to each word of the lyrics of the songs being played back. As for the hoofers and dancing chorines, they would have to repeat their choreographed dance steps for each new angle of the dance number that the director needed and would shoot. To double check himself, Merrill said Thalberg reached for a nearby phone and called the head of his sound department, Canadian-born Douglas Shearer, who happened to be his brother-in-law. Thalberg's idea made sense to Doug Shearer who said he didn't see any reason why it shouldn't work. And it did and the rest is history.

Beaumont did as instructed by Thalberg. Playback speakers were installed and Beaumont moved his camera in closer, up on the stage or wherever required to get the additional coverage. No need to rerecord the musical soundtrack. When the film editors received the new version in color, they cut all the new shots together using the original musical track as their guide. The final edited version of "The Wedding of the Painted Doll" musical number now lived up to Thalberg's vision and production standards.

What happened to Beaumont's original long, wide shot of "The Wedding of the Painted Doll," the shot recorded by the camera in the middle of the theater showing the audience, the orchestra as well as the dancing and singing on stage? It never made the finished film. Just before the number begins the film cuts to a theater program. We, the movie audience, read that the next number is "The Wedding of the Painted Doll"; then, the film cuts to a full shot of the stage with the opening of the number.

The Richard Barrios book confirms for me that playback was created during the filming of *The Broadway Melody* but not as he describes it in his book. Certainly, Douglas Shearer as head of MGM's sound department was consulted and involved with making it work, but the concept didn't originate with him. It was the brainchild of his brother-in-law, Irving Thalberg. As I write this I am certain it is the first written documentation of the how, why, and when playback and its follower, lip-synching, really came to be, as revealed to me by the man who was there, Merrill Pye.

The three stars of *The Broadway Melody* strut their stuff in the Best Picture of 1928/1929. (L. to R.) Anita Page, Charles King and Bessie Love backed up by a row of dancing chorines. Behind them is the very modern skyscraper backdrop designed by Merrill Pye. *Photofest*

Once playback became an every-day tool, singers would pre-record their songs with a full orchestra accompaniment on the recording stage of their studio. Then each singer was given the song just recorded on a vinyl record. At home, they could play the record and practice their song as often as needed to perfect their lip-synching technique. Then when they actually filmed the musical number at their studio, the same pre-recorded track as on their practice record would be played back. The singer, practice perfect, would confidently mouth the song's words as he or she was photographed singing or even singing and dancing to the music. There remain today in many studio archives not only copies of practice records of songs performed and filmed, but practice records of music numbers that were pre-recorded and filmed but for one reason or another were cut from the final film. In addition, there are songs pre-recorded that never even made it to a soundstage, never were played back to be lip-synched before a movie camera. Some day some enterprising musical aficionado will investigate all those pre-records and movie lovers will have a new insight to many musicals of the past and to the talents of the singers who sang on those prerecords.

For many years it was a dirty secret in Hollywood circles and never ever spoken aloud in fear that the movie public would discover the truth, that many of Hollywood's singing stars couldn't sing a note. And what we heard wasn't them singing. That was true of Columbia Pictures gorgeous musical dancing star, Rita Hayworth. Harry Cohn, Rita's gruff boss at Columbia growled that Rita's own singing voice just didn't matched her voluptuous beauty and the sexual image he knew her public expected. To achieve the singing quality he desired playback was the answer. The singing voices of experienced professional vocalists like a Marnie Nixon or an Anita Ellis were auditioned. The vocalist whose voice was deemed the best to enhance Rita's image and seemed natural to her, that vocalist was hired to prerecord Rita's songs for her next movie. Then Rita was given records of all those songs to take home. One by one, in the privacy of her home she would practice lip-synching to the vocalist's recorded voice. When that song was filmed and then shown in theaters throughout the world, the audience seeing Rita in all her singing and dancing glory never doubted that it was she who was actually singing up there on the silver screen. Think of Rita singing "Put the Blame on Mame" in *Gilda* (1946). Hot! Very hot! The perfect blending of voice, movement and beauty!

And if you've ever wondered why a singer in a movie musical isn't out of breath during an arduous song and dance, it's because their singing voice is pre-recorded.

In 1952 for the movie *The Band Wagon* (1953) Cyd Charisse was filmed lip-synching to a song called "Two-Faced Woman" pre-recorded for her by India Adams. The number was cut from the film. Later that year Joan Crawford returned to her home studio of MGM for a film called *Torch Song* (1953) and the unused recording of "Two-Faced Woman" by India Adams was resurrected. It was Crawford's turn to lip-synch to it. To compare the two actresses lip-synching the same song, check the DVD of the film *That's Entertainment 3*.

SOUND: WHEN MOVIES BECAME TALKIES

Here's India Adams surrounded by the two stars that lip-synched to India's pre-recorded version of the song "Two-Faced Woman." To her left, Cyd Charisse with her co-stars Oscar Levant, Jack Buchanan and Fred Astaire in *The Bandwagon*. To her right, Joan Crawford as she appeared in *Torch Song*. Both lip-synched to India's pre-recorded version of the song "Two-Faced Woman." *Movie Collectibles*

Before she became an international star in Hollywood films, Sophia Loren began her movie career in her native country Italy. Sophia has said the role that made the movie world notice her when she was only 19 years old was the part of Aida in a 1953 Italian movie version of Verdi's great opera. Singing opera was not among Sophia's many talents. At first it was announced that the great soprano Renata Tebaldi would herself sing and act Aida in the movie, but Tebaldi reconsidered and dropped out. The part was next offered to voluptuous Gina Lollobrigida with the announcement that Aida's arias would be from recordings of *Aida* by Tebaldi. Lollobrigida would be lip-synching to playbacks of Tebaldi's recordings. But that didn't sit well with Lollobrigida. According to Sophia, Lollobrigida said she didn't want to be "dubbed" which was the wrong terminology for the process. She should have said she didn't want to "lip-synch."

I suspect "dubbing" was on the lovely Lollobrigida's mind because in those days Italian films didn't record the scripted dialogue spoken by the actors. The reason? Many of the actors weren't Italian or weren't fluent in Italian. After all the filming was completed, in post-production in a sound recording studio, Lollobrigida and the other Italian speaking actors would dub in their own dialogue trying to match their words to their on-screen lip movement. Italian voice actors were hired to dub in the lines for those actors not fluent in Italian.

Sophia gladly took the role of the beautiful Ethiopian princess and turned in an exceptional performance. Her lips did not betray she was lip-synching to Tebaldi's vocals.

Another technique used to bolster a singing performance that has its roots in playback was the blending of two pre-recorded voices. That's what the producers decided was necessary for some of the songs that Rosalind Russell as Mama Rose sang in the Warner Bros. film *Gypsy* (1962). Although Rosalind had won a Tony award in 1953 as Best Actress on Broadway for her singing and acting in the musical *Wonderful Town*, ten years later her voice was deemed not strong enough for the score of *Gypsy*. So the producers had Lisa Kirk, a Broadway and cabaret musical star, record many of the songs. The technicians in the sound department carefully blended Rosalind's pre-recorded voice with that of Lisa's for the best musical presentation. And those are the vocals we hear when we see Rosalind lip-synching Mama Rose's songs in *Gypsy*.

Once the dirty secret was out that in a particular movie musical the leading lady wasn't warbling her songs but was lip-synching to a pre-record by some unknown singer especially chosen for her vocal talents, the public insisted on knowing who the unknown was. The studios obliged and released that singer's name. On the other hand, if a movie star who was not known as a singer actually did sing her songs in her film, to give credit where credit was due, as the final end credits rolled by the truth was told. Such was the case in 2011 in the movie *My Week with Marilyn* based on the true story of a real-life affair Marilyn Monroe had in England with a young Englishman seven years her junior. The affair occurred while she was filming *The Prince and the Showgirl* (1957) with Laurence Olivier directing and playing the part of the Prince. To belie any rumors to the contrary and to let the world know that Michelle Williams cast as Marilyn did her own singing in the movie; the final credit scroll read "Michelle Williams' Songs Sung by Michelle Williams." In both her singing and acting in the film, Michelle's performance was charismatic. Some thought she was actually channeling the late Miss Monroe.

If there had not been lip-synching would music lovers the world over been the fans of Milli Vanilli, the pop dance music group who won a Grammy as Best New Artist in 1990? At a live MTV concert in Connecticut as the duo sang "Girl You Know It's True" the record jammed and kept repeating the same lyric over and over again! As a result of this incident the two singers, Fab Morvan and Rob Pilatus, were revealed not to be singing live but to a prerecording. Then it was revealed they weren't even singing to their own prerecorded voices, but were the front men for a pop/dance project using three or four other vocalists prerecorded by their music company. The concert audience didn't seem to care. But Milli Vanilli's career was kaput. Their Grammy was revoked!

Luciano Pavarotti twice refused to sing "Nessun Dorma" at the 2006 Winter Olympics opening ceremonies in Italy because the winter air was too cold for his voice. But the Olympic Committee persuaded him to pre-record and everyone, Pavarotti, the orchestra, and the conductor performed, faking it to the pre-recorded aria.

Most singers on Dick Clark's *American Bandstand* TV show in the 1960s lip-synched to their own hit records. That was what their teenage audience was familiar with and wanted to hear. What about singers riding and performing on floats in the annual live TV broadcast of Macy's Thanksgiving Day Parade? Those performers are either lip-synching to their pre-recorded musical arrangement of their song or if they are singing "live" it's to a pre-recorded musical background. There's no place in or on their floats to house or hide the orchestra or band playing the music. Sometimes when musicians are seen performing on the float, they too are doing it to their own prerecording.

It is said that in the *Motown 25: Yesterday, Today, Tomorrow* (1983) television special celebrating the record company's 25th anniversary that the late Michael Jackson lip-synched to his hit song *Billie Jean* as he made his spectacular moves and it didn't lessen the impact of his performance or his audience's appreciation.

Over the years performers like Brittany Spears, George Michael, Queen and Faith Hill have been known to use playback when their voices weren't in top form. With the high-energy staging of their concerts and the arduous physical demands on them as performers in those shows, rather than strain their voices or give a bad performance, they gratefully rely on a pre-recorded vocal track. Audiences who have paid high prices for their concert tickets expect to hear and see a good show and get their money's worth. Playback helps the performers do just that. All due to the Boy Wonder, Irving Thalberg!

Just as Jolson's first words and song in *The Jazz Singer* were recorded live, over the years that still occasionally occurs in a movie. In 1967, Barbra Streisand asked her director William Wyler if rather than pre-recording the emotional song that closes *Funny Girl*, she could sing it live. The song was "My Man." Wyler said "Yes" and Streisand's live performance is a highlight of the film.

In 1975, Peter Bogdanovich, wanting to showcase his girlfriend Cybil Shepherd, produced, directed and wrote a musical movie called *At Long Last Love*. All the songs in the film were by Cole Porter as was the title song. This was the first movie musical since the early 1930s to record "live" all of its musical numbers rather than having the singers lip-synch to a pre-recorded score. There was no technical necessity to do it "live." It was just a choice made by Bogdanovich. Perhaps he thought by singing the songs "live" his two leading players, Cybil Shepherd and co-star Burt Reynolds, not known for their singing ability, would give the songs a deeper, more emotional, heartfelt reading. Unfortunately, that didn't happen. Critics attacked Bogdanovich for what they considered an ill-advised stunt. In attempting to record "live" the cost of the film went way over its budget. Other players in the film, such as Madeline Kahn and Eileen Brennan, were proficient singers who had sung in films and on Broadway, but still the film did not ignite the viewing public and it closed quickly. Perhaps prerecord, playback and lip-synching might have saved the film!

Shame, a 2011 film about sexual addiction, was far from a musical. It starred Michael Fassbender and Carey Mulligan and was directed by Englishman Steve McQueen. In the film, Carey plays a small-time nightclub singer. She sings one song in the film; the Fred Ebb-John Kander hit "New York, New York," the signature song of Liza Minnelli. Unlike Liza, who is known for her charismatic, very upbeat version of the song, Carey sings it very slowly, very quietly, very bluesy. I saw the film at the Arc Light Cinema in Sherman Oaks, California, at a special screening for the *Los Angeles Times* "The Envelope" project. As I listened to Carey singing the song I had the feeling that she was actually singing it "live." There was immediacy to it, naturalness. In a Q. & A. after the screening the director was asked about Carey's song. He said that he had prerecorded Carey singing the song and used the prerecord in the establishing shot as she began singing. The next time the director cut to her singing it was in a very, very tight head shot, a close-up of just her face, chin to hair. When the camera rolled, instead of just mouthing the lyrics, Carey began singing the song aloud, slow and bluesy and in character. Surprised, the director asked Carey if she was up to singing it live instead of lip-synching to the prerecord. She said "yes" and that's what we hear, a live performance. And as Carey sings the song, its lyrics become a metaphor for her character's hopes and desires. Though she sings "If I can make it there, I can make it anywhere," the heartbreak in her voice underscores that she knows she'll never make it in the big time! It was stunning! Carey's singing performance was as emotionally thrilling for me as Al Jolson's performance in *The Jazz Singer* must have been for the audiences of his day.

When it was announced that Madonna and company would be the star attraction at the 46th Annual Super Bowl Halftime show on a Sunday in February, 2012, there was as much excitement and anticipation about seeing her perform as there was seeing the New England Patriots and the New York Giants battle for the football championship. Just as the Giants took their time in winning the game and title, Madonna paced her self brilliantly, bedecked in gold and leather, bringing to the show her own special pop flair, turning cartwheels, singing her signature songs as well as introducing a new song, dancing and strutting with a hundred or so dancers and athletes, all exuding high energy. The not-so-secret secret was that Madonna was lip-synching to her songs as her pre-recorded musical performance was played back. Madonna is a fabulous entertainer in excellent physical shape and health. But she is human and performing so strenuously she certainly would have run out of breath, been wheezing and gasping for air had she been singing live. For the thousands of fans in the stadium and those viewing it at home on TV, it was the outstanding spectacle that mattered. The costumes, the choreography and seeing 53 year old Madonna at the top of her game. For Madonna, playback was the natural answer! Does Madonna, who is a member of the Directors Guild of America, and a movie director herself, even know that the playback she relied on during her Halftime show was invented for the movies by "The Boy Wonder" when the first musical movie was being made? Thank you, Irving Thalberg! Thank you, Merrill Pye!

LOOPING

"Looping" is the term that describes the process used to correct recorded sound that is defective or inaudible. It takes its name originally from the "loop" of film that contains the bad or unintelligible sound. It could be just one word, one line or an entire scene with dialogue between two or more characters. For the looping session, the technicians make a working print of just the visual section with the questionable sound. The working print is then spliced end to end, forming a continuous loop of film. The loop is then threaded on a projector to be played and replayed as often as needed, until the new dialogue is successfully re-recorded.

When the actor or actors involved are called onto the looping stage, the process works this way: The actor wears earphones and stands before a microphone. In front of him or her is a movie screen on which the looped film with the scene to be corrected is projected. The actor also has a script with the correct dialogue in front of him. When looping begins, the actor hears a voice in the earphones reading the correct word or line or dialogue. Then there is a "get ready" beep and up comes the piece of film. The actor will try to match his or her speech and feeling to the scene on the screen. The actor, having heard the new line, repeats the line in synchronization with his image on the screen. Sometimes the correction is made in one take. Other times it may take several tries before the looping director is satisfied the synchronization and appropriate feeling is achieved.

Looping is an art, no question about it. Some actors love it. Some detest it. Here are two actresses with different reactions to looping. Both occurred when they were performing on *Rod Serling's Night Gallery* television series being filmed at Universal

Studios in 1969. I enjoyed working on the show as a second assistant director.

KIM STANLEY

Kim Stanley, the Tony Award-winning Broadway actress, was in mortal fear of looping. "It isn't acting," she said to me. Although Kim was seen frequently on television screens during the "Golden Days" of live TV drama in the 1950s in New York City and on Broadway in dramatic plays, she rarely did feature films. Her most famous film role was in *The Goddess* (1958), in which she played an ambitious small-town girl who becomes a Marilyn Monroe-like movie star. She also played Pancho Barnes, pioneer woman aviator and stunt pilot, in *The Right Stuff* (1983), the story of the original US Mercury 7 astronauts and their macho, seat-of-the-pants approach to the space program.

I had met and performed with Kim Stanley when I attended the University of Michigan. Every spring the University sponsored four weeks of professional Broadway plays in a season called The Ann Arbor Theater Festival. Kim Stanley and Lillian Gish were brought to Ann Arbor in May of 1954 to perform in the play *A Trip to Bountiful* with Miss Gish reprising her Broadway role. As a student I volunteered to perform as an "extra" in the play. I appeared in the bus station sequence when Miss Gish was in line to buy her bus ticket for her trip to the town of Bountiful. I was stationed stage left, reading a newspaper, a man waiting for his bus. Kim Stanley, playing Miss Gish's daughter-in-law, rushes into the bus station angry, hell bent on diverting Miss Gish from her trip. As Kim entered, I looked up from my newspaper and looked directly at her. Kim saw me looking at her and returned my look. I felt she really saw me standing there, a man in the bus station eyeing her as a woman. Each time we rehearsed the scene that day, I gave her my look. Each time she reacted and acknowledged me with a glance.

For some reason, whether I was too tall, a distraction, or just a bad actor, at the next day's rehearsal I was recast from being a man waiting for a bus standing stage left to a man selling newspapers in the bus station kiosk, stage right. Now when Kim entered the scene she passed right by the kiosk. I don't think she even noticed me in the kiosk when she made her entrance. She was moving fast, anxious to confront her mother-in-law, Lillian Gish.

After playing her very high-strung scene she had to exit the bus station, reversing herself and passing by me in the kiosk. Frankly, I'm not sure how many people in the audience even knew that I or someone was in the kiosk.

I decided to try a little experiment. If I stared hard enough at Kim as she made her exit, would she actually see me as she had before when I was standing on the other side of the stage as a man reading a newspaper? Would she do the same now, as she exited?

At every performance from that rehearsal on, each time she walked by I stared as hard as I could at her, looking directly into her face. Wonder of wonders! From then on, each time she passed by, whether it was rehearsal or performance, she did react to my look. Not as Kim Stanley, but as her character, a southern woman embarrassed that she had just created a "scene" in public. Only I could see that look since her back was to the audience and as I said, she was moving fast.

For me, here was a great actress using every ounce of sensitivity she possessed to create her character. It was beyond just acting. It was Kim Stanley creating her reality in her performance. No wonder she has been called the "female Brando."

In 1971, Kim was contracted to act in "The Fear of Spiders" episode of *Rod Serling's Night Gallery*, the *Twilight Zone*-like television show that had been begun by Rod Serling and was now filmed and produced at Universal Studios. The director of this segment was actor John Astin, who most people remember as Gomez, the husband to Carolyn Jones' Morticia, in the 1960s TV series *The Addams Family*. Directing this episode of *Rod Serling's Night Gallery* was Astin's first opportunity to direct a major TV show. Again, I was the second assistant director on the show.

Kim Stanley was a very talented actress, but often a very difficult one. A student of Lee Strasberg's Method school of acting, she was very into herself and her method. In one master shot for the episode there were lit candles on a table. When the director turned the camera in the reverse direction to get a close-up shot of

Kim, she insisted the candles be lit, even though they weren't in the shot, just because they were still in her eye line.

The next day word came down from the sound department that Miss Stanley was needed for looping for the candle scene we had shot the previous day. Per Universal policy, all looping must be accomplished while the actor or actress was still on salary. If they had to be called back at some later date to loop, they would have to be paid another day's salary. Not desirable from the standpoint of the money boys in Universal's headquarters building, affectionately called "The Black Tower" because it was sheathed in black glass.

When I told Kim that she was needed

The very talented Kim Stanley.
LARRY EDMUNDS

for looping, she wasn't pleased. To ease her distress, I said I would escort her to the looping stage in the sound department. Once there, she pleaded with me to stay with her. She just wasn't comfortable parroting lines back to the screen. Looping wasn't acting as far as Kim Stanley was concerned.

Luck was with Kim that day. As soon as I saw the piece of film that required looping, I knew it wasn't necessary. After John Astin had finished filming the candle scene, he had one more shot on his shot list, an overhead trick shot using a wild camera. The wild camera had been rigged to the top of the set with its lens angled downward to achieve a special overhead shot director Astin wanted. A wild camera is one that usually makes a loud, whirring noise because there's no casing around the camera to mute the noise made as the gears turn and the film rolls through the camera. It is the angle of the shot that is important, not the sound or dialogue in the scene.

With the wild camera rolling overhead, Kim and her fellow actor, Patrick O'Neal, ran the scene once again and did recite their lines. That night, when the sound department checked the soundtrack from the wild camera, the technicians couldn't hear any clear dialogue, just the whirring of the camera obliterating whatever words the actors were saying. To them that meant looping.

Having been on the set when that scene was shot the previous day, I knew that all the dialogue for the scene was already recorded in the master shots and close-ups that had been filmed prior to the overhead wild shot. It would be that sound, if needed, which would be laid onto the footage filmed by the wild camera.

I asked Miss Stanley to wait in the sound department while I went back to the *Night Gallery* stage and explained the problem with the wild camera to John Astin, adding that Kim Stanley was petrified of looping. John called the looping department and the looping session was cancelled. Kim Stanley was saved from what she felt was a fate worse than death.

ZSA ZSA GABOR

For Zsa Zsa, looping was a snap. Zsa Zsa also did a TV episode of *Rod Serling's Night Gallery* that same season and she, too, was required to do some looping. To my way of thinking, looping was close to her acting technique. During the filming of her segment, whenever she had a line to say, she would ask the script supervisor, "Dahlink, vat do I say now?" The script supervisor would read Zsa

SOUND: WHEN MOVIES BECAME TALKIES

Zsa Zsa in a *Rod Serling's Night Gallery* episode. *Movie Collectibles*

Zsa the line, she would repeat it to herself, and then when the camera was turning and the director called "action," she repeated it again beautifully in her own inimitable acting style.

So when Zsa Zsa was called onto the looping stage she was in her element. With the headphones on, she was fed the line and then she repeated it to her image on the screen. She looped all her lines in one take, and then left the looping stage all smiles, thanking all the "dahlinks."

A year later, I was working on a feature film for MGM called *Every Little Crook and Nanny* (1972), a comedy starring Lynn Redgrave as the Nanny to gangster Victor Mature's ten-year-old son. The company was at the Los Angeles International Airport filming late in the evening. During a lull in the shooting, I spotted Zsa Zsa in a crowd of passengers just arriving in Los Angeles.

Delighted to see Zsa Zsa, I thought I'd be friendly and greet her. I wasn't sure that she would remember me from the *Night Gallery* TV episode, but I'd say hello anyway. To my surprise, Zsa Zsa thought I was there to meet her and said, "Dahlink, Ve vould have called you, but didn't know your phone number."

I explained to her that I was at the airport working, shooting a movie for MGM. There were two men arriving with Zsa Zsa. I recognized one of them, a distinguished gentleman with white hair. He was Frank Stanton, formerly the President of the Columbia Broadcasting System. Stanton asked me what the name of the movie was. "Every Little Crook and Nanny," I responded, "directed by Cy Howard."

When Stanton heard it was Cy Howard, he was elated. He knew Cy Howard from CBS radio days when Howard had written and produced *My Friend Irma* and *Life With Luigi* for CBS radio and then later, when both shows made a successful transition to CBS television. Stanton turned to Zsa Zsa and said, "I'd like to say hello to Cy."

Zsa Zsa replied, "Not me. I dated him vonce."

Stanton did go speak with Cy Howard.

Zsa Zsa didn't. She went her way.

DUBBING

Dubbing isn't to be confused with "looping." Looping uses the voice of the actor whose face and form appears on the screen. "Dubbing" uses the voice of a different actor. The most common form of dubbing is when producers want to release a foreign-language film, say Italian, in an English-speaking country. An English dialogue script is written. Actors are hired whose voice quality seems to fit the faces on the screen and the characters being played as well as their facility with the dubbing process. In a similar set up as in looping, the sections of film to be dubbed are screened for the actors and then their English dialogue is dubbed over the Italian faces on the screen. Very often when the quality of the dubbing is poor, the audience viewing the film can tell it's dubbed because the quality or sound of the voice coming out of the face on the screen doesn't quite match the look or size of the actor on the screen. Or more often in a bad job of dubbing, the sound has stopped and the lips are still moving or vice versa.

In 1991, Universal Studios' epic *Spartacus* (1960) was restored and re-released. In the restoration, it was decided to include a scene with Laurence Olivier and Tony Curtis that had been cut from the original release because of the scene's homoerotic overtones which now would not be objectionable. The soundtrack for the scene was missing, but there was a copy of the script. Tony Curtis was still available to record his voice. Sir Laurence Olivier had passed away. According to Olivier's widow, actress Joan Plowright, British actor Anthony Hopkins of *Silence of the Lambs* fame did the best vocal impersonation of her late husband. On the recommendation of Olivier's widow, Universal hired Hopkins to dub in Olivier's lines. No one knew the difference, according to my friend, the late Nick Singer, who was working in the sound department at the time.

Another very active use of dubbing occurs in many animated and now 3-D animated films such as *Shrek* (2001) and *Kung Fu Panda* (2008). Top "A List" movie stars are delighted to add their voices to the very popular animated movies. Shrek was the highest-grossing animated film since Disney's *Snow White and the Seven Dwarfs* (1937). It led to three equally as successful sequels. Canadian-born comedian Mike Myers played Shrek in all four films. Also repeating their roles in the sequels were Cameron Diaz as the very beautiful Princess Fiona who falls in love with Shrek and comedian Eddie Murphy as Shrek's sidekick, "Donkey." The first *Shrek* won an Academy Award Oscar in 2002 as Best Animated Feature. For an animated film to be considered for Best Animated Film, the Academy of Motion Picture Arts and Sciences states that a significant number of the characters in the film must be animated and that at least 75% of the film's running time be in animation. That applied to *Shrek*.

Joining the cast of *Shrek 2* (2004) was Spanish actor Antonio Banderas playing the fairy tale character Puss in Boots. The swashbuckling, romantic character was so popular he was written in to the two sequels that followed and then had his own spin-off as the star of his own animated film called *Puss in Boots* (2011) nominated for a 2012 Oscar.

In the *Kung Fu Panda* films comic actor Jack Black played the hero, "Po," beauteous Angelina Jolie voiced "Tigress," action star Jackie Chan provided the voice of "Monkey," and Academy Award Best Actor for *Rain Man* (1988), Dustin Hoffman, voiced the wise "Shifi."

To dub a foreign movie, the scene of the filmed actors speaking their lines in a foreign tongue is projected without sound on a screen. Then the actor or actors hired to dub the new dialogue for the scene stand at microphones in front of the screen, looking at the projected film. They are holding the script with the new dialogue. On cue they recite the new dialogue, attempting to synchronize their words to the mouth movement of the actors on screen. The director overseeing the dubbing is there to help the actors achieve synchronization and to perform the emotion or attitude needed for the scene. When the new script to be dubbed is written, a prerequisite for the writer is to write new dialogue in the exact number of words that come out of the mouths of the actors on the film. A perfect dubbing session would make the dub seem seamless, the spoken words and mouth movements matching perfectly.

For animated films, the actor playing each character first records the written lines. Then the animators make the cartoon characters mouth movements coincide with the prerecorded dialogue. Before the animated film is completed there is always time to make last-minute adjustments, animated retakes if you will.

Would you believe that dubbing is also vital in musical films to make sure we hear every click-clack, every tap-tap-tap that a Fred Astaire or a Gene Kelly makes as they entertain us with their dancing agility on the big screen? If when first filmed the taps made by a dancer's tap shoes aren't crisp and clear or didn't record properly, then that dancer will redo the dance steps in the dubbing studio on a surface similar to the floor where those taps were originally filmed. A microphone is placed at foot level to record the new taps. If the dance star is unavailable, then a professional dancer who has learned the routine will be hired to tap-in for the unavailable star and match tap-tap-tap for the tap-tap-tap of the dancer dancing on the film as it is seen on the dubbing room's movie screen. Thalberg probably never envisioned this!

ACTORS, ACTORS EVERYWHERE

What is it about the actors and actresses we see on the movie screen that fascinates us so? For the men is it only their chiseled good looks or in the case of the women only their beauty and voluptuousness? Periodically, there are newspaper stories of stalkers so enraptured with the on-screen persona of an actor or actress that they are unable to distinguish between the on-screen fictional character and the off-screen real person. Many times this leads to tragedy in real life for the performer. Beyond the physical charms that an actor or actress possesses, that may loom large in our individual fantasies, it's their humanity and the vulnerability captured on film that makes for a successful performance.

It is with their humanity we in the audience identify and with their vulnerability we empathize. We recognize ourselves in the situations the actors portray on screen. That was evident when I was working on *Bewitched* in 1966, the TV series starring Elizabeth Montgomery playing a witch who marries a mortal man. Each episode revolved around the conflicts that might arise in such an unusual marriage. One of those conflicts was the on-going animosity between the mother-in-law and her son-in-law. With gifted actors like Dick York playing the mortal son-in-law and the great dramatic actress Agnes Moorehead as the meddling mother-in-law witch, the comedy had a very human face that actors could play and viewers identify with.

But not every actor or actress has "human moments" written for their character to play. In *Bewitched* octogenarian Marion Lorne portrayed Elizabeth Montgomery's dithering, befuddled Aunt Clara who because of her advanced age is losing her magical powers and forever causing mix-ups.

Marion Lorne as Aunt Clara unexpectedly finds her magic powers have landed her in a huge metal drum to the disapproval of her niece Samantha played by Elizabeth Montgomery in *Bewitched*. *Photofest*.

Marion was born in Pennsylvania and made her New York stage acting debut as an ingénue in 1905. She had a flourishing career in both America and Great Britain. While performing in London she married Englishman Walter Hackett, a playwright. Together, they were manager/owners of their own theater, the Whitehall, where Marion performed in plays written especially for her by her playwright husband.

Alfred Hitchcock, when asked, said Marion Lorne was "an institution" in London's theatrical world even though she was born in America. Hitchcock cast Marion in her first feature film in *Strangers on a Train* (1951). Marion played a wealthy but addled matron, the mother of Robert Walker, who was the film's psychotic killer.

One day in the kitchen set of *Bewitched*, Marion and Elizabeth Montgomery had a very short scene together. Not more than a page of script. The scene was about a niece's concern for her beloved aunt who because of her advancing age is not mentally the woman she once was. Much of the comedy surrounding the character of

Aunt Clara on *Bewitched* was based on just that, the fact that she was always making mistakes when she cast one of her witches' spells. For Marion, the concerns expressed by Elizabeth in the scene about the character's failing abilities probably was just as true for Marion off screen as it was for her character on screen since she was in her 80s and had moments of forgetfulness. As I stood and watched the scene being performed, I was moved by her performance. It seemed a very real, very human, moment for Marion. Afterwards, I went up to Marion and complimented her on the scene. With her great big eyes suddenly saddened, she said to me, "I don't get those opportunities very much anymore." She, of course, was referring to a scene scripted to show her human side, rather than the wide-eyed, dithering, addled old lady she played for comedy. The following year, 1968, Marion died. That same year she received a posthumous Emmy Award from the National Television Academy of Arts and Sciences for Best Supporting Actress in a Comedy. Elizabeth Montgomery accepted for her.

Magic in a sitcom like *Bewitched* was usually a trick in the editing of the film. If Agnes Moorehead as Endora, Elizabeth's witch mother, wanted to magically disappear she'd say some magic words, make a gesture and the cameraman would film her action then lock the camera off so that the background wouldn't change. Agnes would physically step out of the scene and the cameraman would roll a few feet of film of the same setting but without Agnes. In the editing room by cutting the two pieces of film together with the identical, unchanged background, it would appear that Agnes magically disappeared from the scene. If the next scene was to show where Agnes reappeared, the filming would be in reverse. First a few feet of film showing the new setting without Agnes in it. Then the camera is locked off. When Agnes steps into the new setting, the cameraman rolls film and the new scene is played with Agnes magically appearing out of nowhere. Again, the editing makes the magic work!

This was a film trick that was discovered accidentally in 1896 by Frenchman Georges Méliés, acknowledged as one of the first and most innovative of the early filmmakers. While filming a simple street scene in Paris his camera jammed. Later, when he developed the jammed strip of film, he discovered that as he had played with the camera, trying to get it to work, stopping and starting it, attempting to eliminate the jam, the new scenes filmed were missing elements that were in the scene just a few minutes before. Méliés, a man of many interests, was captivated by the art of conjuring and appeared himself on stage performing as a magician. Because of the accidental jamming, he realized that he could manipulate and distort time and space simply by stopping and starting his camera and removing or adding elements to the scenes he was filming. In 2011, Academy Award-winning director Martin Scorsese produced and directed *Hugo*, a 3-D film in which he paid homage to Méliés and showed several of Méliés early works, including the delightful *A Trip to the Moon* (1902) in which a group of astronomers go on a voyage to the Moon in a rocket ship that lands smack in the left eye of the Man-in-the-Moon.

In movies today, directors create their magic using many of the old tricks, but have a new trick at their command thanks to computer technology known as Computer Generated Images (CGI). With CGI, filmmakers now can imbue their films with amazing scenes of fantasy and instill their non-human figures with movement and human qualities. Perhaps the best example of that is in James Cameron's 3-D mega film *Avatar* (2009). In that film the hero played by Sam Worthington is sent into an alien world. Once there he assumes the physical look of the people of that world. That look is the results of CGI. The actor as he performs is outfitted with a series of electrodes attached to his face and body to monitor his physical acting movements or expressions. That information is sent to a computer and stored as digital computer information. Then the computer artist translates those facial and physical action inputs into the facial and physical action of the imaginary visual CGI character created for Worthington. The result in *Avatar* is a fantasy figure, the blue, elongated alien image that we see on the movie screen.

Before CGI technology became a useful tool for moviemakers to create otherworldly characters or an animal with human qualities, they hired an actor and dressed him in a costume befitting the character and created a face or head mask with special makeup. That's what they did in the original *Planet of the Apes* (1968), based on Pierre Boulle's book published in 1963, which 20th Century-Fox produced and Franklin Schaffner directed.

In that film actors Kim Hunter and Roddy McDowall played talking, human-like apes for which they wore ape costumes and heavy ape makeup and head gear. The most recent film in the series, *Rise of the Planet of the Apes* (2011), is a prequel, telling what occurred before the first movie's story. A young scientist is developing a drug to cure Alzheimer's disease and is using live apes as test animals. The drug was given to a female ape when she was pregnant. When her baby ape was born the scientist soon realizes that the new born he names Caesar, inherited the power of the drugs given to his mother during her pregnancy. The scientist realizes that a side effect of the experimental drug increases brain power. Though the drugs hadn't been administered to him directly, it soon becomes apparent that Caesar seems to understand everything in the world about him as if he were human. He only lacks the ability to expressing himself verbally, to talk. When he matures, he can communicate with his fellow apes and leads them in a revolt against the human world.

Englishman Rupert Wyatt, who directed *Rise of the Planet of the Apes*, has said that although the human actors in the previous ape movies gave excellent performances, their physical appearances were not accurate for the simian world. Apes have long torsos and short legs. In comparison, humans have short torsos and long legs. Whereas apes with their long arms can touch the floor easily, humans with their shorter arms have much more difficult touching the floor. CGI creates an ape so realistic, so true to its species, that we don't doubt he actually exists in our world.

Rise of the Planet of the Apes takes computer-generated films out of the age of green screen backgrounds. In green screen technology, the actor would be filmed doing his or her action in front of a large backdrop curtain colored green, stretched taut from floor to ceiling.

During the winter of 1967, I worked as the second assistant director on Screen Gems' *The Flying Nun* starring Sally Field. To give the illusion that Sally was actually flying, beneath her habit she wore a hidden harness attached to a crane which hoisted her into the air with only the green curtain scrim behind her. Then a wind machine was turned on blowing at her, giving movement to her nun's habit. With her body in a prone position and her arms waving like the wings of a bird in flight, who would not believe this was, indeed, a nun in flight! Then in post-production the flying Sally on film would be superimposed over a real aerial view on film. By combining the two shots, the aerial view replaces the green of the green curtain, but does not cover up Sally. The petite actress appears to be actually flying high in the sky.

Now with actors wearing motion-capture suits or leotards and helmets with electrodes attached to their faces and bodies, sending digital signals to a computer, the actor can move about performing the real action scripted whether on a stage set or in an actual outdoor locale. No green screen is needed! With the digital information collected from the motion-capture suits transferred to the computer image of the ape created by the visual effects or computer operator, a very life-like Caesar the ape appears in the film *Rise of the Planet of the Apes*. Once an actor's movement is recorded, the visual effects artists begin their digital artistry on the image, turning the human actor into the ape or whatever character the script calls for. The CGI ape, through the wonder of technology, reflects a high degree of emotional resonance and humanity that the viewing audience can relate to. We look into the ape's eyes and he seems alive! We sense there is intelligence in there! "Digitized Acting" is the term used to describe a human actor's portrayal of non-human or fantasy creatures.

The human qualities captured and then reproduced in the movements and attitudes of Caesar the CGI ape, as in the latest ape movie, is a reflection of the very unique acting of an English actor named Andrew Serkis who specializes in non-human roles. He is the Gollum in *The Lord of the Rings* (2001) and the great gorilla King Kong in the recent remake of that film in 2005. Serkis spends time at a zoo observing the real animals he is to portray so when he dons the motion-capture outfit, he is ready to give his best performance as that animal, giving the animal an interior life all the while moving as the animal would in real life. The challenge for these actors is to have the movie audience understand that the emotionality of the non-human character on screen is not provided by the animators, but by the actor in the motion-capture outfit. As more films are made using this CGI technique there is a greater emphasis on facial performance as opposed to just bodily movement. There is also growing support to allow such performances to be considered for Best Acting Oscars when Academy Award time rolls around. Time will tell!

No matter how talented they are actors and actresses are still real human beings dealing with real situations in their daily lives, whether at home, at the studio or on location. I observed many of them in their off-screen moments when I was working with them as their assistant director. What one person might think was normal; another might say was just crazy. But all is forgiven when we are moved to laughter or tears by their wonderful on-screen performances.

BARBARA HERSHEY
and Her Stunt Man

Where have I seen this before? That was my feeling as I viewed director Richard Rush's wonderful movie *The Stunt Man* (1980), a black comedy about a production company in the midst of filming a movie. It starred Peter O'Toole as a brilliant director, Barbara Hershey as the actress starring in the movie-within-the-movie, and Steven Railsback who takes a job as a stuntman with the movie company but in reality is a fugitive hiding out from the cops, using his work in the film as his cover. In one of the subplots, the characters that Railsback and Hershey play are attracted to one another and have an affair. The movie company is on location, and just as a real movie company on location, everyone is housed in a local motel. In the film, when O'Toole unexpectedly wants Railsback on the set to do a stunt, the assistant director character in the film has to locate him quickly. Since Railsback's infatuation with Hershey was common gossip among the crew in the script, the assistant director knew exactly where to find Railsback. He telephones Barbara Hershey's motel room.

In that scene, she and Railsback are in her bed. The phone rings. Hershey answers it and gives the phone to Railsback. After hanging up the phone, Railsback makes a hasty departure heading for the movie set, wondering how the hell the assistant director knew where to find him.

Déjà-vu! In the spring of 1968 I was the second assistant director

David Carradine as a cruel rancher in *Heaven with a Gun* (1969) brutally strikes Barbara Hershey's Indian girl before raping her. Off screen they had a much more loving relationship. *Photofest.*

on a western film called *Heaven with a Gun* (1969) starring Glenn Ford, Carolyn Jones, David Carradine and the very same Barbara Hershey. *Heaven with a Gun* was the second MGM film starring Glenn Ford that I worked as an assistant director; the first was *Day of the Evil Gun* (1967). In *Heaven with a Gun* Ford played a peace-loving preacher forced to return to the world of violence when danger threatens his church and his town. The outdoor scenes were filmed on location in Tucson, Arizona. David Carradine played the villainous son of a local rancher. Barbara Hershey was a local Indian girl who is viciously raped by Carradine. In fact, that was the very first scene that the two were scheduled to film together on the very first day they worked together.

As in *The Stunt Man* script, the *Heaven with a Gun* movie cast and crew were housed in a local motel. Seated one Sunday afternoon at the motel swimming pool, I was talking to David Carradine and Richard Carr, the film's writer. As we spoke, Barbara Hershey approached the group. Not knowing if the other men had already met her as I had, I introduced Hershey to the others. Carradine arose from his chair and if ever I saw a man smitten by a woman that was it. I could almost hear the bells ringing and see the fireworks going off. It was the classic "love at first sight" movie scene, only in real life! And I sensed his feelings towards her were not unrequited.

From then on Carradine and Hershey were a constant twosome. Even after the film was completed and we all returned to California, they continued their relationship. It was in that idealistic, flower child period of the late 1960s that Hershey bore David a son, who they named Free, in the spirit of the times. In adulthood, Free changed his name to Tom Carradine.

What's all this got to do with *The Stunt Man*? The key, of course, is Barbara Hershey.

For the morning work call on location, one of my many chores as an assistant director was making sure the actors are on time for their call and are taken to the location in their assigned cars.

On *Heaven with a Gun* if the car was ready to leave and either Barbara or David were not on time, I knew where to find them both. Just like the character of the assistant director in the film *The Stunt Man*, I would phone Hershey's motel room first. If there was no answer, I dialed Carradine's. In a few moments, they both would be in their car heading for their day's work. For me, that scene in *The Stunt Man* will always be a case of *art imitating my life*.

For a short time in 1969-1970 Barbara also changed her name. For her it was her last name from Hershey to Seagull. The next movie she appeared in after *Heaven with a Gun* was director Frank Perry's *Last Summer* (1969), adapted for the screen by Perry's wife Eleanor from a novel by Evan Hunter about four teenagers coming of age on Fire Island, NY. During the filming Barbara blamed herself for the accidental death of a seagull used in the film. Her guilt prompted her to change her last name to Seagull. Time passed and she returned to using her original name.

As in many westerns, *Heaven with a Gun* had a saloon with beautiful dance hall girls. One of those gals was Angelique Pettyjohn, whose figure rivaled Marilyn Monroe's. When Angelique was cast she had agreed to film a sexy bedroom scene with her clothes on and then repeat the scene topless for the foreign market.

Angelique felt free about her voluptuous body. Several times when I knocked on her dressing room door to call her to the set she was topless when she opened the door. A pretty sight, indeed.

One day when shooting was over and we had called a wrap for

Here I am happy to be surrounded by the beautiful dance hall girls in *Heaven with a Gun* (1969). (L. to R.) Bee Tomkins, Angelique Pettyjohn, my dinner date, myself, and Jessica James. AUTHOR'S COLLECTION.

the day, Angelique came over to me and asked what I was doing for dinner. Nothing special, I replied. She asked if she could join me. Of course, I said, I'd be delighted. During a very lovely dinner and after a bottle of vino, Angelique was relaxed enough to tell me why she had asked to join me for dinner. The director of the film was

Lee Katzin, a rather conservative, seemingly straitlaced man who affected a pipe to smoke and always, even in the hottest weather, wore a tie and a suit jacket while filming. Angelique told me that Katzin had asked to take her out to dinner that night and because she sensed it would be more than dinner, she had told him she was busy. And I was "that busy." But not that busy, she said looking at me flirtatiously. The director's loss was his assistant's gain!

KIRK DOUGLAS
Goes For a Ride

When it was produced in 1960, *Spartacus* was considered one of the most expensive movies produced in film history: a whopping 12 million dollars. It was an epic spectacle based on historical fact about the rebellion of the slaves against Republican Rome led by the slave Spartacus. The film was directed by a 29-year-old Stanley Kubrick and had an outstanding cast of actors, including Laurence Olivier, Charles Laughton, Jean Simmons, Peter Ustinov, Tony Curtis, John Gavin, Woody Strode and Kirk Douglas as Spartacus. In 1961 Ustinov won an Oscar for Best Supporting Actor for his role, and the film won three other Academy Awards, for Best Art Direction, Best Cinematography and Best Costume Design.

There are many perks that actors enjoy on films. As star and executive producer of *Spartacus*, Kirk Douglas was assigned a studio car and driver to pick him up at his home in Beverly Hills each day and drive him to the studio or to the shooting location. The first driver who was given the duty was told that Mr. Douglas preferred no conversation in the car. "Don't talk to Douglas," the driver was told by his teamster captain.

On the first day the driver swore all he said was, "Good Morning. I'm your driver." Whatever the reason, the next day Douglas had a new teamster driving his studio car. Foster Phinney was a second assistant director on *Spartacus*. I worked with Foster at Universal on the TV series *Banacek* starring George Peppard. According to Foster, the new driver, who we will call "Ray," was a man who held his tongue. Unless Douglas spoke first, Ray was silent. He didn't even look in his rearview mirror to check the backseat. Unless he was told otherwise, Ray drove his passenger to the shooting site or at the end of the work day, drove Douglas back to his Beverly Hills home. Silence reigned in that car.

One day after work, plans were changed. Instead of Beverly Hills Ray was to drive Douglas to Palm Springs where he and his wife Anne owned a second home for many years. Recently the City of Palm Springs named a street in his honor, Kirk Douglas Way, which wends its way near the city's international airport.

As Douglas' car headed southeast to Palm Springs on I-10, he rested in the backseat, still dressed in his Roman toga costume. About halfway there Ray had to stop for gasoline. In those days you didn't pay for your gas at the pump but had to go inside to the office or at least up to a window off the office. While Ray went up to pay the bill, Douglas, unseen by the driver, got out of the car and headed for the men's room.

With the bill paid, the gas tank filled up and the oil checked, Ray returned to the car. Not realizing that Douglas was no longer in the backseat, he drove off. Moments later, still wearing his short toga, Douglas came out of the restroom and found his car and driver gone. Until Ray arrived in Palm Springs, he didn't know his passenger was missing. He assumed Douglas was asleep in the backseat the whole time.

Kirk Douglas was in a predicament! What to do? There were no cell phones in those days to make a quick call. Had he been wearing his street clothes he might have had his wallet with him and money to use a payphone. But he was wearing his toga. No pockets! No wallet!

Resourceful Douglas stepped out onto the highway and raised his thumb in the universally known gesture that means "I need a ride!" In a famous scene in the 1934 film *It Happened One Night*, Claudette Colbert finds herself and Clark Gable in a similar situation; rather than thumb it Claudette raised her skirt and showed her shapely leg. A car came to a screeching halt, the man driving eager to give her a lift. But why did a car stop for Douglas? Could it have been curiosity? Why was that hitchhiker wearing those funny clothes? That was the very reason given by the young girl driving the car that stopped for him. When she and her passenger, another young girl, recognized that dimpled chin and that famous face they

Kirk Douglas as Spartacus in the toga he was wearing when he hitchhiked on I-10. *Photofest*

were thrilled. They happily drove Douglas to the front door of his house in Palm Springs.

To his credit, Douglas understood the mishap and Ray wasn't fired. But from then on, there was a bit more communication between driver and the man in the backseat.

Besides playing the leading role, Kirk Douglas was also the film's executive producer. His company, Bryna Productions, was named in honor of his mother and bore her name in its title. *Spartacus* was produced by Bryna Productions in cooperation with Universal Pictures. Douglas was not only heroic and brave as the slave in the film; he was equally brave as the executive producer. Against the prevailing thought of the time, he gave screen credit to the man who wrote the script, Dalton Trumbo.

Trumbo was one of the "Hollywood Ten" blacklisted for not cooperating with the 1947 House UnAmerican Activities Committee investigation of Communists in the movie business. Trumbo had refused to do the committee's bidding; he wouldn't name names and implicate his friends. He was found in contempt of Congress and sentenced to a year in a federal prison.

After his release from prison Trumbo was technically persona non grata in the film industry. The major studios would not openly hire him or any of the "Hollywood Ten." But on the sly, Trumbo was offered writing jobs and continued to write scripts that were produced. He was paid, but his name never appeared in the official screen credits. Instead, for many of the blacklisted writers like Trumbo, "a front" was used as the script's author and "the front" was named on screen as having written that film.

This reached the height of hypocrisy four years before *Spartacus*, before Douglas' brave decision to give Trumbo an on-screen credit. In 1956 Trumbo wrote the script for a King Brothers MGM feature film called *The Brave One*, which won the 1957 Academy Awards Oscar for Best Original Story.

Trumbo wasn't in the audience waiting to rush up on the stage to accept the award. The name officially credited as the writer of the script was a "Robert Rich." That name wasn't a pseudonym that Trumbo had dreamed up. It was the name of the brother-in-law of the producers of the film, the King Brothers. Rich often was employed by them, working in their office at MGM. When I was assigned to the King Brothers film, *Heaven With a Gun*, I met Rich, a very affable gentleman. Using Robert Rich's name was a convenient subterfuge for the King Brothers, a convenient "front." Not until 1975, a year before he died, through the efforts of Motion Picture Academy president and Hollywood producer Walter Mirisch, did Trumbo finally receive his Oscar statuette for writing *The Brave One*. In 1960 while he was still alive, Trumbo received the Writer's

Dalton Trumbo on a movie location. LARRY EDMUNDS

Guild of America (WGA) award for Best Written American Drama for *Spartacus*. In May 1993 the Academy presented Trumbo's widow with a belated Oscar for the Best Original Script that Trumbo had written for *Roman Holiday* (1953) starring Audrey Hepburn and Gregory Peck.

No "front" for Kirk Douglas when it came to *Spartacus*!! By giving Trumbo full credit, Douglas singlehandedly ended the "Hollywood Ten" blacklist that had sullied the reputations, indeed destroyed the livelihood, of so many talented people in Hollywood. Douglas' action off screen was as heroic as the character he portrayed on screen in Spartacus.

In 1976 Martin Ritt directed a movie called *The Front* starring Woody Allen and Zero Mostel. It told the story of a cashier played by Woody who fronted for several blacklisted screenwriters until he had to take a personal stand on the issue. Like Warner Bros. movies of the 1930s, the plot of *The Front* was ripped from the headlines of the day!

ROBERT MONTGOMERY
and His Rage

In 1941, MGM released *Rage in Heaven*, an adaptation of the James Hilton novel set in England. The film told the story of a pathological steel mill owner who plots an unusual murder-revenge scheme. The female lead was played by Ingrid Bergman in her second film in America on loan-out from David O. Selznick Productions. The lead role was assigned to a long-time MGM leading man, Robert Montgomery.

Montgomery was a fine, versatile actor who could play elegant, debonair gentlemen as he had in the 1930s opposite Garbo and Crawford as well as brutal killers. In 1937 he had had a major success in his career playing the killer in Emlyn Williams' *Night Must Fall*. Montgomery was also the father of actress Elizabeth Montgomery who would become a major TV star herself in the 1960s playing nose-twitching witch "Samantha" on the situation comedy series *Bewitched*.

One morning in the 1970s I was listening as I usually did to Michael Jackson, not the late singer, but the talk show host, on KABC-AM Talk Radio in Los Angeles. The knowledgeable, erudite Jackson is the son-in-law of the deceased Paramount star Alan Ladd, Michael's wife was named Alana Ladd after her dad. That morning Jackson was interviewing Gottfried Reinhardt, a longtime

A young Ingrid Bergman and Robert Montgomery in a scene from *Rage in Heaven* (1941). *Movie Collectibles*

MGM producer. Reinhardt's father was the legendary European theater director Max Reinhardt. Jackson was asking Reinhardt about the MGM movie he had produced years before, *Rage in Heaven* with Robert Montgomery cast in the lead. Reinhardt told Jackson that Montgomery hated the script. He absolutely did not want to play the part, but he was a contract player at MGM and had to accept roles he was assigned. His only alternative was to refuse and go on suspension and thereby lose his weekly paycheck. Reluctantly, Montgomery chose to play the part, but at the outset of filming, Reinhardt told the radio audience, Montgomery said he would not be very cooperative during shooting.

Montgomery reported to work each day and played the part, but gave it no emotion or depth of feeling; he was like an automaton, a robot. Reinhardt even switched directors three times thinking a new director might have a better rapport with Montgomery and get a better performance out of the actor. But, no! Montgomery continued to perform without emotion. Reinhardt tried to reason with him, but to no avail. Representatives from the Screen Actors Guild were called in to view Montgomery's performance. They agreed that it was a flat performance, but when it came to artistic interpretation, it was a difficult call. After all, Montgomery could simply say that was his artistic interpretation of the role. If Reinhardt was displeased with Montgomery's performance, he could fire him and replace him with another actor under contract to MGM. Reinhardt said that was not an option for him because the majority of the movie was already filmed and being edited. Replacing Montgomery would make the budget soar.

Finally, *Rage in Heaven* was completed. Reinhardt was desolate. The film just didn't work. He attributed its failure to Montgomery's lackluster performance. Distraught, seeking advice, perhaps a way to make the film work, Reinhardt asked a friend who was a screenwriter to view the film. To Reinhardt's surprise, the writer felt the film could be saved. He suggested that a new scene be written for the beginning of the film in which a doctor in a mental hospital informs the police that a male mental patient has escaped. The doctor should tell the police that to the untrained eye the escapee will be difficult to detect because he seems to be as normal and as sane as anyone. But because the escapee speaks without emotion he'll be easy to spot and a cinch for the police to capture.

That scene was filmed and spliced into the beginning of the movie. To Reinhardt's delight, the movie now worked. The curse had been taken off Montgomery's flat performance. The audience was forewarned that he was playing against type as a mentally disturbed individual. They would not be seeing the Robert Montgomery they knew and loved; instead, an actor revealing another side to his talent.

When the film was previewed in Pasadena, Reinhardt said Montgomery was in the audience, and, to Reinhardt, he appeared quite jovial, probably Reinhardt suspected, positive his performance had sabotaged the film's success. But the audience enjoyed the film and thought Montgomery's acting was on target. Montgomery stormed out of the preview scowling. He learned the hard way what many other actors have discovered: film is the producer's and the director's medium to shape and cut to their vision and not the actor's.

PAUL NEWMAN
and the Lady Reporters

In the spring of 1969 I was walking on Las Palmas Avenue in the heart of Hollywood and passed by the famous newsstand just below Hollywood Boulevard. At that newsstand you were overwhelmed by the myriad of newspapers and magazines from countries all around the world. If you were looking for your hometown newspaper, chances are it was on those racks along with dozens of magazines you never even knew existed.

A headline on the front page of the then-infamous gossip paper *The National Enquirer* caught my eye. It read, "My Love Affair with Paul Newman." Alongside the headline was the photo of a very cute young woman whom I will call Miss Kewpie Doll.

I recognized the "Kewpie Doll"—but from where? I opened the paper to her story. Perhaps something that I read would jar my memory. Not surprisingly, the headline turned out to be more provocative than the story. Obviously, the headline had been written to entice the reader to buy the paper. The story was rather bland. If the reader expected the words on the page to describe in steamy detail two people in the throes of a love affair, that wasn't what was written! Like many women in those days, Kewpie Doll's "love affair" was with the blue-eyed, handsome image of the actor projected bigger than life on the movie screen. Perhaps she had written the story on speculation or had convinced the editor she had a new slant on Newman's appeal to women. She arrived on location in Taxco, Mexico, ready to interview Paul while we were filming *Butch Cassidy and the Sundance Kid* (1969).

Taxco! Of course! Then I remembered Miss Kewpie Doll. I had been a second assistant director on *Butch Cassidy*. In the fall of 1968 the company had spent several weeks in Colorado filming the Hole in the Wall Gang campsite and the train holdup scenes. When they returned to Hollywood for two weeks of shooting on the 20th Century-Fox and Warner Bros. back lots, the original second assistant director, Randall, left the film and I was hired to replace him. I had previously worked well with the unit manager, Lloyd

Anderson. Seeing my name on the DGA Availability List, he hired me. The unit manager on a film is the liaison between the shooting company and the management or production company. He oversees all aspects, but especially the financial goings-on. He's there to resolve any problems that might occur and be one step ahead of the shooting company and trouble.

The first assistant on the film was Steven Bernhardt, whose father, Curtis Bernhardt, had been a film director in Germany using his birth first name of Kurt. Fleeing Hitler's anti-Semitism, Kurt came to America and anglicized his name to Curtis. His first American movie was *Million Dollar Baby* (1941) for Warner Bros. starring Priscilla Lane and future President Ronald Reagan. Curtis went on to direct films with such stars as Bette Davis and Rita Hayworth. For his son, Steven Bernhardt, the movies were also a family business. He would go on to produce another film I worked on, *Get to Know Your Rabbit.*

All the shooting on the 20th Century-Fox back lot for *Butch Cassidy* was scheduled for the evening. One night when Paul Newman knew he wouldn't be needed for several hours, he asked to leave the lot. He wanted to head to Studio One, then a very popular disco in West Hollywood. The director, George Roy Hill, was loathed to let him go; he didn't want to incur a delay in his shooting schedule if Newman was suddenly needed but wasn't there.

Newman wracked his brain, seeking a way to overcome Hill's objection. Then, it hit him. Like himself, Hill was a gambling man. Like Newman, he was competitive and loved nothing better than a challenge between gentlemen! It was common knowledge that Newman was a race car enthusiast. Around town he drove an ordinary, seemingly undistinguished Volkswagen—which translated from the German means "people's car." The VW was designed for speed on Germany's autobahn and was affectionately known as "The Beetle." Paul's beetle had a secret. Hiding in the rear of the car, replacing the original rear end, rear wheel drive, four-cylinder boxer engine was a very high-powered Porsche engine! Give it the pedal and it practically flew!

So Newman made Hill a gentleman's wager. From the moment he got the call that he was needed on the set, Newman bet it would take him no more than twenty minutes to drive from Studio One

Fun in the brothel! Paul and Cloris getting acquainted in *Butch Cassidy and the Sundance Kid* (1969). *Photofest*

back to the studio. When he was needed, director Hill sent me to the phone. I was to write down the exact time I made the call. That was my specific instruction from Hill. Newman won the bet. He was back in eighteen minutes, burning rubber all the way!

Cast in the film that week was character actress Cloris Leachman hired to play Agnes, a call girl in the local brothel favored by Butch Cassidy. Director Hill preferred working with actors who came from a theatre background. He felt they had the ability to improvise within a scene more so than actors who were strictly film actors and had never performed on a theatrical stage. Paul Newman had a long list of credits in theatre and on the Broadway stage. So had Cloris. When casting the part of Agnes, director Hill specifically asked for Cloris.

Married and raising five children, Cloris was well known and respected among Hollywood's professionals, but was not yet a familiar face with the movie-going public.

She loved acting and took every job that came her way whether it was a feature film, a TV show, a TV series or a theatrical play. In

1972 she would win the Best Supporting Actress Oscar for playing Ruth Popper in director Peter Bogdanovich's black-and-white sleeper *The Last Picture Show* (1971).

Cloris would gain full recognition as a comedic actress when she appeared as Phyllis Lindstrom, Mary Tyler Moore's kooky neighbor, in the 1970s TV series *The Mary Tyler Moore Show* and then in her own TV series Phyllis (1975–1977). In 2008, when she was 82-years-old, Cloris scored a major personal success amazingly as a dance contestant on ABC-TV's long-running, very popular TV show *Dancing with the Stars*. And when last I checked she was playing kooky grandmother "Maw Maw" on the Fox-TV's series *Raising Hope*.

Being privy to the contracts of day players, I knew that the contract Cloris had signed to perform in *Butch Cassidy* stipulated she was to work one day and be paid one thousand dollars for that day. I also knew that, according to the Screen Actors Guild, each additional day actors worked beyond what their contracts called for they would receive the same pay as agreed to for that one day. Cloris, though costumed and in make-up and ready, hadn't worked on Monday, her first day, nor on Tuesday, Wednesday, or Thursday of that week. All that time she sat in her dressing room knitting or reading, awaiting her call. When I finally came to her Friday evening about 8 p.m. to say we were finally going to film her scenes, a hairdresser came along with me to check on her period hairdo. As the lady attended to Cloris' hair, she expressed her sympathy that poor Cloris had had to sit around for five long days until the company was ready to shoot her scene. Cloris slyly smiled at me. Both she and I knew that her contracted one thousand dollars had blossomed into a hefty five thousand dollar paycheck. And she'd had had time to get some knitting done!

Reading Miss Kewpie Doll's "love" story in *The National Enquirer* that spring day brought back to my mind that she had been on the set of *Butch Cassidy*. We were on location in Taxco, Mexico, a colonial city high in the Southern Sierra Madre Mountains, known as the silver capital of Mexico, where tourists flocked to buy silver jewelry. That day on the set there had been not one but two lady reporters interviewing Paul Newman, Miss Kewpie Doll and a slightly older, more staid dark-haired woman.

An important duty of the second assistant director on any film is preparing the call sheet for the next day. The call sheet is a shooting company's daily bible. Reading it, all the actors and the crew will discover what the shooting call is for the next day, what time they are needed in the make-up department and on the set and what scenes the company is planning to film. Accordingly, everyone is expected to prepare, actors to know their lines, crew members to know what special equipment or props will be needed. In the confines of the studio, normally the call sheet is prepared in the morning, checked over by the first assistant or unit manager, and then sent to the production department to be printed. Sometime in the afternoon the printed call sheets are returned to the set to be distributed by the second assistant to all concerned.

If an actor is on call for the next day and is not on the set, it is the second assistant's responsibility to telephone that actor and notify him the time of his call and the scenes he will be doing. If it's a new actor who has not worked on the film before, the casting department or agent knows to give out that call. If extra crew members are required it is the responsibility of each studio department to read the call sheet and provide the additional crew.

It falls on the second assistant's shoulders to order the background performers, in movie lingo the "extras" that surround the principle actors, the people who make each scene look like real life. Prior to shooting, the director discusses with his first assistant where and when he wants background action. This information is passed on to the second assistant, who, when ordering the extras, will specify the exact number required, the gender breakdown, their age range, how they should dress and if they need to bring a change of clothing as well as any other special requirements needed for the scene, some which may earn the extras additional pay.

This particular day in Taxco, though the call sheet had been prepared early in the day and had been printed in the production office in the hotel, it was necessary to make some corrections. The director decided to redo a particular scene so I was writing in the new details for those who the changes would affect. Although this was one of the best hotels in Taxco, in 1967 it did not have telephones in the rooms. Though there was a bulletin board for the company where I would post tomorrow's call sheet, it was my practice to deliver each corrected call sheet personally to those cast and crew affected.

The shooting day was over. Everyone was dismissed. They were on their own, back in their hotel rooms or out on the town for dinner. I was revising the call sheets standing at the front desk of the hotel. The hotel had an unusual layout. The main entrance to the hotel's lobby was not on the side of the hotel facing the street but at the back of the hotel. As I stood at the front desk to my left was a hall leading to rooms, among them Paul Newman's. To my right was the main entrance to the hotel.

Finished correcting Paul Newman's call sheet, I walked down the hall to my left to deliver it personally. I could have just slipped it under his door, but that wasn't my style. I wanted to see it in Paul's hand. I knocked on his door. After a moment the door opened. Paul was only wearing blue jeans; he was bare-chested and bare-footed. No shirt. No shoes. From the expression on his face when he opened the door, I felt that I had interrupted something. What I had interrupted I had no idea, but I felt embarrassed! I wanted to get out of there as quickly as possible! With haste, I handed him his call sheet. He thanked me, closed the door and I returned to the front desk to adjust call sheets for other cast members.

A few minutes later, as I was still at work at the hotel desk, I heard a door open and voices down the hall. I looked up. There was the dark-haired, more staid, lady reporter coming out of Paul's room. Aha! She had been in the room when I had handed Paul his call sheet. Was that why I felt I was interrupting something? She walked past me to the entrance of the hotel, waved her hand and from the right a taxicab drove up to her. She opened the cab's door, stepped inside and the cab drove off to the left. Then almost as if it were in a movie script, as soon as the first cab cleared the scene, quick as a flash, another taxicab drove in from the right and stopped in the entranceway. Out stepped Miss Kewpie Doll. She paid her fare and with a smile on her bright red lips entered the hotel lobby. She sashayed past me as I stood at the front desk, not nodding or even acknowledging me. But I had my eye on her!

She knew exactly where she was headed! Straight down the hall to my left where Paul Newman's room was located. She stopped at his door, adjusted her dress, smoothed her hair, and then briskly knocked on the door. The door opened. She stepped inside. The door closed behind her! Now, I must confess, I have no idea of what did or did not go down in Newman's room that evening when either of those two accredited female reporters were in his room alone with him. As I stood on Las Palmas months later reading Miss Kewpie Doll's article in *The National Enquirer* (I did not buy a copy), I wondered if Miss Kewpie Doll's story might have had a different headline, might have been written in another tone, if she had known she had been the second, not the first, lady reporter in Paul Newman's room that evening!

When 20th Century-Fox first purchased William Goldman's script about the legendary outlaws, it was titled *The Sundance Kid and Butch Cassidy*. Goldman gave the story a Robin Hood twist. The heroes were bumbling bandits who though they robbed banks were really trying to help people. None of that was true. When Newman first read the script, he saw himself as The Sundance Kid. The studio was having difficulty casting the part of Butch Cassidy. Marlon Brando turned the movie down. Robert Redford was sent the script, told to read the part of Butch, but when Redford met with director Hill Redford said he wasn't interested in playing Butch. He saw himself as Sundance. Redford's enthusiasm must have convinced Hill. He liked the idea; all he had to do was to convince the studio and convince Newman to play Butch. At first, Newman was hesitant, but when he came around so did the studio. Now that Newman was willing to switch parts, the director had Goldman change the title to *Butch Cassidy and The Sundance Kid* giving Newman not only top actor billing but also putting his character first.

Another change was made because director Sam Peckinpah was releasing a western that same year called *The Wild Bunch* (1969), starring William Holden and Ernest Borgnine. The Wild Bunch was the real name for Butch's gang. To avoid confusion, Butch and his cohorts were renamed The Hole in the Wall Gang.

Conrad Hall was the director of photography on *Butch Cassidy*. He won his first Oscar for *Butch Cassidy* in 1970 and would go on to win two more, for *American Beauty* (1999) and *Road to Perdition* (2002). In 1932, his father James Norman Hall with Charles Nordhoff had written a bestselling adventure novel *Mutiny on the*

Director George Roy Hill in a pleasant moment. LARRY EDMUNDS

Bounty, a true story on the mutiny aboard the *H.M.S. Bounty*, a British Royal Navy ship sailing the South Seas in the 18th century. The book was made into a classic film in 1935 starring Clark Gable and Charles Laughton. The original destination of the *Bounty* was the island of Tahiti in the South Pacific. Conrad Hall was born in Tahiti, perhaps while Daddy was researching and writing the book with his co-writer Nordhoff.

While filming *Butch Cassidy* Conrad Hall had a close relationship with the film's leading lady, Katherine Ross, who played Etta. One day she expressed her interest to Conrad to sit in the camera operator's seat on the camera dolly, to place her eye in the viewing aperture and hit the switch and actually film a scene when the command "Roll Camera" was called. Conrad let her do it when they were filming an easy shot with the camera stationary. George Roy Hill had been looking at the scene when he called "action" and the camera rolled. He hadn't noticed that Katherine was actually operating the camera. When he looked back to get the okay on the shot from the camera operator, he saw that it wasn't the camera operator but the lovely Katherine in the cat bird's seat. He blew his Irish stack! Stomped his feet and yelled out an expletive! Conrad quieted Hill down. Katherine Ross never played camera operator again.

THERE'S MANY A SLIP
Between The Script and The Screen

William Goldman won three major awards for writing *Butch Cassidy and the Sundance Kid*: the 1970 Oscar for "Best Writing, Story and Screenplay Based on Material Not Previously Published or Produced," the 1970 Writers Guild of America Award for Best Original Screenplay Written Directly for the Screen, and in 1971 the BAFTA, the British Academy of Television and Film Award for Best Screenplay. But the film that won all those accolades was not the film he originally wrote.

It's no secret that after a film has finished shooting, when it gets into the film editor's hands or the movie has been previewed before an audience, the producers and director, trying to improve the film, may change the order of the scenes, adding some or cutting some. In Goldman's original script Etta Place, played by Katherine Ross, is a young woman who loves both Butch and Sundance. She's with them when they flee to South America to continue their robberies. But she's uneasy. One night, as the three lie there awaiting sleep, Etta announces she may go back to the States ahead of Butch and Sundance. The boys repeat what she has said and they all go to

Here are our three stars, Paul Newman as Butch, Katherine Ross as Etta and Robert Redford as Sundance, arriving in Bolivia, South America. *Photofest*

sleep. In Goldman's original script this was foreshadowed when Etta said earlier she wouldn't stick around waiting to see the boys die.

In production a scene was filmed showing the three principles at a railroad station waiting for Etta's train. She's leaving Bolivia, going back to the States. They have a few free minutes. There's a silent movie playing in a large tent set up near the station. They buy tickets and go inside the tent. When the movie is projected onto a makeshift screen, the name of the film appears. It reads *The Hole in the Wall Gang*. Surprise! It's about them! The very next title card says that the real Butch and Sundance are now dead. Reading that is more than enough for Etta. It reinforces her fears. She gets up, exits the film tent and boards the train, leaving the boys behind to their fate.

When the movie was released, that entire sequence at the railroad station and the showing of the silent film was cut; instead, there is just the nighttime scene in the jungle as the three are going to sleep as Etta casually mentions she may be leaving. After that we never see Etta again.

Why was Etta's leaving Bolivia and the silent film sequence cut? I can only imagine that although it was a beautiful scene, well filmed and well acted, the producers and director felt it was redundant. We knew Etta's fears that the boys' lifestyle might lead to their death which she didn't want to witness. It didn't need to be hammered home with the silent film saying they were dead! Once the sequences were cut, they weren't missed.

The movie winds down with Butch grousing that he's through with robbery in the jungles of Bolivia. There's not enough money to be made. Next, they stop in a small town café for some food. We are now into the final sequence of the film. Butch and Sundance are recognized as the "Yanqui Bandidos." The Mexican Federal troops arrive. A final shoot out battle ensues between the troops and the "Yanqui Bandidos." Butch and Sundance bravely face their attackers but they are overwhelmed, mowed down, killed by a volley of rifle fire. Or are they?

The final scene as filmed by George Roy Hill was his special creation. It is a combination of live-action film and a dissolve to a very wide-angled still photograph of the scene as the two men race out of their hiding place, firing away in a last desperate attempt to escape capture. A special still camera, equipped with a special lens that could capture a very wide scene, was placed alongside the main film camera. Its mission was to get several still photographs of the same action. In post-production the action on the film was frozen with Butch and Sundance caught in mid-air firing away. As the film freezes, the scene goes from full color to sepia brown. At that exact moment in time there is an undetectable dissolve to the same moment in the photograph, already in sepia brown, that had been captured by the still camera set up alongside the main movie camera. Then in post-production another camera optically filming the sepia brown photograph continued the zoom out, revealing a much larger view of the small café and its surrounds. As the view widens, the two figures of Butch and Sundance are still frozen in their final action. The effect of the dissolve is to extend the freeze frame beyond the capability of what could have been captured on motion picture film. These last moments of Butch and Sundance, frozen in mid-action, their guns blazing, firing away became an iconic image for the film!

Butch and Sundance in the final freeze frame at the end of the film. Frozen in space, still alive, still firing away! LARRY EDMUNDS

In real life it is believed that at least Butch did not die in South America. Butch's sister, Lulu Betenson, in *The San Francisco Chronicle* in 1970, claimed Butch lived until he was 69 and died a natural death in 1936. Is that why George Roy Hill ended the film with a freeze frame of the two "Yanqui Bandidos" still in an upright, alive position? In my opinion, probably. But I can never ask Hill and get an answer to my question. He died in 2002.

Thankfully, the silent film of *The Hole in the Wall Gang* originally planned to be seen by Etta, Butch and Sundance in the movie tent near the railroad station did not end up on the cutting room floor. Wisely, the creative forces decided to use it to good effect during the beginning of the film alongside the opening credits with only the whirring of a silent camera providing background noise.

When *Butch Cassidy* was filming in Mexico, the custom was for a Mexican director to be assigned to work with the American director. It was purely a ceremonial position unless the American director was open to suggestions from a peer. The Mexican director assigned was Gabriel Rodriguez. During the big final shoot-'em-up sequence that is the ending of the film, when the Mexican Federal soldiers were trying to mow down Butch and Sundance, there originally were stunts showing Federal soldiers being shot and falling from a wall twenty feet high. To achieve one of those falls, the lead stuntman from Hollywood, James Arnett, put on a Federal soldier's uniform and plotted his stunt. He would be shooting his rifle when a bullet from Butch would kill him. Then he would fall off the wall to the ground some 20 feet below. To cushion his fall Arnett built a bed of cardboard boxes on the ground that he would fall onto, that would break his fall and absorb the shock to his body. The boxes spanned a 12-by-12-foot area and were two boxes deep. The Mexican director, seeing this set-up, went over to Arnett and cautioned him. He thought, as the stunt was set-up, that Arnett might possibly injure himself. Arnett was confident. This was the exact same way he would do this stunt if he were in the States. But, said the Mexican director, "These are not American cardboard boxes. They are Mexican cardboard boxes!"

Arnett went ahead with the shot as he had planned it. When the camera rolled and action was called, he took a bullet as he stood on the top of the wall, then fell gracefully into the boxes, which were out of camera range. The boxes collapsed under his weight as planned. But, to Arnett's dismay, his fall was not the only thing broken; broken also was his leg.

The Mexican director was correct. He knew Mexican cardboard. Arnett's leg healed quickly. In a few months he was back before the movie cameras performing stunts.

ORSON WELLES
and the Magic Rabbit

Get to Know Your Rabbit (1972) was a quirky comedy I was assigned to in 1971 at the Warner Bros. Studios in Burbank, California. It starred Tommy Smothers of the Smothers Brothers comedy act doing a solo acting performance without his brother Dickie. I reminded him that I had worked with him and his brother on their short-lived television sitcom *My Brother the Angel.* He agreed with me that the show didn't catch on because the film editors couldn't capture the Smothers Brothers' off-beat comedic timing. It was that delayed reaction that the Smothers Brothers were noted for, that drew the audience's laughs in their stand-up routines or on TV variety shows. Perhaps less editing might have salvaged their humor. Also starring in *Get to Know Your Rabbit* was John Astin, who I had worked with when he directed Kim Stanley in *Rod Serling's Night Gallery*, and Katherine Ross, who had been the leading lady in *Butch Cassidy and the Sundance Kid* For me, it was old home week.

Brian De Palma, who directed the film, was among the young American directors who were a part of "The New Hollywood" changing American cinema in the 1970s. That group included Martin Scorsese, Francis Ford Coppola, George Lucas and Steven Spielberg. De Palma often said he wanted to be the American Godard, the French director who had taken the film world by storm with his New Wave film *Breathless* (1960) starring France's Jean-Paul Belmondo and America's Jean Seberg. De Palma in the years to come would direct some very important films, including *Scarface* (1983) with Al Pacino, *The Untouchables* (1987) with Kevin Costner, and the first *Mission: Impossible* (1996) with Tom Cruise.

Before he came to Hollywood, De Palma had built his reputation filming documentaries and comedies in New York City. Robert De Niro, not yet known nationally, appeared in several early De Palma films, including *Hi, Mom!* (1970), which caught the attention of the producers of *Get to Know Your Rabbit*. The plot of Rabbit was anti-establishment, in keeping with the anti-Vietnam War feeling that was expressed by many people throughout America in the late 1960s. Tommy Smothers played a guy caught in the corporate trap. Even his apartment entraps him; it's laid out like a maze from which he cannot escape. He's not the only one in this situation. To emphasize this, De Palma had the art director design the kitchen in Tommy Smother's apartment with a window on both the east and west walls. Looking out either of those windows one looked into the kitchen window of an identical apartment next door. In each kitchen there was a neighboring blonde, buxom wife wearing a white blouse and black skirt exactly like the white blouse and black skirt that Tommy's blonde, buxom wife wore in her kitchen! The husbands in the neighboring kitchens were outfitted in gray businessman's suits just like the gray businessman's suit that Tommy wore.

Tommy's imagination is set on fire when he learns that if he enrolls in the Delasandro School of Magic his life will be changed forever. He'll bid adieu to the humdrum world of corporate chicanery for the glamorous world of showbiz by becoming—YES!—a tap-dancing magician! Cast to play Mr. Delassandro, the owner of the school and magician extraordinaire, was the legendary Orson Welles. Casting Welles was in itself sort of an inside gag. During World War II, Welles had his own magic act which he performed at military camps for the America's serviceman. Among his many tricks was sawing glamorous Marlene Dietrich in half. As Mr. Delasandro, Welles admonishes his students that to be a first-rate magician they must "get to know your rabbit"—hence the title of the film.

When Welles appeared in *Get to Know Your Rabbit*, his glory days were long past. He first achieved national fame in 1938 with his radio adaptation of H. G. Welles science-fiction novel *War of the Worlds*. Thousands of radio listeners panicked thinking it was a real news show reporting an invasion of extraterrestrials intent on destroying America. Welles solidified his fame by starring in and directing *Citizen Kane* (1941), a thinly disguised story about the life and loves of famed newspaper publisher William Randolph Hearst. *Citizen Kane* is still considered by many the greatest movie ever made. Late in his life Welles achieved additional notoriety and is remembered for television commercials he did for Paul Masson wines in which his rich voice proclaimed, "We sell no wine before its time."

Though Welles was often hired as an actor in Hollywood films, he could never get Hollywood studio backing for films he wrote or wanted to produce and direct. He was always searching for funds to finance his films independently. Technically, according to the standard Screen Actors Guild contract, Welles should not have accepted work on *Rabbit*. He was already signed and committed to act in another movie that was already in production. And he had already acted for the film. When his agent was contacted about the availability of Orson Welles for only one day of work on *Rabbit*, that one day coincided with the several days that Welles knew he was not on call for that other film. Although it was illegal for him to do so, Welles accepted the job on *Rabbit*. If for some reason the other movie had needed him on the one day he had a call to work for us, there would

Orson Welles wearing his own black clothes as he explains the art of being a tap-dancing magician in *Get to Know Your Rabbit* (1972). *Photofest*

have been trouble. His first obligation was to the other company. But apparently the additional paycheck for *Rabbit* was reason enough for Welles to take the risk and overlook the SAG rule. Fortunately, the other movie company did not need him that day. Everything went smoothly. Almost.

The magic school set was built in an apartment above Frederick's of Hollywood, the famous sexy lingerie store on Hollywood Boulevard in the heart of Tinseltown. The previous day we had filmed a scene in the store itself, surrounded by all the provocative lingerie. On this day we were upstairs where the art director had dressed the biggest room as the magic school. The smaller rooms served as dressing rooms for the actors. Mr. Welles had been unable to come in for a fitting for his costume, probably because he was at work on that other movie. So our wardrobe man obtained his sizes from Welles' agent and brought several outfits for Welles to try on. Welles was a huge man, considerably overweight. When the wardrobe man showed him the outfits, he refused them all saying he'd wear what was on his back, what he wore every day, a huge black shirt jacket and black pants. That was okay with Brian De Palma, the director.

De Palma was in awe of Welles. When De Palma was in college his major was physics. He was so blown away when he saw Welles' *Citizen Kane* that he switched his major to filmmaking. Welles was his hero.

The scene was lit and the director was ready for Mr. Welles. As the second assistant director I went to his room to bring him to the set. He was seated. He looked up at me and said he didn't think he could make it. He wasn't feeling well. Concerned, I immediately asked him if there was something I could get him. What was wrong? Did he need a doctor? He just waved his hand as though dismissing me and didn't say another word. My responsibility then was to notify the first assistant that Mr. Welles was not responding to the call. I hurried back to the set and just as I reached the side of the first assistant, a voice in stentorian tones boomed out from the entrance to the room, "Here I am, good people!" It was Welles. He walked onto the set and for the next hour or so performed beautifully.

Why had he played games with me? As a director himself, he knew full well what my duties as a second assistant were. There had been no wink of his eye to say that he was kidding. Or any other gesture.

I once related this story to a psychoanalyst friend of mine. His diagnosis was that Welles was acting out the self-destructive side of his personality. He was a brilliant man idolized by many, yet a man

Tommy Smothers helps homeless John Astin cross the street, walking towards the camera. Tommy hadn't noticed that John had dropped his pants. So I sent a lady extra to cross over in the other direction. I told her to make sure as she passed them that she looked down at John's bare legs. Tommy got the message and played the moment. She earned an extra fee in her paycheck that day. AUTHOR who by his nature was often his own worst enemy. He couldn't find a way to produce or direct within the Hollywood system, was angry with that system and probably because of his anger lashed out at me, a very minor cog in that system. Maybe so. But I'm still in awe of his talent, love his films and envy him for having married Rita Hayworth.

John Astin played Tommy's boss, Mr. Turnbull, who keeps following Tommy wherever he goes. Tommy just can't shake himself free of Astin. His compassionate nature prevails when he discovers Mr. Turnbull has also left the corporate world and is now a homeless bum and a drunkard. In his attempts to help his former boss recover his self-esteem, Tommy convinces John to dry out, straighten up. He does and as a result of his recovery, they both fly right back into the corporate world, much to Tommy's annoyance.

While he was in *Get to Know Your Rabbit,* Astin was courting actress Patty Duke, herself an Oscar winner at age 16 for portraying Helen Keller in *The Miracle Worker* (1962). They married in 1972 when *Rabbit* finished shooting. John adopted her months-old son by a previous marriage, giving the little boy his family name. That child, Sean Astin, grew up to be an actor in such films as *The Goonies* (1985), *The Lord of the Rings* cycle (2001, 2002, and 2003) and the title role in *Rudy* (1993). Duke and Astin had their own son, MacKenzie Astin, who also became an actor. Another family in show business.

A character actor named Allen Garfield appeared in *Get to Know Your Rabbit.* Garfield had worked in New York with De Palma in two films, *Greetings* (1968) and *Hi, Mom!* (1970). He had a line in *Get to Know Your Rabbit* written by scriptwriter Jordan Crittenden that always stuck with me. Allen's character "Vic" befriends Tommy Smothers and takes him to a three-day party to meet girls. It's standing room only at the party, in fact, there's such a crush of bodies between them that there isn't an inch to move, let alone exhale. A very beautiful girl stands next to them. To Vic's eye she isn't wearing a brassiere. Vic is brash and crude and refers to any girl who doesn't wear a brassiere as a cheap broad. The girl only has eyes for Tommy. She looks at him and says,

"My name is Susan."

"Susan," Vic exclaims, "Hell! Where do girls get names like that?"

Cover girl Samantha Fox, as Susan, gets fitted for a bra by Allen Garfield as Tommy Smothers looks on. The scene from *Get to Know Your Rabbit* (1972) was filmed in Frederick's of Hollywood, the famous lingerie store in Hollywood. *Movie Collectbles*

It still makes me laugh!

Allen was also a character off screen. One evening the producer took a group of the cast and crew out to Chinese dinner at a restaurant on the Sunset Strip. I was included. At the conclusion of the meal, the producer asked for the bill. When the waiter brought the bill for the ten of us, he also brought Garfield a Chinese dinner-to-go, charged to the producer. No wonder there's such an outcry about the escalating costs to make a movie.

When *Get to Know Your Rabbit* finished shooting, Tommy rejoined his brother Dick in their nightclub act, fulfilling an engagement at Caesar's Palace in Las Vegas. To my delight, as a "thank you" gift for working on the movie, Tommy invited me and my significant other to see the show. Graciously, he paid for our night's lodgings at Caesar's Palace as well as a table for two to see the Smothers Brothers perform. Outstanding! The room, the meal and the show!

BARBARA EDEN
and The Harper Valley P.T.A.

Phil Borack was in the movie distribution business in Cincinnati, Ohio. After purchasing the rights to Jeannie C. Riley's hit song "Harper Valley P.T.A.," he raised money to turn it into a movie. He came to Hollywood, interviewed producers and hired George Edwards. George had produced several movies, including *Games* (1967) with Simone Signoret and *Ruby* (1977) with Piper Laurie. George wrote the script, taking the song's lyrics as a starting point and then extended the plot. In the song, the mother of a junior high-school student gets a letter from the Harper Valley Junior High School PTA. They admonish her for wearing miniskirts, being a party girl and a bad example for her young daughter. From then on the fun loving mom, Stella Johnson, played by Barbara Eden, along with her best friend, played by Nanette Fabray, seek comedic revenge on the PTA board members, whom they call Harper Valley hypocrites.

One of Barbara's comedic acts of revenge centered on Otis Harper of the founding Harper family. Otis was played by comedian and satirist Pat Paulsen who was a regular on *The Smothers Brothers Variety Show* on CBS-TV in the late 1960s. One of his more famous bits on that show began in 1968 and continued every four years thereafter. As Americans were choosing candidates for the presidency of the United States, Paulsen himself ran as a presidential candidate in a campaign more comedic than political. He even got some actual write-in votes because of his anti-Vietnam rhetoric, popular at the time.

In *Harper Valley P.T.A.* Paulsen's character Otis was played as a man who drank too much alcohol. He was always a bit tipsy. There's an old saying, "Seeing pink elephants," which is a euphemism that claims when drunks are in an alcoholic stupor they imagine they see pink elephants. So Barbara and Nanette Fabray rent elephants painted pretty-in-pink. The elephants crash through the walls of Otis' bedroom as he lies in bed in a stupor after coming home three sheets to the wind. Drunken Otis, seeing the pink elephants, is

Barbara Eden and Nanette Fabray enjoying their pranks in *Harper Valley P.T.A.* (1978). LARRY EDMUNDS

frightened out of his wits. He runs to the safety of his wife's arms and swears he'll never drink again. Oh, yeah!

The pink elephants also had an effect on Nanette Fabray. As we were shooting the beginning of the sequence outside Otis' home, the elephant handler warned the crew and the actors that elephants have poor eyesight. No one was to stand directly to the side of the elephant's eye. A fearful elephant, the handler said, not clearly seeing what was there might lash out with his trunk in a defensive gesture to protect himself, hurting anyone who stood there.

In the rush of setting up the scene, Nanette happened to hit the wrong spot in relation to the lead elephant. The fearful elephant knocked her to the ground. Nanette said she was okay, but the producer had someone drive her home and Nanette took the next day off. When she returned to the set, she was fine, just a bit bruised. We assured her there would be no elephants on the set when she returned. Nanette laughed and said, "Thank heavens! Though if there was, I was planning to bring a bag of peanuts to let him know all was forgiven!"

ACTORS, ACTORS EVERYWHERE

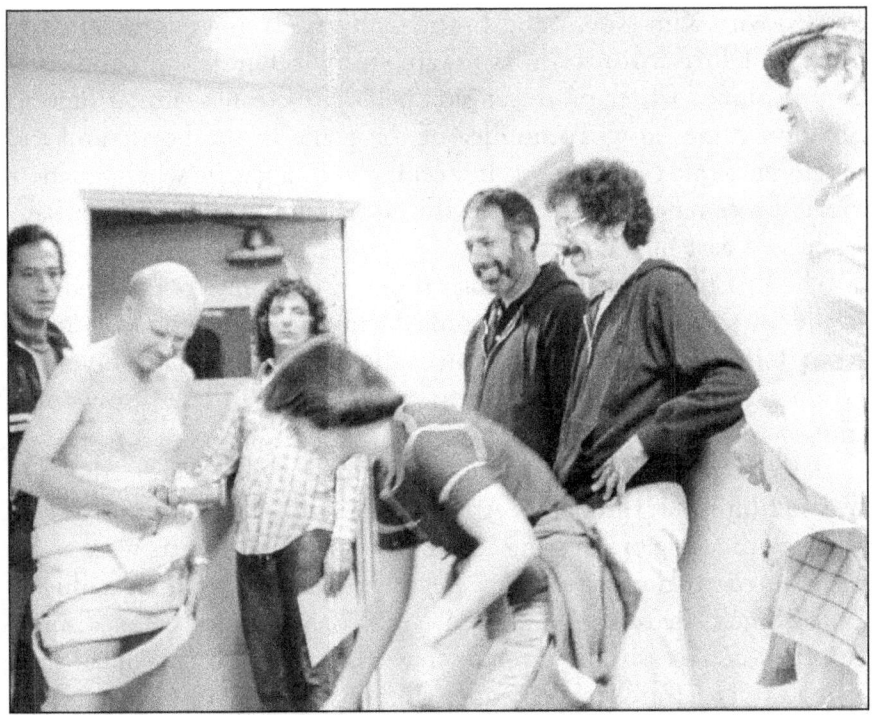

Actor John Fiedler being "dressed" with the fire hose by the crew so he can leave the motel. Watching from (R. to L.) are the director of *Harper Valley P.T.A.*, Richard Bennett; the producer, Phil Borack; myself and crew members. It gave us a good laugh! AUTHOR'S COLLECTION

Another Harper Valley board member was Bobby Taylor, played by John Fiedler, who lusted after Barbara's character, sexy Stella Johnson. Stella playfully leads him on. She makes an appointment to meet him in a local motel. He's over the top, thinking he's finally going to have an afternoon love tryst with her. But it's not to be! Once they are alone in the motel room and Bobby has undressed, Stella has her revenge. She scoops up his clothes and exits the room with them leaving a stunned Bobby stark naked. To get out of the hotel he hides his nudity by draping a fire hose wrapped strategically around his middle.

Barbara Eden, who had been a starlet in 20th Century-Fox films, hit the big time when she portrayed the genie in the bottle in the Screen Gems TV comedy *I Dream of Jeannie*. Screen Gems had had great success with their sitcom *Bewitched* about a civilian marrying a witch, a spin-off of Columbia's movie *Bell, Book and Candle*

(1958) with Kim Novak and Jimmy Stewart. Trying to replicate the appeal of *Bewitched* with its magic and witchcraft, Screen Gems commissioned writer-producer Sid Sheldon to create a similar sitcom. Sheldon came up with the idea of the genie in the bottle and the magic the genie can perform. In keeping with a female witch Sheldon created a female genie with an invisible belly-button and Barbara Eden was cast in the part.

The first two weeks of filming *Harper Valley P.T.A.* were scheduled in the town of Lebanon, Ohio, some twenty-five miles north of downtown Cincinnati so that producer Borack's Cincinnati investors could have the thrill of visiting a movie set and see how their money was being spent.

Barbara arrived in Lebanon on a Sunday afternoon, the day before filming was to begin. Arriving the same day was a box of tee-shirts with a slogan referring to the movie. The tee-shirts were to be distributed to the crew and were the brainchild of the producer, Phil Borack. Because she arrived late, Eden had not eaten dinner. As the second assistant director, I was asked to go to a local inn, The Golden Lamb, to pick up a dinner for Barbara. The inn was historic. When English author Charles Dickens toured Ohio in 1842, he had slept in the very same inn with his wife.

I had placed the order with the maître when I saw a handsome, square-jawed man with a shock of hair wearing the newly arrived *Harper Valley P.T.A.* tee shirt. As far as I knew it had not yet been distributed. The man was walking with a very lovely young woman. He had his arm around her waist and from the way they were talking and giggling, it seemed to me something extracurricular was on the man's mind. The couple walked out of the lobby and I lost sight of them. My order was ready. I paid for it and went back to Barbara's motel, all the while wondering who that man was and why he was wearing the *Harper Valley* tee-shirt. I found out the next day.

He was Barbara Eden's new husband, Charles Feigert, her second husband. He had arrived with her and must have seen the tee-shirts and been given one. I kept my knowledge of what I had seen to myself, until now, when it really doesn't matter anymore. Barbara divorced Feigert a few years later. In Barbara's biography, *Jeannie Out of the Bottle*, she recalls that when she first met Feigert her intuition told her to stay away from him. Even her mother didn't like him. But he was such a charmer, so good looking, so persistent that Barbara fell in love with him and accepted his marriage proposal. Would she have believed me if I had brought back a side of gossip along with her meal that night and ratted out her bridegroom? I doubt it. As they say, love is blind even if you are a genie with special powers!

Harper Valley P.T.A. was a funny movie and earned back its investment for Phil Borack and his Cincinnati investors. It was so successful that in 1981 a television series based on the movie was licensed by Borack to Universal Studio. Universal produced it as a sitcom for NBC and hired Sherwood Schwartz and his son Lloyd as producers. Schwartz had created two of the most commercially successful sitcoms in TV history, *Gilligan's Island* and *The Brady Bunch*. Eden repeated her role of Stella Johnson. Success was written all over it. After the first season Schwartz and company left the show and without their input, the show's ratings took a nose dive. After the second season it was cancelled. But Phil Borack's original Cincinnati investors got a good return for their investment.

JON VOIGHT'S
Lucky Break

Some 60 miles east of San Francisco is Vacaville, California, where Warner Bros. was filming *The All-American Boy* (1973) starring Jon Voight as a struggling professional boxer with family problems. I was assigned to the film as a second assistant director. With Jon on location was his agent Saul David. I mentioned to Saul how much I had enjoyed Jon's performance in *Midnight Cowboy* (1969). What a great career break for a young actor. It made him a star! Saul smiled slyly and with a glint in his eye said to me, it almost didn't happen. Jon wasn't the first actor chosen to play Joe Buck. *Midnight Cowboy* was a great success. It was the first X-rated film to ever win the Best Picture Oscar. John Schlesinger who directed the film won the Best Director Oscar and the writer Waldo Salt, Best Adapted Screenplay. Jon was even nominated for Best Actor along with his co-star Dustin Hoffman. Getting the role of the naïve male prostitute, Joe Buck, who, with his sickly friend Ratso, desperately tries to survive on the mean streets of New York City, didn't come easily for Jon.

Saul David told me that as Jon's agent when he tried to get Jon an audition for the role he was told nothing doing! Saul was persistent. Every time he ran into the agent he would talk up Jon's talent and how perfect he'd be for the role of Joe Buck. After the third encounter the casting agent finally relented and agreed to schedule a screen test for Jon, probably just to get Saul off her back. Jon was thrilled. He thought the filmed test went well. But several weeks later the casting agent called Saul. Jon had not been cast as Joe Buck. The director and producer had chosen a young Canadian actor who was under contract to Universal Studios, the very talented Michael Sarrazin.

What Saul wasn't told because it was of no concern to him, was that there was a financial problem in casting Sarrazin. He was under contract to Universal Studios. When an actor was under contract to a studio, as Sarrazin was, he was paid a fixed weekly salary by the studio. Loaning the actor out to another studio or production company was an opportunity for the studio to make a profit on their player. They might charge five times his weekly salary and keep the difference between that amount and the weekly wage they were paying the actor. Studios were notorious for profiting on their loan-outs.

The producer of *Midnight Cowboy* was Jerome Hellman. He and director John Schlesinger weren't pleased to be paying Universal what they thought was a very inflated price for Sarrazin, but despite their concerns, after viewing all the screen tests for the role they thought Sarrazin was their best choice. On a Friday morning they phoned him and told him the part of Joe Buck was his, that he should go home and have a happy weekend. On their agenda that afternoon was a review of Sarrazin's screen test.

Sitting in the screening room with them that afternoon was a young secretary who was privy to their concerns about the monies Universal was asking for Sarrazin. Hellman signaled the projectionist to run the screen test. To everyone's surprise, Jon Voight's test came up instead of Sarrazin's. It seems both Jon's and Sarrazin's tests were spliced together on the reel. The projectionist had to run through Jon's test to get to Sarrazin's. So they all sat there looking at Jon's

An anxious Jon Voight as hustler Joe Buck on the mean streets of New York City in *Midnight Cowboy* (1969). *Photofest*

test. As it unreeled the young secretary piped up, "He's cute. There's your Joe Buck. I like him. Bet you can get him for less money."

What she said hit a nerve, a financial nerve. Schlesinger and Hellman asked the projectionist to replay Jon's test one more time. Maybe the secretary was right. Monday morning they cancelled Sarrazin, called Saul David and hired Jon Voight. Saul told me Jon's salary for the entire movie was fifteen thousand dollars, a nifty sum for a young actor like Jon, but far less than they would have paid Universal for Sarrazin. Jon Voight's performance as Joe Buck made him a bankable movie star and propelled his career into high gear.

FAYE DUNAWAY
Certainly Did It Her Way

There's a mansion overlooking the Pacific Ocean, a few miles north of the City of Santa Monica on the coast highway leading into Malibu that for years many people assumed was the home of oil billionaire J. Paul Getty. It wasn't. Getty's home was located a bit further inland and was unseen from the highway. In 1972 I was working in that mansion when Universal Studios was filming a movie-of-the-week about the abdication of England's King Edward VIII so that he could marry an American divorcee from Baltimore, Wallis Warfield Simpson. Faye Dunaway played Mrs. Simpson, Richard Chamberlain played King Edward and the TV movie was titled *The Woman I Love.*

Because Getty's home, about a mile inland, was overflowing with his collections of ancient Roman, Grecian and Etruscan antiquities, he ordered another building constructed nearby to house just his treasures. It would also be unseen from the Pacific Coast Highway. In 1974 the new building, styled as a Roman villa modeled after the Villa Papyri in ancient Herculeum, was opened to the public. It was called the Getty Villa. Not only would it house all his ancient treasures, it would also be a learning center dedicated to the art of ancient cultures. After Getty died in 1976, the Getty Foundation used the vast fortune derived from Getty's oil holdings to erect a bigger museum complex called the Getty Center on a hilltop further south in the Pacific Palisades area of Los Angeles. This was in addition to the Getty Villa which would continue to operate.

The mansion mistaken for the Getty home and the Getty home itself had only one thing in common. They were both built by very wealthy men. When motorists driving by on the Pacific Coast Highway looked up at the mansion, they couldn't help but notice that the two-story building had a very distinctive feature. At the northernmost corner of the grand house as it faced the Pacific was a two story round structure that seemed an unusual appendage to an otherwise rectangular building. Once I was in the mansion my curiosity drew me to the round rooms. On the first floor the round

Faye as a very elegant, black-haired Wallis Warfield Simpson in the TV movie *The Woman I Love* (1972). *Photofest*

room served as the mansion's main dining room with a glorious view of the ocean. On the second floor the round room was a sitting room ringed with windows that provided an equally glorious view. The mansion had been built in the late 1920s by a rancher from Montana who made his millions raising sheep. To commemorate the source of his fortune, the head of a sheep was carved into the lower end of the wooden banister of the grand staircase leading to the second floor.

Only the interior of the mansion was filmed for the TV movie. It was chosen to represent the French Riviera villa to which King Edward and Wallis Simpson had fled in 1936 to escape the tumult about them making headlines in England. It was from that villa that Edward stunned the world when he broadcast his abdication speech "for the woman I love!"

Whoever now owned the mansion rented it out to movie companies even though it was in a neglected state. To film the 30 foot high living room Universal had to replace the frayed drapes that covered the very high windows as well as furnishing the room in the correct period. In the living room was an ornate, antique desk that was part of the sheep rancher's original furniture for the room. In a desk drawer I found an *Architectural Digest* magazine from 1928 with a picture story of that very mansion and that very room in its heyday.

Faye Dunaway had done her homework. She knew that the favorite flower of Mrs. Simpson was the fragrant white stephanotis also known as Madagascar Jasmine. Faye asked to have that flower on the set and so every morning a local florist delivered a bouquet of stephanotis to the property manager to be placed in vases near Faye or to be pinned in her hair or on a dress. A little extravagance to please Faye.

Mrs. Simpson had very black hair. Faye did not. She was a tawny blonde. Every morning, before shooting began, her hair stylist would run a black rinse through Faye's hair that would then be washed out at the end of the day. Faye was a brilliant actress. She would go on to win an Oscar in 1977 for her galvanizing, ruthless performance in the movie *Network* (1976). Perhaps Faye was accustomed to a more leisurely schedule when she acted in feature films as compared to the fast-paced grind of movies made for TV. If her work call was for her to be ready and on the set at 8 a.m., she was invariably late, holding up production and costing bucks. As the lead she was in practically every scene and it was difficult to schedule an early morning scene without her.

One day, the director and the morning make-up people had a conference. The outcome was that instead of asking Faye to be in make-up at 6 a.m. for her 8 a.m. call, they would add on some extra time. Surely that extra half hour would give Faye enough time to accomplish everything needed to get ready to perform at 8. I was instructed to tell Faye her call for the next morning was 5:30 a.m.

Faye arrived promptly at 5:30 a.m. But she was even later than usual that morning to the set. When she arrived, she was very apologetic. She explained that with the extra time she had asked her hair stylist to dye her hair black that morning, rather than just give it a black rinse as they had been doing every day of the shoot. Naturally, the dye job and styling took more time than usual. Smiling, Faye assured the director that with her hair now dyed black it would speed-up her time spent in make-up and hairdressing each morning.

Had Faye figured out the director's game and decided to twist it her way? Certainly, I never asked her. From then on in the grand tradition of keeping your star happy, the director accepted Faye's apologies and her late arrivals on set were never again a topic of concern.

LOUIS B. MAYER
and Mama's Chicken Soup

He was the powerful head of studio operations and a Vice-President at Metro-Goldwyn-Mayer in Culver City, California. He was credited with starting the star system in Hollywood. At MGM he boasted "they had more stars than there are in the heavens" under contract. To some of those actors Louis B. Mayer was a loving father. To others, he was a tyrant. He was the stereotypical Hollywood mogul, short, feisty, cigar-chomping, self-made man who ruled his movie kingdom with an iron fist for 27 years. Under his rule during the Great Depression of the 1930s, MGM was so successful it was the only Hollywood studio to declare dividends to its investors. Mayer was the first American in history to earn over a million dollars in salary, more than the President of the United States was being paid that same year. And he earned over a million from 1937 on for nine years straight.

Louis B. Mayer in his executive office in the Thalberg Building at Metro-Goldwyn-Mayer during World War II in the early 1940s. To the far left on the wall behind him is a cloth with stars indicating four MGM employees killed and 951 still fighting for their country in the war. *Movie Collectibles*

In the golden days at Metro-Goldwyn-Mayer, an invitation to eat lunch in the studio commissary was much sought after by movie fans. In the commissary, a visitor could catch a glimpse of their favorite stars, perhaps in costume for their latest film, eating lunch just like mere mortals. At MGM's commissary, the really big stars, like Gable, Garbo and Garland, were assigned their own reserved tables. The various professionals and craftsman who worked at the studio also had tables reserved for their categories. If they chose, they could sit with their peers at a table reserved just for directors, or for assistant directors, another for the directors of photography, and so on. Though they were working on different films and on different soundstages, the craftsman could compare notes and discuss their problems over lunch or just enjoy each others company.

A favorite item on the MGM menu was chicken soup. But not just any chicken soup, a delicious Jewish chicken soup that was Louis B. Mayer's tribute to his mother and his heritage. It was a favorite, made from the finest, plumpest chickens that could be bought.

Art director Merrill Pye, under contract to MGM at the time, and I were eating lunch together in the MGM commissary when he told me about a crate of chickens that was delivered on a weekend to the studio. Though it was addressed to Louis B. Mayer, the big boss, the guards at the gate sent the chickens down to the property department, assuming they were intended for use in a film. Monday morning, the receiving clerk in the Property Department was puzzled. He wasn't expecting any chickens. He couldn't find any paperwork indicating that chickens had been ordered for a movie then being filmed on the lot. The clerk assumed they had been sent his way by mistake. Chickens being food, his best guess was they were meant for the commissary. A lover himself of "Mama Mayer's Chicken Soup," as it was billed on the daily menu; he had the crate of rather scrawny, odd-looking chickens redirected to the commissary's kitchen.

What no one knew was that these were very expensive, very rare specimens of a Chinese chicken that the boss himself, Louis B. Mayer, had purchased for breeding purposes. Mayer was known as a breeder of race horses, but not chickens! You guessed it! When the commissary chefs received the crate of chickens addressed to Louis B. Mayer, they assumed they were intended for that day's chicken soup. Into the pot they went. That day lovers of Mama Mayer's Chicken Soup had an exceptionally tasty and costly bowl of soup.

ACTING TAKES MORE
Than Talent and Ambition

Mecca for aspiring young actors interested in a career in the theater has always been the Broadway stage in New York City. If those hopefuls imagined their talent unreeling on silver screens throughout the world, then Hollywood was their goal. Many went west and succeeded. Many never made the grade. Was it that they lacked the talent or didn't have enough endurance to overcome the obstacles? Perhaps they just didn't get a lucky break? Or perhaps their lucky break broke the wrong way!

That happened to my friend, actor Eldon Quick. He had the talent, the ambition, and the confidence and was cast in a television sitcom that had success written all over it—and then the bottom fell out of the project and his big break vanished!

Eldon was appearing in the touring company of Ira Wallach's stage comedy, *The Absence of a Cello*, which was playing at the Huntington Hartford Theatre in Hollywood, the last stop on the tour. One night an actor's agent caught the show and was blown away by Eldon's performance. He rushed backstage to introduce himself and persuade Eldon to allow him to be his film agent in Hollywood. Because he was still performing nightly in the play at the Huntington, he agreed to let the agent send him out during the day on auditions. After all, his days were free. Eldon hit it big.

Filmways, the producers of two mega CBS sitcoms, *Petticoat Junction* and *Green Acres*, had signed an unusual deal with CBS. Based on their successful track record, Filmways wouldn't even have to go through the exercise of filming a pilot. CBS bought the show just by reading the proposal submitted by the writers. CBS gave the new show called *Doc* a definite, guaranteed place in CBS-TV's schedule for the fall of 1967. Instead of filming a pilot, they would jump ahead and film the first episode of the show.

Doc was about a small-town doctor who had reached the age of retirement. When he couldn't attract a young doctor to take over his practice, the townspeople raised enough money to send one of their own hometown boys to medical school. That was the leading role Eldon was cast to play. Eldon told me he thought he was cast because of the self-assertion he displayed in the audition scene he did with veteran character actor John McIntyre, who was playing the older doctor. The producers liked the way Eldon stood up to the older doctor when the older man questioned the younger man's sincerity and desires.

In that first episode when time flashed forward and Eldon returned with his medical degree, a full-fledged doctor, the comedy arose from the fact that he stumbled all over himself, was prone to injury, even breaking his leg as he got off the train when he arrived home. The older doctor, seeing how inept the younger man could be, knew it wasn't the right time to retire. He had to stick around a while longer to keep his eye on the newly-minted young doctor. That would be the hook, the continuing storyline in each episode of the series. Though a bumbler, the way Eldon played him the young doctor was lovable. Best of all, the viewing audience could identify with him and laugh at his self-inflicted misfortunes.

Filmways had had all the actors including Eldon sign contracts for a full season of shows. If they were only filming a pilot, the actors would have signed a contract just for the pilot with options should CBS pick up the show for a full season. Because it seemed such a sure thing since the show had a firm commitment from CBS, Filmways anticipated a long run for *Doc*. What could go wrong?

To insure its success, *Doc* was scheduled at 8:30 p.m. Monday evenings. Preceding it at 8 p.m. was the popular *Gilligan's Island*, a surefire lead-in. Following *Doc* at 9 p.m. was *The Lucy Show* with Lucille Ball, the biggest hit on CBS-TV. What more could a producer want! *Doc* was sandwiched between two proven audience pleasers. Surely that would rub off on *Doc*. It was pure gold scheduling.

Desilu Productions, owned by Lucille Ball and her ex-husband, Desi Arnaz, had produced another show for the upcoming season that CBS had made a commitment to air. It was a detective show

ACTING TAKES MORE THAN TALENT AND AMBITION

called *Mannix* starring Mike Connors. CBS scheduled it for 9 p.m. Saturday evenings. To program it at that time CBS had to cancel the show that had been broadcast in that hour for many years, namely *Gunsmoke*, the much-loved western with Jim Arness. Though *Gunsmoke* was still very popular, still earning top sponsor dollars, to justify the cancellation CBS-TV blamed their action on demographics. Gunsmoke attracted an over 40-year-old audience when they would have preferred that time period attract a younger demographic, an age group that would buy more of the sponsors' products.

Gunsmoke's cancellation set up a hue and cry from the public that swamped the CBS headquarters at both CBS Studio City in Hollywood and on Madison Avenue in New York. Not only were fans appalled, but even sponsors vehemently protested. CBS executives went to Desilu and said they had reconsidered. They were going to keep *Gunsmoke* in its 9 p.m. Saturday time slot. When mid-season came, no doubt there would be several low-rated shows that they would be canceling. CBS assured Desilu that *Mannix* would be the first new program scheduled at mid-season.

Desilu would have none of it. They argued to keep *Mannix* as programmed Saturday evening at 9 p.m. Not wanting to anger Desilu (read: Lucille Ball, their top star) CBS looked for another option. Someone suggested leaving *Mannix* at 9 p.m. Saturdays and moving the one-hour *Gunsmoke* into the 8 p.m. hour preceding *The Lucy Show* on Monday evenings. Sure, they would have to cancel *Gilligan's Island*, but it was running out of steam anyway and they'd cancel that new show, what was its name, oh yes, *Doc*. And that's what CBS did to please Desilu, Lucille Ball and Desi Arnaz.

Eldon and his wife Susan found out about the cancellation of his show as the movers in New York were loading their furnishings onto the moving truck headed for Hollywood. For them, logistically, it was too late to turn back. They made their move to Hollywood. Eldon had signed a run-of-the-show contract. Filmways honored that contract and paid Eldon half of what he would have earned had he actually filmed all the contracted episodes. It was a whopping sum and more than enough money to help Eldon and Susan set up their home in Hollywood. As an additional mea culpa on their part, Filmways promised to cast Eldon in a major motion picture they were producing, *Ice Station Zebra* starring Rock Hudson. It was being filmed at the MGM studios in Culver City at that very time. That never happened.

When *Doc* was cancelled, Eldon had lost what might have been a lifestyle change. Had the show become a major hit for CBS, the very fact that he was in a TV show everyone was positive would be at the top of the charts, no question about it, Eldon would have been pushed into the celebrity spotlight! That celebrity might have made him an actor in constant demand, offered the choicest of roles. Perhaps another series. Perhaps a major feature film. Without a doubt, had *Doc* run several seasons and gone into reruns his bank account would have grown quite healthy! Perhaps he and his family would have been set financially for life! Eldon had the ambition, the talent and he was ready to give the performance the show required. But it was not to be.

Eldon and Susan both continued acting. They are among the ninety-nine percent of the Screen Actors Guild membership we call working actors, not the one percent called movie stars. You've seen Eldon and Susan in many commercials, on TV shows and in feature films. They raised a son, but the fame and fortune that might have been Eldon's wasn't to be. Was Eldon bitter? Not at all. Rejection, in any form, is part of an actor's life.

When I was majoring in Radio and Television in the Speech Department at the University of Michigan in the 1950s, I became friends with another student in my public speaking class named Gordon. Where my goal was radio and TV production, his was acting. And he was a good actor, appearing with considerable success in many college productions. To his advantage, he had leading man good looks.

I had been in Hollywood over a year working as an assistant director when I got a call from Gordon. He had just arrived in Hollywood gung ho about acting in the movies. Like many newcomers in his shoes he was taking acting classes. There was an attractive blonde in his class named Marilyn Devin. She had an agent who was sending her out on auditions. She was getting favorable reactions not only on her beauty but on her acting ability. Her agent suggested that for future auditions she prepare a scene to perform with another actor. She asked Gordon to be that actor.

Gordon didn't have an agent and wasn't being sent out on auditions. He did read the trade papers and hit as many open auditions or cattle calls that he read about. Performing with Marilyn by default gave him the appearance of having an agent. One callback was at Warner Bros. for a movie called *First to Fight* (1967). Actor Chad Everett was cast in the lead role, playing a Marine in World War II, the sole survivor in his squad of a Japanese attack on Guadalcanal, a jungle-covered tropical island in the southwest Pacific. Because of his heroism, he is awarded the Medal of Honor. He returns stateside a hero and is assigned to training new recruits for the Marines. Once home, he falls in love with a girl named Peggy, the part Marilyn Devin was auditioning for. Training recruits and marriage have an unsettling affect on Chad's Marine. He misses the life of a marine in battle. He requests a transfer back to the front lines. But once back in combat he finds that he's a changed man. Marriage and his life at home mean more to him then the glory of battle.

Marilyn got the part. The casting agent told Gordon there would also be a part for him in the film and there was. It was only one scene but an important one because it contained a story point that affected the plot. Gordon, wearing his Marine uniform, was driving a jeep, telling his story point to his passenger, a high-ranking officer being played by veteran actor Dean Jagger. On the day he was to shoot, he reported to Warner Bros. studios in Burbank and was driven down to Camp Pendleton, the Marine base north of San Diego, where his scene would be filmed. All of Gordon's friends were excited for him. This was his lucky break!

When Gordon returned to Hollywood, I phoned him. He wasn't very excited. It had been a tough day of shooting for him. Beyond that, he didn't say any more. For him the issue was closed. The following morning Gordon received a call from Warner Bros. Would he please come into the studio on Monday; the director, Christian Nyby, wanted to reshoot part of his scene. He thought it would play better in an office than on the road in the jeep. Gordon went into the studio and the scene was reshot. For Gordon it meant two additional days of pay, money he was glad to bank.

I assumed that Marilyn's agent would now add Gordon to the roster of actors he represented. But he didn't. When *First to Fight* was released, I went to see it on the big screen at the Warner Theatre on Hollywood Boulevard.

There he was driving the jeep, his image a mile high on the big screen, his every expression magnified a thousand times! Gordon looked good in his uniform, but, watching it, there was something about the scene that made me feel uneasy. It was because Gordon was uneasy. You could see it in his eyes—anxiety, fear. Whatever you call it, it wasn't in the script! Was he having a problem driving and saying his lines? Whatever it was, Gordon didn't seem to inhabit the role and make us forget he was acting. Instead, his face registered his personal anxieties. Quite often an actor will dig deep into himself, his memories, his psyche, to find an emotion appropriate to the character at that moment. No deep digging was required for this part. Though Gordon had talent and talked as though he had the ambition, it seemed he just couldn't pull it all together on this his first big chance.

I suspect that was what the director saw when he screened Gordon's scene that night in the dailies. In order to save the scene and its story point important to the film, the director broke the scene in two. He kept a minimum of the uneasy Gordon driving the jeep and played the important dialogue in conversation standing in an office. Gordon now appeared at ease, but he must have realized he wasn't ready for the big time. He left Hollywood, went back to New York, and carved a career for himself as a dresser to actors in Broadway shows, in charge of their costumes and wardrobe changes.

TO BECOME A PRODUCER

When I made the long trek cross-country from the East to Los Angeles in my tiny, rear-engine, baby-blue GM Corvair, laden with all my worldly possessions, the ride was on a wing and a prayer. Would the Corvair make it without breaking down and more important, was it the right move for me? Would I find work opportunities in Hollywood? I had a membership card in my pocket for the Directors Guild of America which meant I could work as an assistant director. But I was new in the town! I introduced myself to the people at the Director's Guild headquarters on Sunset Boulevard who could help me find work. It took a while but I did get my first job at the Four Star Studios in Studio City, Ca, working on the Smothers Brothers' sitcom show during pilot season in late 1965.

When the pilot season was over I returned to the world of the unemployed, picking up an occasional job as a stage manager in live TV as winter turned to spring. Then, in June of 1966, I received a call to work on a new show, *The Monkees*, a takeoff on that other four-boy musical group that was rocking the nation, The Beatles. From then on, I was able to keep working through my connections or simply being on the DGA availability list.

There were feature films, situation comedies, westerns, pilots for TV, commercials. I never said no! As the years went by I watched as other assistant directors were given the opportunity to direct. Usually they got their chance on an upcoming episode in the series that they were currently working on as a first assistant. The producers would take into consideration three things: Most important, did he have the desire to be a director and had he asked to direct an episode? Second, did he have a good working rapport with the show's actors, and, third, did he have an understanding of the show's format? If the answer to all three was "Yes," then the producers would be inclined to give him the opportunity.

As for me, that was not a road I saw myself on. Although I'm a highly visual person, there were some aspects of my personality that I thought weren't suited to success as a director. Some of those traits might be better suited to another position in the film industry, that of a producer. As the next few years went by and as I worked from one assistant director assignment to another, I kept my eyes open for stories I might produce; stories that might make a great film. In 1970 one landed in my lap. And so I optioned it. What I didn't realize at the time that even though I was attempting to change the role I was playing in Hollywood, from assistant director to producer, I was still playing in the clutches of crazy, crazy Hollywood!

For me, finding a property to produce for a movie is instinctive. When I read it, see it or am told about it, something clicks in my head. Perhaps it fits into a genre of proven movie hits. Perhaps it has a provocative storyline that speaks to an issue facing society that day. Perhaps it has starring roles that cry out for and will attract topnotch actors with proven box-office success. Or perhaps it's a bestselling book and the author is a good friend of yours.

That's the how and the why that I optioned the 1969 bestseller *The Peter Principle, Why Things Always Go Wrong* written by Dr. Lawrence J. Peter and Raymond Hull. Larry Peter and I were friends. It wasn't simply because we were friends that I took an option, but because it was a humorous book with serious intent that seemed to resonate with peoples across the world. I truly believed it could be adapted into a funny, satirical movie.

Larry and his co-author had written *The Peter Principle* when Larry was a citizen of Canada, living there with his wife Irene. Offered a teaching job at the University of Southern California (USC) to create prescriptive programs to develop competent teachers and teacher educators, he moved to Los Angeles and set up residence. That's when I met Larry and Irene through a mutual friend. While he was still in Canada, he had submitted the book to publishers in Canada and the United States. On his desk Larry had a stack of rejection slips. No interest at all!

One night a writer he met at a party laughed out loud when

Larry told him what the Peter Principle was, namely that "in a hierarchy every employee tends to rise to his level of incompetence." In other words, competent employees are rewarded for their competence by being promoted to the next level. Eventually, they are promoted to a position at which they are no longer competent and that's where they remain, being unable to earn further promotions. And because of their incompetence in that last position that's "why things are always going wrong!" The writer loved it, saying he was sure everyone knew someone like that, who was forever screwing things up because he was in over his head.

With Larry's permission, the writer submitted an article about a professor at USC who had this crazy, funny theory that rang true. The article appeared in the magazine section of *The Los Angeles Times*. An editor at William Morrow publishers in New York read the article, wrote Larry asking if there might be a book in the idea. Larry sent him the book and a publishing phenomenon was born. Larry, by himself, wrote several other books taking off from *The Peter Principle*. His second book was *The Peter Prescription or 66 Formulas for Improving the Quality of Life,* combating why things always went wrong. The book contained many humorous quotations by famous folk. Some of the lesser-known quotes really came from Larry's wit and wisdom. Rather than attach his name to all of them, just for fun, he attributed them to his friends. Turn to page 141 of *The Peter Prescription* and you'll read, "Jumping to conclusions seldom leads to happy landings," attributed to yours truly.

Once I had the *Peter Principle* legally optioned with the help of my lawyer Dixon Dern, I set my strategy. I needed a great comedy writer. I telephoned Elaine May in New York. In my opinion, she was a great comedy writer. A woman with a heavy dialect answered the phone. I said I was hoping to speak to Miss May. The woman responded that Miss May was unavailable. So I left a message with her giving my name with the reminder I had worked with Miss May on the movie *Luv*.

The heavy dialected woman said, "Yust ah moment." The next voice was that of Elaine May.

"Hi, Steve. What can I do for you?" Elaine said in her most mellifluous tone. She wasn't interested in doing a script based on *The Peter Principle* when I explained my reason for the call, but she said she knew someone who would be just perfect to adapt it to film. A wonderfully talented writer, Charles Gordone.

Who, I said to myself? I did not believe my ears. Charles Gordone was a pioneer in a form of race-conscious theater, best known for his 1969 play, *No Place to Be Somebody*. That play was the first drama by an African-American playwright to win a Pulitzer Prize, the first to win the coveted prize before it was even produced on Broadway. I had seen one of three touring companies performing it at the Huntington Hartford Theatre in Hollywood. A wonderful play, but not the work of a comedy writer. The play was about disappointment, despair and death that lie in wait for African-Americans who think they'll find success in the big city. No laughs there.

I thanked her for the recommendation and said I'd mull it over and hung up, wondering if she even knew what *The Peter Principle* was! Had I heard right. Gordone? It wasn't until several years later when Elaine May was directing a movie called *The Heartbreak Kid* and had cast as the lead in her film an actor named Charles Grodin that I realized my mistake. Then it hit me. Grodin! Not Charles Gordone. She had said Charles Grodin! He was a comedy writer just blossoming into a comedic actor. That's who she meant! I promised myself I'd get my ears cleaned without delay! I had misunderstood her. Too embarrassed to call her and confess my misunderstanding, I opted for a dish of ice cream from the fridge.

Fortunately, my good friend designer Leonard Fisher phoned me soon after. He thought he could help me find a writer if I came to New York. I flew out that Friday. He met me at the JFK airport with a chauffeured limousine and we drove out to one of Long Island's very fashionable beach communities. Leonard had arranged for us to be weekend guests at Baby Jane Holzer's legendary and leviathan mansion in Southampton, Chestertown House, which had originally had 60 bedrooms and was on 14 beachfront acres. Much of the furniture in the house was early American that had been handmade for export to England in the early 1800s. A previous owner had purchased the furniture in England and had it all shipped back to their land of origin to be displayed and used in Chestertown House.

In her sun room we sat on a set of what I thought was white

wrought-iron furniture, but was actually hand-cut wood, carved to look like wrought-iron, then painted white. It had been presented to England's Queen Victoria by her loyal subjects in India. Wow! For me this was what some might say was living in high cotton!

Baby Jane was the "it" girl of the '60s, beautiful with a halo of blonde hair, her every action written up in the society columns. She loved confusing the columnists who reported on what she wore to parties by changing outfits as she was being chauffeured from one party to another. She was also known as Andy Warhol's first superstar, appearing in his underground films. Because we were Baby Jane's guests we were invited with her to an outdoor cocktail party. Baby Jane knew that among the guests that summer evening would be Peter Stone, a playwright who had written the screenplays for *Charade* (1963) with Audrey Hepburn, *Sweet Charity* (1969) with Shirley MacLaine and the thriller *The Taking of Pelham One Two Three* (1974). Stone was charming and pleasant, but didn't think *The Peter Principle* was his cup of tea.

The next day as Baby Jane, Leonard and I lolled in the sun at the water's edge, I wondered out loud if a Woody Allen might be interested in writing it. Brilliant idea, Baby Jane exclaimed. She knew Woody and had had a personal relationship with him several years before. It was well known that Woody and his jazz band performed at a restaurant on Manhattan's East Side on Monday evenings. Since Monday was the very next day, Baby Jane said she'd call Woody and arrange for us all to meet him there the following evening.

Back in Manhattan on Monday I was strolling along Sixth Avenue at the corner of 57th Street. To my surprise coming towards me on Sixth Avenue was Larry Peter arm-in-arm with his wife Irene. Neither one of us knew that the other would be in New York. Very excited, I told the Peters what I had been up to that weekend on behalf of the movie version of his book and that I was going to meet Woody Allen that evening to get Woody involved with my project. Instantly, I knew what I should do. I invited Larry and Irene to join me that evening when we were to meet Woody. Having them there would be a major plus and show how serious we were about getting Woody on board. The Peters were delighted to come along since they were both fans of Woody and his films.

Leonard and I with the Peters were the first to arrive. Next, Baby Jane entered the restaurant all by herself. All heads turned to look at her as she walked to our table. The room went silent as though the very air had been sucked out of it. By God, she was a star! Woody soon joined us and was pleased to meet Larry Peter. He explained he had just purchased the rights to *Everything You Always Wanted to Know About Sex (But Were Afraid to Ask)* and was busy writing that. Though he found *The Peter Principle* amusing, he usually liked working on his own original ideas. He thanked us for thinking of him, but declined.

I was confused! *Everything You Always Wanted to Know About Sex (But Were Afraid to Ask)* was not his original idea but that of Dr. David Reuben, who wrote the book. It was a bestseller and actually a sex manual, the first of many to come. In 2011 in a biographical documentary on Woody's career airing on PBS, Woody admitted that adapting that book and directing the film was not his proudest moment, indeed a mistake in his career.

Disappointed that Woody wasn't interested in *The Peter Principle*, we stayed for dinner, drinks and Woody's music. My time in New York was over and I flew back to the west coast.

I was getting antsy. My option time was running out fast. What to do? Perhaps if I had a script that I could show around. I ran an ad in *Daily Variety*, a Hollywood trade paper.

> "Wanted: A successful WGA writer with comedy experience to write a motion picture from a best-selling, humorous non-fiction book."

I received twelve replies. Everything from a man who had won an Academy Award for a very popular comedy film to someone who thought I was a stand-up comedian looking for a gagster to write jokes for my Las Vegas act. What had he read or what had he smoked?

One of the replies was from a man named Alfred Golden. Although I did not hire him, he became a good friend. Al Golden had an interesting background and career. In the 1930s he had written a play which was produced on Broadway. As a result of that 20th Century-Fox brought him out to Hollywood to write scripts, but after a year they dropped his option and he went back east. Eventually, Golden found success in the insurance business promoting insurance as a life's necessity. He was the person who invented what came to be called "third-party marketing." It works as follows: A letter is sent to every customer of a company which says because the recipient is a valued customer of said company he or she is being offered a special deal on insurance. At one time or another we've all received an offer like that for a variety of products. Golden's product was always insurance. His first client to reap "third-party marketing" benefits was the American Express credit card. "Third-party marketing" soon became a staple in the sales world. Not only were Al Golden and I good friends, I regarded him as my "intellectual father"!

The man who answered my *Daily Variety* ad that I hired to write the script for *The Peter Principle* was Maurice Richlin. Maurice and his partner Stanley Shapiro had won the 1960 Oscar for writing *Pillow Talk* (1959), the racy comedy starring Doris Day and Rock Hudson, which was a box-office bonanza. The director of that movie was Michael Gordon, the "furniture director" I assisted on *The Impossible Years*.

Maurice wrote what I thought was a very funny script based on the Peter Principle. He captured the concept with some wild and crazy scenes. Larry Peter read it and gave it his stamp of approval. Maurice knew I was a novice at producing and had a limited number of connections in the business. To be helpful he arranged an appointment for me with his agent Irving Lazar, arguably the most flamboyant, famous talent agent in Hollywood at this time. Humphrey Bogart gave him the nickname of "Swifty" after Lazar contracted for Bogart five movie deals in five hours. Lazar preferred representing writers because they worked alone and didn't need as much of his time as actors who he said were needy requiring constant attention and reassurance.

Swifty was a short man, barely over five feet tall. Did he have a Napoleon complex? I didn't know, but I thought he might when I met with him. His office was a long narrow room. He sat behind a very big desk, his back to a large window so that he was back lit and his face was in semi-shadow. He shook my hand and indicated I should sit down in one of the two sumptuous Lawson easy chairs situated in front of his big desk.

When I sat down in the chair, surprise! Like Alice in her Wonderland I went down, down, down! At first I thought the chair had been pulled out from under me. But that wasn't the case. I was still seated in the Lawson! Whoever designed or ordered that chair for Swifty's office did so with a special purpose in mind. The chair was constructed so the sitter would be sitting so much lower than Swifty, that height-challenged Swifty on the other side of the desk would give the illusion that he was a much taller man than he really was. Who was his decorator? Alice's Red Queen?

Swifty heard me out and said he would forward Richlin's script to the gifted Carl Reiner: actor, producer, director, and writer. I was delighted. Less than a year before I had worked as a first assistant director to Reiner on a sitcom pilot he was directing at Warner Bros. I was a fan of Reiner's. When I was in college in Ann Arbor, Michigan, in the early 1950s if I didn't have a Saturday night date I was just as happy to stay home and watch television, to see Reiner on *Your Show of Shows*, playing second banana to Sid Caesar and Imogene Coca. When Swifty sent my script to Carl, I took that as a positive sign because we knew each other!

When Richlin's script got to Reiner he was producing *The New Dick Van Dyke Show* at the CBS Studios in Studio City. It was a new comedy series to bring Dick back to weekly TV. Several months later the script was returned to me. Not interested. Disappointed, I tried getting the script out to other people who I thought might find it to their liking.

That fall when *The New Dick Van Dyke Show* was about to go on air, I saw a television promo for it. The ad contained a scene with Dick and toilet commodes. To me it looked very much like a scene in Maurice Richlin's *Peter Principle* script that I had sent to Reiner. I rushed to Dixon Dern, my lawyer. Since the episode was already filmed and on the CBS-TV fall schedule to be broadcast, if I believed I had legitimate grounds for plagiarism, I could prevent that episode from airing by serving the producers with a legal halt and desist order. To do so, I would have to post a bond for $50,000. Not having that amount of money, I let the issue drop, although I did send the Dick Van Dyke office a letter stating my suspicions.

Several months later I was at Warner Bros. Studios on the set of Columbia's TV series *Police Woman* starring Angie Dickinson visiting a friend. To my surprise, Carl Reiner was also on the stage. Before either one of us said a word or even a "Hello," Reiner recognized me, walked over to me and said, "I never read that script."

To this day, I want to believe Reiner. I just couldn't help wondering why when he recognized me that day the first thing he thought of saying to me was "I never read that script." Suffice to say, *The Peter Principle* property was never made into a movie. Perhaps it was never meant to be a movie. Years later, after Larry and his wife had died, his estate did allow a British company to produce a British sitcom based on the book starring Jim Broadbent.

Though I had a script that I thought was funny and true to *The Peter Principle*, I hadn't been able to find financing or a major studio interested in producing it with me. With regrets, I didn't renew my option.

THEN ALONG CAME THE "DAVIDS"

The desire to become a producer still burnt within me. The world was changing. No longer did people spend an entire lifetime working for the same company or on the same job. Society was mobile. Wherever one's heart and desire took them they could travel. It was never too late to abandon an old job for a new career! One day in 1978 I picked up the June 6 issue of *Esquire*. Above the name of the magazine there was a line of copy that leapt out to me promoting an article inside the magazine: "Rescuing David from the Moonies... a father's story by Warren Adler."

Here was a story that fit my criteria for a provocative film. The Moonies were a controversial issue in the late 1970s. There were articles about them almost every day in the nation's newspapers, discussions on talk radio. It was a topic that troubled not only families here in America, but families of various nationalities in other parts of the world. The right movie on this issue could be an international moneymaker! I was hooked! Once again I was wading into the deep, deep crazy waters of Hollywood! Would I be in over my head?

Warren Adler was then and still is a very successful novelist who has written over 30 novels. Over the years several have been made into successful movies, one being *The War of the Roses* (1989) starring Michael Douglas, Kathleen Turner and Danny DeVito. It wasn't about the historical English civil wars in the mid-1400s but about a hysterical American war of divorce between two, no-longer-consenting adults. That film was a major success for 20th Century-Fox. Another book that Adler wrote was called *The Sunset Gang*. It was a collection of short stories about seniors living in a retirement village in Florida. Warren got the idea for the book from the anecdotes his mother, a resident of that community, told him. "Yiddish," the first story in Warren's book, was about seniors in that community who were trying to recapture memories of their youth as well as their heritage by learning how to read and speak Yiddish, the everyday language of Jews around the world. Coincidentally, my mother's 88-year-old cousin, Yankel, lived in that same retirement community. Yankel or Jack (in English) had founded the Yiddish class. He was the first teacher and probably taught Warren's mother. A delightful, unexpected coincidence!

In *Rescuing David*, Warren Adler was telling the true story of his eldest son, David Adler. His David, the first of my two Davids, was in his early twenties. After graduating from the American University in Washington, D.C., at the age of 22, David was the founder and publisher of the *Washington Dossier*, a magazine that covered power, society, politics and social entertaining in the nation's capitol. The start-up money for the magazine was provided by his parents, Warren and Sonia. His mother Sonia worked on the magazine as its editor.

David devoted himself entirely to making the magazine a success. Not having taken a vacation since the magazine was first published David was finally planning a skiing holiday in Aspen, Colorado; his first time away from the magazine. Coincidentally, the night before he was to leave, he received a phone call from a long-time good friend who said he had met some wonderful people on the West Coast who were changing his life and invited David to join him. David, still in that youthful state of mind, still questioning his place and purpose in life, changed his plans and flew off to San Francisco.

What David didn't know was that his friend was in a Korean-based religious cult gaining daily prominence in the United States. His friend was a member of the worldwide Unification Church founded by the Reverend Sun Myung Moon. Because of their allegiance to Sun Myung Moon, his followers were called Moonies.

Reverend Moon claimed that in 1935, when he was a young preacher, a vision of Jesus came to him and chose him to continue Jesus' teachings here on earth. One of the more unusual rituals of the Unification Church was a mass marriage ceremony. As their spiritual leader his followers allowed him to arrange their marriages, often between two people previously unknown to each other, meeting for the first time at the wedding ceremony. The marriage rites would then be performed by Reverend Moon himself at a mass wedding with hundreds of marrying couples reciting their vows before him and the world.

Several hours after David landed in San Francisco he was whisked off to Boonville, California, to a Moonie camp euphemistically called the Ideal City Ranch. Warren and his family realized something was amiss when they spoke with David on the phone. He seemed hazy and uncertain about where he was and what he was doing. Actually, David was being brainwashed, fiercely indoctrinated into the political and religious beliefs of Moon's Unification Church. He was love-bombed by his new friends, enjoying the newfound adulation they professed for him. He didn't suspect that they had an ulterior motive. His new loving friends even warned him that the parents who he thought loved him might be in league with Satan and try to take him away from their happy world. They even used the words "kidnap him" and "deprogram him."

Why had they chosen David? Warren remembered that a young Korean woman, whom he did not know, once sat in the *Washington Dossier* reception room without an appointment waiting for him for six hours. When he arrived, she happily volunteered to do a food and cooking column for their magazine. No pay required. Warren was put off by her aggressiveness and unusual proposal. He thanked her, but turned down her offer.

Were the Moonies through the young lady food columnist trying to get a foothold in Washington via the *Washington Dossier*? Probably. When that didn't work, it seems their next plan was to recruit David himself, turn him into a follower of the Reverend Moon and convert him to their way of thinking! That was exactly what David was told when he was in Boonville. His new friends said his publishing venture could be tremendously important to the church and the Heavenly Father's cause.

If that was their plan, Warren and his family by rescuing David from the cult's clutches definitely thwarted their scheme! Years later, the Reverend Moon and his church purchased *The Washington Times*, a right-wing, conservative newspaper. At long last Reverend Moon had an outlet in the nation's capitol for his cult and his radical beliefs. In 2010 the Reverend's family cut off the thirty-five million dollars they pumped annually into the newspaper to keep it going and sold the paper for one dollar to a group sympathetic to Reverend Moon's teachings and beliefs.

Warren, his wife and middle son Jon, flew out to the West Coast in desperation. Warren's story in *Esquire* told of how they eventually rescued David from the Moonies by outwitting the very insecure young lady named Berthie, assigned by the Moonies to guard David at all times. To their surprise, David was allowed to meet his parents in a hotel in San Francisco. There were a series of desperate scenes with David fluctuating between returning to Washington, D.C., or remaining with the Moonies. When Warren threatened to commit suicide, David's love and concern for his father came to the forefront. David finally agreed to fly home to Washington, D.C., with his parents. He asked only one condition. That his Moonie friend, Berthie, should fly with him. Warren happily agreed. Unbeknownst to Berthie, Warren only bought her a one-way ticket. If she did or did not get back to Boonville was not his concern. On the flight Warren managed to keep Berthie separated from David. Upon arriving at the Dulles Airport he whisked David into a taxicab when Berthie wasn't looking. Realizing she had lost control of the situation she became frightened. Warren and his family had succeeded in their mission. They had their David back.

As more and more families were faced with rescuing their offspring from cults like the Moonies, a new occupation suddenly appeared on the horizon—people calling themselves "deprogrammers." Parents were so distraught about having their child involved with what everyone considered a cult, they would do anything, pay anything, to get their offspring away from the Moonies. First the deprogrammers had to free the youngster from the cult. Kidnapping was not unknown, especially if the child would not come away on his or her own. Once the young person was "rescued" he or she would be closeted in some offbeat motel room, locked away from normal daily activity. Then the deprogramming began. By constant repetition and a more positive form of love-bombing, the deprogrammers aimed to rid whatever propaganda the Moonies had ingrained into the victim's mind and to bring the victim back to reality. Deprogramming was frequently a slow and costly process and quite often left a very troubled, confused former believer. For David the deprogramming opened him up to his real emotions. It was many months before he could turn off the light in his bedroom and sleep in the dark.

I phoned Warren Adler. We met and he gladly gave me an option on the *Esquire* story. Rather than spend money to have a script written as I had done with *The Peter Principle*, I decided to first try to interest a major studio or a big-time producer with a two-page treatment that I wrote, backed up with a copy of the original magazine story.

One day Warren phoned me. Did I know a Peter Guber? Someone from Guber's office had called Warren's agent expressing interest in optioning *Rescuing David*. The agent explained the property was already optioned.

Yes, I replied. I knew who Guber was, not personally but by his work and reputation. Guber was a big-time player in the Hollywood scene with offices for his Filmworks company in a producer's building near the Hollywood Way Gate on the Warner Bros. lot that was shared with Columbia Pictures. Guber had a three-year deal with Columbia to produce films. In 1978 he had produced Peter Benchley's *The Deep* with a very revealing wet tee-shirt on the well-endowed leading lady, Jacqueline Bisset. Guber would boast that Jacqueline's wet tee-shirt had made him a millionaire. He also had executive-produced *Midnight Express* (1978), the true story of a drug deal going bad in Turkey and the dealer, a young Californian, being tossed into a hellhole of a Turkish prison. In the future Guber would be associated with such winning films as *The Color Purple* (1985) with Whoopi Goldberg, *Rain Man* (1988) with Tom Cruise and Dustin Hoffman, and several in the *Batman* series. It was said he was more of an executive producer than a hands-on, there-every-day producer.

Warren Adler suggested I call Peter Guber's office. Perhaps I could work with him. So I contacted Guber's office at Columbia on the Warner Bros. lot. First, I met with one of Guber's assistants. The next thing I knew I was invited back to meet with Guber. Another man joined us in Guber's office. We were introduced. His name was David Puttnam. The name didn't mean anything to me. Later, I would learn that this David, the second of my Davids, was a very pleasant Englishman who had been the producer of *Midnight Express* for Guber. Puttnam would in 1982 win the Best Picture Oscar for producing *Chariots of Fire* (1981), a story of bigoted rivalry between two English track athletes in the 1924 Olympics.

The meeting went very well. We three came to an agreement that if a movie was made of *Rescuing David* I would work in a producing capacity along with Puttnam. Floating on a cloud I went back to my day job which was working as a first assistant director on a TV movie called *Transplant* (1977) with my favorite director William A. Graham. *Transplant* was the story of a hard-working executive whose heart is failing and he opts for the risky operation of a heart transplant. Billy Graham, myself and other crew members went fact finding to the hospital in Palo Alto, California, where heart transplants were being performed. Billy noticed that the head surgeon wore a colorful bandana on his head during the operation. Had Billy not seen the bandana, probably the surgeon in our film would have worn the standard white hospital cap. Oh, how the times were a-changing!

The heart transplant patient was played by Kevin Dobson and his wife by Melinda Dillon, a favorite actress of mine. Playing his 16-year-old daughter, in for just a few days of work, was a very professional, talented teenage actress named Helen Hunt. Years later I was delighted when she was in full bloom of her talents and won the 1998 Best Actress award for her role in *As Good As It Gets* (1997) costarring Jack Nicholson.

A couple of weeks after my meeting in Guber's office I received a contract from Guber confirming that I would be getting a producer's credit and salary on a Moonie movie inspired by *Rescuing David*. I happily signed my John Hancock wherever it was required on two copies of the contract and sent both copies back to Guber's office. The next step would be for Guber to sign the two contracts on behalf of his company. He would keep one copy and return a copy to me, which I intended to frame and display conspicuously!

Time passed. Then I received a phone call from David Puttnam. He was meeting Adler's agent in New York and he asked me to join him. Gladly, I flew out. Met David for breakfast at his hotel and off we went to the agent's office. Once we were seated, Warren Adler, unexpected by David and myself, joined us. Somehow, I sensed this didn't please Puttnam. He said as much after the meeting as we two boarded the down elevator to leave the building. I returned to California and back to work, still floating on a cloud.

A month went by and I had not received a signed contract nor had David Puttnam been in touch with me. I was uneasy. I smelled there was something rotten in Denmark, as they say. Yes, there was something rotten. I discovered what it was in an April issue of *New York* magazine, not to be confused with *The New Yorker*. On the cover of the magazine, no less, was the big story of the day, the breakup of the professional relationship between David Puttnam and Peter Guber. Puttnam would later say that he saw himself as a hands-on producer, a lover of the true art-of-cinema whereas he saw Guber's natural bent was for hype over substance; anything was good if it put more cash in his pockets.

Guber after leaving Columbia Pictures had partnered his company Filmworks with Neil Bogart's Casablanca Records, a hot record company. Both men were aggressive, always seeking a more lucrative deal. They found one when Polygram International, a German company with deep financial pockets, bought an interest in Casablanca Filmworks. It was under the Polygram flag that Guber finally produced a movie about a Moonie-like cult. It was called *Split Image* (1982), directed by Ted Kotcheff. The plot focused on deprogramming someone indoctrinated with the cult's philosophy. It wasn't very successful. When Sony Entertainment purchased Columbia Pictures Entertainment and the Metro-Goldwyn-Mayer Studios in Culver City, Peter Guber and his new partner Jon Peters reentered the picture. It is said in tandem they seduced Sony into hiring them for the very lucrative job of running the motion picture arm of Japan's mega electronics corporation.

David Puttnam was a *"mensch,"* the Yiddish word which in simple translation means "a man." But when it is applied to a person it means he is a person of integrity. And David Puttnam was, threefold! He phoned me one day and asked me to come to his office now at Warner Bros. He had a deal with Warners to develop several story ideas. Warners had first refusal on anything he developed. In exchange they gave him office space and financing and the opportunity to do his thing and develop winners. This was an arrangement studios often made with producers with proven track records.

David Puttnam, to whom I shall always be thankful for his belief in me. *Photofest*

Puttnam said that one of the projects he was developing for Warners was a Moonie script. Not from Warren Adler's story. Instead, he had hired a young English woman who herself had been a victim of the Moonies in England. From her personal experiences she was to write a script about the cult. If it went into production Puttnam assured me I would work with him on the film as a producer. In the movie business, especially in England where Puttnam had started, he was known for giving newcomers their big chance, perhaps their first opportunity to write or direct or produce. He was graciously extending to me my big opportunity!

A few weeks later when Puttnam had brought the woman writer to Hollywood, he invited me to meet her at a lunch at Warner Bros.' commissary. Also at the table was a young man who Puttnam said would be directing the film. Again, I was elated. How exciting to be involved with these very bright, very enthusiastic people. I was getting another shot at my dream. I was one step closer to being a producer.

But, once again, it was not to be. There are many scripts written and many movie projects planned that never get the go ahead to begin actual production. The reasons are as varied as there are people on the face of the earth. And perhaps it's just a big crap shoot for all the elements to come together. Puttnam's career continued on a spectacular rise what with the success of *Chariot of Fire* and other projects he would develop for the movie screen. For a time he was head of production for Columbia Pictures.

In my efforts to produce a movie about David Adler's entrapment and his parents' confrontation with the Moonies, I didn't think I was in waters over my head. Just the opposite. As I waded in, in spite of my best moves, the waters of possibility receded like the evening tide, first flowing towards me then quickly changing direction and flowing out, withdrawing with it my last possibility to be a producer. Even David Puttnam, a seasoned player in this crazy world of Hollywood gamesmanship, couldn't reverse the tide for me.

WHAT HAVE I MISSED? TV, OF COURSE!

So far my crazy recollections have come primarily from the feature films I worked on during my years as an assistant director. And my attempts to produce films. There must have been some crazy, crazy stories that happened when I worked on shows for television, on the sitcoms, the westerns, the TV movies-of-the-week, even the commercials! There must have been. But why don't they come to mind? Perhaps they weren't as cataclysmic as those on the features and didn't lock themselves into that part of my brain set aside for memorable retentions. Nevertheless, here are a few I do recall.

THE DEBBIE REYNOLDS SHOW (1969)

When Debbie decided to do a weekly television comedy, she hired the best. Namely, Jesse Oppenheimer as her producer. Jesse had been the original producer of *I Love Lucy*. In fact, as a writer and producer he came up with the winning concept for the show. It was very simple. Desi Arnaz playing Lucy's husband (on and off screen) was a successful bandleader (on and off screen) who loved nothing more than to come home and spend time with his family and wife. On the other hand, his wife Lucy, played by Lucille Ball (on and off screen), wanted to be more than just a housewife. She wanted to be in show business like her husband. That's where the fun came in. Jesse also was the first to suggest filming a show like *I Love Lucy* with three cameras in front of an audience. This technique allowed continuous action and laughs. An episode could be filmed in a few hours in one evening with three cameras. Up until then television

Debbie listening to her sister, played by Patricia Smith, on *The Debbie Reynolds Show* (1969). Patricia was "Ethel" to Debbie's "Lucy." Seated behind Debbie is Tom Bosley, playing her brother-in-law. *Photofest*

sitcoms used only one camera as was the practice in filming movies since day one. There were some sitcoms like *Bewitched* and *The Flying Nun* that still used one camera and scheduled three days for shooting each episode rather than in one evening.

Jesse Oppenheimer was truly a talented and gifted gentleman and a gracious one. For his participation as producer and head writer of *I Love Lucy* he received 20 percent of the profits, a sizable sum when you think of the longevity and worldwide popularity of the show. Jesse gave 5 percent of his 20 percent to his long-time associates and the show's writers, Madelyn Pugh and Bob Carroll, Jr.

For *The Debbie Reynolds* Show Jesse used the same concept that had been so successful on *I Love Lucy*. Debbie's husband, played by Don Chastain, was a successful sportswriter for a major newspaper and loved being at home with his family. Debbie was the housewife who yearned to be successful outside her home as a newspaper reporter and would do anything to get a good story. And that's where their fun began.

A footnote on Jesse Oppenheimer: Not only was he successful in television, he was an accomplished inventor. He held 18 patents for as many inventions, one being for the words of a script to appear in the lens of the camera filming the actor. All the actor had to do was to look into the lens and he could see and read his line, if necessary. It was another form of the widely used TelePrompTer.

Debbie was not only fun to work with but she was the "hostess with the mostess." In the first four months of shooting her sitcom at the MGM studios we had four parties. The first to celebrate finishing the first episode, the second honoring Debbie's sponsors, a third at her spacious home in Beverly Hills, and the last, a wrap party when we shut down for the summer. It was at the supper party in Debbie's home; Chinese delicacies were served because her cook was Chinese, that her teenage daughter Carrie sang for Debbie's guests. Did anyone even know that Carrie could sing?

All this predated Carrie's novel, *Postcards from the Edge*, in which Carrie gave a fictional twist to life with a movie star mother. In the movie Shirley MacLaine plays the movie star (read: Debbie) and Meryl Streep plays the daughter (read: Carrie). At a party Shirley asks her daughter, Meryl, to sing for her guests. Daughter Meryl isn't happy with the request, but rather than cause a scene in front of everyone, she does sing. Ditto the real Carrie Fisher the night I was at Debbie's house. Momma Debbie asked and daughter Carrie sang. What a deep, rich, beautiful singing voice she had even at 13 or 14-years-old. That shouldn't have been a surprise. Her father was the 1950s singing sensation Eddie "Oh My Papa" Fisher. Everyone remembers her mom Debbie singing with Gene Kelly in *Singin' in the Rain* in 1952 and starring and singing in the musical *The Unsinkable Molly Brown* in 1964. To be able to sing beautifully was surely a dominant gene Carrie inherited from both parents. She did follow in her mom's movie footsteps. When she was only 21-years-old, she gained international fame as Princess Leia in the original *Star Wars* trilogy.

Unbeknownst to me, when I heard Carrie sing, she and her brother Todd had already performed and sung on stage with their mother when they were teenagers. And later on, Carrie was in the chorus when Debbie starred on Broadway in 1973 in the revival of *Irene*, a 1920s vintage musical.

Debbie and teenage Carrie off to London shortly after Carrie sang for our supper. *Photofest*

People always ask those on the inside of show business if such and such a performer is really a nice person. When it comes to the unsinkable Debbie Reynolds, what you see is what you get. A real, warm person who loves her work and the wonderful life her talent has brought her. One Saturday evening when I was working on Debbie's show I was enjoying dinner with friends in a very chic Italian restaurant on Little Santa Monica Boulevard in Beverly Hills. I noticed that Debbie was having her dinner in a back booth shielded with curtains. I excused myself from my friends and went over to her table to say "hello." She was as gracious as ever. To my delight, when she and her party were finished eating and were exiting the restaurant, she made a point to stop by my table for another word or two to kibitz with me. Were my friends impressed? You betcha. Was I thrilled? You betcha. Was that typical of Debbie? You betcha. Oh yes, what did I eat at that fine Italian restaurant? Fegato alla Venezia! Liver Venetian style with onions. Delizioso!

THE WILD WILD WEST (1969)

I only worked on a few episodes of *The Wild Wild West* being filmed at the CBS Studios in the San Fernando Valley. Ross Martin played Artemus Gordon to Bob Conrad's James West in this lighthearted, action-packed late 19th-century Western adventure. Both gentlemen were secret agents for President Ulysses S. Grant. Their mission was to rid the western frontier of evil. As Conrad's sidekick, Martin's specialty was to invent tricky gadgets to help them outwit and overcome the villains.

One day at lunch in the CBS commissary, Ross told a story on himself to those members of the crew at the table. That included me. It was about his first big break in films in *Experiment in Terror* (1962), directed by Julie Andrews' husband Blake Edwards. A suspense thriller, the film starred Glenn Ford, Lee Remick and Stefanie Powers. Ross played the villain, Red Lynch, who threatens Remick, a bank teller. If she doesn't help him steal twenty thousand dollars from her bank he'll kidnap and kill her younger sister, played by Powers. Part of the trickery of the film was to keep the villain unidentifiable. So Ross' face was filmed in deep shadows. They wrote the character as suffering from asthma causing him to breathe very heavily and speak very slowly, which made him seem even more menacing. And the final touch to keep Ross unidentifiable as the villain, he didn't receive a credit in the opening titles. The name "Ross Martin" did not appear.

Ross's mom lived in Brooklyn. The day *Experiment in Terror* opened at a first-run movie palace in Manhattan Ross said his mom happily boarded the BMT subway bound for Manhattan. She was intent on seeing her beloved son in his big picture as soon as she

Trust me! That's deeply-shadowed Ross Martin as the villain terrorizing Lee Remick in *Experiment in Terror* (1962). *Movie Collectibles*

could. The movie was playing on Broadway in a theater a few short blocks north of 42nd Street. She bought her ticket for the first screening of the day, found a seat and the movie began. She sat there puzzled. Where was Ross? Maybe he comes in later? But as far as she could see, he didn't! She didn't recognize his asthmatic voice or realize that her baby boy was the villain in the shadows. Perhaps as his mom she could never picture him as a villain. Even before the movie ended, even before the final credits unreeled, Mama Martin stormed out of the theater, terribly angry. Had she sat through the final scenes, she would have seen her son's face as he was chased by the police. Had she sat through the closing credits she would have seen a special card on screen. It read "Ross Martin as Red Lynch."

As we all smiled at his story, Ross added the clincher! His Mom never believed he ever appeared in the film, no matter what he said!

MANNIX AND WOMANIX
Working Late (1969-1970)

Friday nights in television production were usually long nights of work. When I was assigned to an action series of a one-hour weekly television show, I never planned any social activities for Friday nights. All I wanted to do on those nights was head home after work and crawl into bed and sleep, sleep, sleep! Why were Friday nights long nights? On weekdays Screen Actors Guild (SAG) rules stated an actor needed a twelve-hour rest period between work calls. Dismissed at 7 p.m. the actor's first call the next day couldn't be until 7 a.m. If the work call was over a weekend, from Friday night to the next Monday morning, SAG required the actor or actress to have 54 hours of rest between the wrap Friday night and the call Monday morning. That meant you could work actors until 12 midnight on Friday and still have 54 hours till their Monday morning make-up call at 6 a.m. If we worked late Fridays, the company had to provide a dinner break and a catered dinner. Very often late Friday nights were programmed into the work schedule and production costs by the unit manager. Some penalties were overlooked or tolerated because Friday nights were often needed as extra time to catch up if there had been delays or problems earlier in the week's shooting schedule.

One Friday night I was working late on the *Mannix* television series with Mike Connors playing the classic hard-boiled private eye in this action-packed detective series. The guest actress was Sally Kellerman who had won instant fame playing Major Margaret "Hot Lips" Houlihan in Robert Altman's 1970 film classic *M*A*S*H*. As the hour was getting late, everyone was growing weary, including Sally. In her best *grande dame* theatrical voice, Sally intoned aloud, "Hurry up, guys! I only have one more take left in me." Whether she was jesting or grandstanding, I'm sure the rest of the crew, including myself, felt the same way. But we worked until the director called a wrap. That was the game!

GUNSMOKE (1970-1971)

I worked for one season on *Gunsmoke*, the 15th season of the beloved western on TV. How do I know it was the 15th season? As a Christmas gift from the producers of the show the entire crew received a two-inch cube of clear plastic with one frame of film imbedded in the plastic showing a very recognizable 6'6" Marshall Dillon walking down *Gunsmoke's* main street. The only lettering on the film was "The 15th season." By then, James Arness, who played Marshall Dillon, wasn't in every show. In some episodes the story wrapped itself around his character. In others he only appeared in the open and close, still others he didn't appear at all, was supposedly "out of town."

The beautiful Amanda Blake, who hit her acting stride in *Gunsmoke* playing the saloonkeeper Miss Kitty, had purchased tickets to see the risqué stage revue *Oh! Calcutta* at the Fairfax Theatre in Los Angeles. The Fairfax was a neighborhood movie house that had been temporarily converted to a legitimate theatrical stage when no other theater would or perhaps was available to house this shockingly, sexy revue that had been a hit in London and New York.

Oh! Calcutta was created by British theatre critic Kenneth Tynan. Some called it the most innocent dirty show. It consisted of a series of sex-related sketches, notorious because the men and women performed absolutely nude in several of the sketches! Quite daring! It was the rage! Voyeurs raced to buy tickets!

Amanda asked her stand-in to go with her, but was loathing attending without a male escort. So she sidled up to me and in a soft, sweet voice wondered if I might accompany the two ladies to the show that everyone was talking about. She had an extra ticket and would be delighted to treat me. I accepted immediately. I was thrilled not only to see the show, but to be seen with two very beautiful women, one on each arm. The show was great fun. Not as daring or as scandalous as the media publicity made it out to be. As far as nudity, I had seen a few nudes in my life! But it was an unexpected perk. Also unexpected was the pewter beer stein that

WHAT HAVE I MISSED? TV, OF COURSE!

Gathered around a table in Miss Kitty's saloon are *Gunsmoke's* leading players the season I worked the show. (L.) to (R.) James Arness as Marshall Dillon, Amanda Blake as Miss Kitty, Buck Taylor as Newly, Ken Curtis as Festus and Milburn Stone as Doc. *Movie Collectibles*

Amanda gave me as a Christmas present with "*Gunsmoke*," the year "1969" and "Miss Kitty" inscribed. Now I had two pewter beer steins, one from Amanda, the other from Paul Newman.

THE PARTRIDGE FAMILY (1973-1974)

The Cowsills were a musical group consisting of four brothers, their mom and later their kid sister and younger brother who gained national recognition performing as a singing family in the 1960s. Producers at Screen Gems, the TV arm of Columbia Pictures, thought the Cowsills singing family would make for a good situation comedy. At first they thought they would cast the Cowsills to play themselves, but some of the children turned out not to have the acting skills. Instead, the Cowsills became the inspiration for *The Partridge Family* television series. Five Partridge children enlist their widowed mom, played by Shirley Jones, to join them in their family singing group. The series revolved around their singing success as well as their own family and teenage trials and tribulations. In each episode the family sang a song. David Cassidy, playing the eldest son, became a teenage heartthrob. His adolescent admirers, teenage girls, would wait patiently each morning and evening at the entrance gate to the Columbia Ranch on Hollywood Way in Burbank where the show was filmed, hoping to catch a glimpse of their idol.

Midway through the fourth season, when I was working as a second assistant to my friend Tom McCrory's First, the producers scored a coup. They scheduled an episode to be filmed aboard the *Fairseas*, one of the Sitmar cruise ships sailing round trip between Los Angeles and Acapulco. We were to film the episode on the four day return voyage from Acapulco to Los Angeles. So it was necessary for our equipment for the show to be preloaded on the *Fairseas* while still anchored in San Pedro, the harbor for Los Angeles, before the cruise ship set sail south for Mexico.

One of our studio's electricians assigned to load the electrical equipment mysteriously didn't hear the call for non-passengers to debark. The ship sailed and so did he. Poor guy, he had to endure four days aboard ship, overeating on cruise ship food, lounging in deck chairs, dancing with the widows and single women as the *Fairseas* headed south to Acapulco. Poor guy, he missed four grueling days of work with the Partridge crew back at the Columbia Ranch in Burbank. The following Sunday the rest of us were flown down to Acapulco and boarded the ship for its return to L.A. As we cruised north back to Los Angeles, we filmed the episode written especially for the cruise which included the cast dressing for a masquerade party aboard ship. If the ship swayed with the ocean so did the crew.

The highlight of the journey for me was when the stars of the show, Shirley Jones and teenage singing heartthrob David Cassidy, entertained us at a performance for just the cast and movie crew. David is Shirley's stepson, son of her first husband, actor Jack Cassidy. The setting for the entertainment was the private dining room the ship's captain assigned us. Shirley's and David's combined songs and patter surely would have qualified as a topnotch Las Vegas nightclub act. And then we all danced!

WHAT HAVE I MISSED? TV, OF COURSE!

Aboard ship. (L. to R.) Irv, the property master, David Cassidy dressed as the Easter Bunny, Shirley Jones in a clown costume, then myself looking elsewhere and finally the back of Dave Madden, bewigged and dressed as a ballerina for the ship's masquerade party.
AUTHOR

Back on shore that same season I was asked to drive an actress guest-starring on *The Partridge Family* from the Columbia Ranch in Burbank to her Hollywood hotel, the Montecito. What fun for me, a fan of the 1939 classic *The Wizard of Oz*. The lady in question was Margaret Hamilton, the green-faced Wicked Witch of the West. She answered as many questions about the Munchkins and the stars of *The Wizard of Oz* that I could fit into the drive time.

When people ask me if Shirley Jones is as nice as she seems in her films and interviews, the answer is an unequivocal "Yes!" Easygoing, friendly and a pleasure to work with. And she doesn't forget you after you no longer work with her day to day.

I was driving my car into a parking lot to attend an afternoon musical concert. I knew that Shirley was scheduled to sing, as were her sons Sean and Patrick Cassidy in a trio with their half-brother David Cassidy. Walking towards me was Shirley, carrying her own garment bag. I rolled down my driver's window and shouted out a "Hello." Without missing a beat, she recognized me and replied, "Hi, Steve. Enjoy the show. How are you doing?" Nice lady. The same when she and her middle son Patrick were starring to great acclaim on Broadway in a revival of the musical *42nd Street* in

2004. This was the first time in Broadway musical history that a mother and son had starred together in the same musical show. After enjoying the show I went backstage to say "hello." Though it was over a quarter of a century, 30 long years before that we had worked together in 1974 in *The Partridge Family*, without missing a beat Shirley greeted me by name. She was still as beautiful as she was on *The Partridge Family*, but just as the years had turned my hair gray, so had they turned her hair gray. Unlike many women of her age she wore her gray locks with pride. A lovely lady!

MOVIN' ON (1975-1976)

Movin' On was a one-hour action series about big rig truckers and the adventures they had hauling cargo on the road. The stars of the show were contrasting buddies: Claude Akins was the folksy, old-timer, rugged trucker; Frank Converse, the handsome, college-educated dude the girls went for.

I joined the company midway through their season. They were in Henderson, North Carolina, filming two shows. Next, we moved to Atlanta, Georgia, and then on to Mobile, Alabama. *Movin' On* was supposed to end the season in the City of New Orleans. The adventure the truckers would encounter would occur as the city celebrated Mardi Gras. However, word came down from the producers in Hollywood that there wasn't enough money in the budget for the trip. Instead, the producers transposed the story to Mobile, Alabama, where we were established and had already filmed one episode. What most people don't know is that the first Mardi Gras in America was held in Mobile in 1702 when Mobile was the capitol city of French Louisiana. The city carries on the tradition to this day. All the necessary Mardi Gras paraphernalia was on hand so we had no problem filming the show in Mobile as scripted for New Orleans.

It fell to Ernie Frankel, a producer traveling with the show and a Henderson, North Carolina boy himself, to break the news to the civic leaders in New Orleans that *Movin' On* wasn't coming to film in their fair city. I was asked to accompany Ernie on the trip to New Orleans. I never really knew why. My guess at the time was to give him visible, physical support in his unenviable task. To my amazement when Ernie was finished explaining the situation to all the civic leaders gathered in the hotel meeting room, the outcry of disappointment that I had expected to hear in the room did not materialize. The angst I was sure I would witness in their demeanor did not occur. Their concern wasn't for themselves or for their beloved city but for Ernie himself! Somehow, in his masterfully phrased speech he had turned the situation around. It was his own disappointment that *Movin' On* would not be coming to New Orleans expressed with such heartfelt sorrow that Ernie's personal grief seemed far worse than their city losing the filming of a TV show. After all, *Movin' On* would not be the last show to want to film in New Orleans.

One by one they came up to Ernie to express their understanding, that they knew it wasn't his fault or his decision. Ernie was a master speaker! In trying to ease any negativity or bad publicity that canceling filming might bring, he turned the situation into a positive for everyone concerned. Even I found myself tearing up as he spoke to the community leaders.

Because we wouldn't be going to fabulous New Orleans as originally scheduled, Ernie Frankel arranged for the producers to pay for a four-day holiday over Thanksgiving weekend for the cast and crew in New Orleans. Travel, hotel and food! Imagine the clerk's reaction when on the road to New Orleans our bus stopped at a Hardee fast food burger restaurant and Claude Akins, the star of the show, went inside and ordered fifty burgers to go!

A SENSITIVE PASSIONATE MAN (1977)

In 1977 I was working on a movie for TV called *A Sensitive Passionate Man*, directed by John Newland, that starred David Janssen as the husband and Angie Dickinson as his wife, in a story of an outwardly happy marriage that is threatened by the husband's alcoholism. Twelve years before, when the DGA gave me my first opportunity in Hollywood by assigning me to the situation comedy *My Brother the Angel* starring the Smothers Brothers, a beautiful woman in her fifties reported for work. She was an extra for a scene around a hotel pool. Her last name was Janssen. On the Q.T.

another extra told me she was actor David Janssen's mother. That was hard for me to believe since she looked too young to have a son as old as Janssen. My informant also told me, soto voce, that when she was sweet 16 she was a showgirl on Broadway. Looking at her then I had no doubts that that was true. She was still a stunner, gorgeous!

In the course of the day we became friendly. She was given a call-back for the following day which meant another paycheck for her. When lunch was called that next day, I headed for the commissary. So did she. I purchased my food and sat down alone at a table. She purchased her meal and came over to my table. Could she join me, she asked. Gladly, I replied. Please sit down!

As we ate we made small talk. She smiled, she giggled, and her eyes glowed. By God, I thought, she's coming on to me! Back then the word "cougar" meant a large, tawny feline found in jungles! Today it colloquially describes an older woman lusting after a younger man. I had dated older women before, though not 25 years older. Since this was my first job as a second assistant director I didn't want to make any moves that might reflect badly on my job performance. Also, this was my first time dealing with extras and their ways and needs.

The job of the extras is to make a scene in a movie or TV show seem like real life. Officially they are background actors because they are the people in the background who are walking on the street, seated at the other tables in the restaurant, in the theater audience, and so on. They are simply making the surrounding scene come alive. Until 1992, the Screen Extras Guild (SEG) founded in 1946 set the pay scales and rules and regulations that the studios had to abide by when hiring extras. Becoming a member of the Screen Extras Guild was beneficial for anyone who wanted to work as a background actor in the movie industry. In 1992, SEG disbanded and the extras were taken under the wing of the Screen Actors Guild.

Since 1925 Central Casting was the primary casting service used by the major studios. There are also several non-union casting services that some non-union producers prefer because the rules aren't as exacting and the pay scales less. An aspiring extra registers with one or more of these casting services. Each extra, man, woman or child, will be categorized by age, gender, height, weight, race, special abilities, and so forth. All their vital statistics will be stored in a vast computer file that will be searched to see if they are appropriate for any of the day's orders for extras. Sometimes an assistant director will ask for an extra specifically by his or her name. Other times the extra is just lucky to have phoned in at the right time and fit the bill! Brad Pitt and John Wayne began their movie careers as extras.

Extras have to be alert to perform their action as preset for them by the assistant director or on a visual cue from the assistant director. Sometimes they work off an action in the scene (for example, cross the room when the actor opens the door to leave). At all times they must act natural and fit in appropriately to the scene being filmed. The work can be tiring because extras may have to repeat and match their action exactly each time a dissatisfied director calls for another take to cover the scene he's shooting. Whether it's a long or medium shot, even a close-up, if the extra is visible in the background he has to be ready to repeat his action.

Anyone working as an extra has to be tough-skinned, persistent and optimistic. If he's working on a show and doesn't get a call back for the next day, or if he wasn't working that day, when 4 p.m. comes, he and every extra seeking work for the next day will make a beeline for a telephone or pull out their cell phone and dial Central Casting. By 4 p.m. every TV show, feature film or commercial in production has already notified their casting service if there are any callbacks for the next day or the number of new extras needed, according to gender, age, race, nationality, etc. If the extra is lucky and gets a job for the next day, he'll be told where to report and may be told a bit about the story. He'll be advised what to wear, whether he should dress down or dress up, whether he should bring a change of clothes. Will they use his car? For many of the additional requests (can he ride a horse, swim, etc.) there probably will be a bump, a whammy, an added fee in his paycheck for that day. If he's performed a "silent bit" that day where he doesn't have any lines but is someone interacting with the star or a principle actor in an action pertinent to the script, again he will have earned an additional fee. Extras live with much anxiety and frustration especially when there is no job for the next day. To ease their lives and to avoid the daily telephone ritual, some extras prefer to work as stand-ins. There's more security in that position.

A stand-in usually matches the gender of the actor he or she is "standing-in for." Short adult stand-ins, over 18-years-old, are hired to stand-in for children. As his actor rehearses the scene, the stand-in watches every move. When the actors leave the set and the director of photography and his crew light the scene, the stand-in duplicates the action of his actor so the scene and the actor can be lit properly. Some stand-ins prefer working for an established movie star. They build a relationship with the movie star and will be alerted by their star to be available for the star's next movie. That way they are guaranteed a job whenever that star works. The more films for the star, the more paychecks for the stand-in!

Other extras seek work as utility stand-ins on a weekly television series, covering the stars of the show and the guest stars hired for each weekly episode. Because a series will be filming multiple episodes over many months and has the possibility of being renewed for the next season, the utility stand-in is assured a run of paychecks now and perhaps next season. If an extra can find a feature film that will be shooting for several weeks or months, working as that film's stand-in would also be a good deal financially. As in a weekly series, on a feature film a good stand-in will also be required to stand-in for other actors and guest stars when his star is not involved. Quite often a stand-in who has acting skills and is a member of the Screen Actors Guild will be given a small acting role and receive Guild pay and perks for the day. Unlike those extras who must call in every day for a job, stand-ins get their next day call from the second assistant director on the show they're working. That makes a more peaceful, secure life for them.

No matter how they get their work call, each extra's aim is to build a strong relationship with the many assistant directors they encounter, hoping the assistants will remember their face and give them a call, if not on the show where they met on another show on another day. Remember me, is their theme. Naturally, doing a good job, being on time and staying out of trouble puts an extra on any assistant director's preferred list. Once in a while, I was asked to do a favor for an extra by giving them a work call. The 70-something-year-old widow of silent screen star Roscoe "Fatty" Arbuckle needed a few more work days as an extra to qualify for her full pension. That was the reason I was asked by a fellow assistant director to give Minna Arbuckle a work call when I was assisting on the TV series *Banacek* at Universal Studios.

For aspiring young film directors, work as an extra is an excellent opportunity to observe and learn firsthand about film production. Usually they are film students studying in one of the top-notch film schools in the Los Angeles area, either the University of Southern California (USC) or the University of California at Los Angeles (UCLA). Two such college students who worked as extras for me and became highly successful directors in Hollywood are Randall Kleiser and Taylor Hackford. Kleiser's first major film was the musical *Grease* (1978), starring John Travolta, produced by the late Alan Carr. Hackford often produces and directs his films. He did both for the movie *Ray* (2004), the story of singing legend Ray Charles with Jamie Foxx playing Ray. Both Kleiser and Hackford are active in the day-to-day affairs of the Directors Guild of America. Taylor has been elected President of the DGA for 2011 through 2013. Working as extras when they were students certainly gave them an edge as they pursued the big time.

Well, was David Janssen's mother really hot for my body on *My Brother The Angel*? Or was she just hot for a third day of work as an extra and for the paycheck she'd pocket if she was called back for another day's work? Was that why I thought she was cozying up to me? I never found out. There were no extras needed for the next day's shooting. And, as fate would have it, when pilot season was over a few weeks later, I was out of work as a second assistant director. Mother Janssen and I never reconnected.

Filming *A Sensitive Passionate Man* with David Janssen and Angie Dickinson was a delight. We were shooting at night inside a large house in the Windsor Square area of Los Angeles. The house was owned by the wife of H. R. "Bob" Haldemann, who was President Richard Nixon's chief of staff and a key figure in the Watergate scandal which forced Nixon to resign from the presidency in August, 1974. Allowing movie companies to shoot in one's home brought the owner a vey substantial fee, plus the written agreement to return the house to its original condition if any changes were made or any accidents occurred.

Angie Dickinson's dressing room trailer was parked across the street from the Haldemann house. One night, when her scenes were finished for the night and she was dismissed, Angie grabbed my arm. Clinging to me, she asked me to escort her across the dark street to her dressing room trailer. Angie had never even touched me before let alone clung to me. The reason? She confided that there was a man lurking in the shadows that she had seen earlier, just hanging around, his eye on her. She thought he might be stalking her and was afraid of what he might do if she was alone. She didn't want to risk it. The perils of being a beautiful star! I gladly walked with her to her trailer, waited until she got out of her costume and into her civvies and then walked with her until she was safely in her car parked nearby and watched as she drove off.

Escorting is not in the second assistant's handbook of official duties, but I was pleased to assist her and ease her mind. A happy actress is a better actress. If that isn't in the handbook, it should be!

GUYANA TRAGEDY
The Story of Jim Jones (1979-1980)

When I was in the fourth grade in P.S. 76 in the East Bronx, I was cured of any desire to act. In a class play I was George Washington, complete with breeches and a white wig. When I banged a gavel on a small pedestal table calling the Continental Congress to order, the table top fell off! It drew a big laugh from the audience, but I was so embarrassed I turned beet red. No more acting for me. That is until 1979 when I was the first assistant on *Guyana Tragedy: The Story of Jim Jones*.

A TV movie for CBS-TV, *Guyana Tragedy* was directed by William A. Graham, who I had enjoyed working with before on several made-for-TV movies. Billy, as everyone called him, became a television director in New York when he was still in his early 20's, working on such live TV shows as the Kraft Television Theater in what has been called the Golden Age of Television. Like many other east coast directors he soon moved out to Los Angeles where there were more opportunities. In 1969 he directed *Change of Habit*, the last movie Elvis Presley ever made. Billy said, "Elvis was the nicest man I ever met in my life. He was the politest man I ever met. He called everyone sir or ma'am, you know, starting with the guard at the gate all the way up to the head of the studio." Personally, I thought Billy was one of the nicest men I ever met.

Guyana Tragedy told the true story of Jim Jones, a self-proclaimed prophet, charismatic and corrupt, who founded the People's Temple. To join his commune, his followers had to sell their homes and donate their entire life's savings to him and the Temple. In 1978 they all followed him to Guyana, the only English-speaking country in South America, where in the midst of the jungle they built from scratch their People's Temple Agricultural Project, which was known as Jonestown. Jones always had a leaning in his teachings towards Communism. Under his leadership the members of his church believed they were building a new order of equality and a better spiritual life. When there were accusations of abuse of temple members in Jonestown, Congressman Leo Ryan of California flew to Guyana to investigate. As Ryan was boarding his plane to leave, taking along several defecting members and the journalists who were with him, Jones' security guards opened fire and killed Ryan and four others. This was the final straw for Jones. He feared the murder of Ryan would result in the US Government destroying Jonestown. Rather than face his accusers, he urged his followers to commit the ultimate sacrifice, to die with him by drinking cyanide-laced grape Flavor-Aid. Nine hundred and eighteen people, including 303 babies, either drank the poison or were murdered for refusing to commit suicide. It was the worst mass murder and mass suicide in history.

The locations necessary for the film were many and varied and had to reflect different parts of the United States. Needed were a small Midwest town where Jones grew up, the Midwest cities and Northern California towns Jones moved to as the number of his followers grew attracted by his message and charisma and finally San Francisco, where he established his headquarters. Also needed for the film was the Jonestown compound he and his followers built in Guyana and government buildings in Guyana's capitol city, Georgetown.

The location manager recommended two locations. The first was Atlanta, Georgia. He felt all the scenes prior to Guyana could be filmed in Atlanta and its surrounding towns and communities. The second location was Puerto Rico, where there were many Spanish Colonial buildings to double for Guyana's government buildings and where there was available land on which a replica of the Jonestown compound could be built. The entire movie could be filmed between Atlanta and Puerto Rico, except for two scenes in San Francisco which were placed at the end of the shooting schedule. For those scenes the company would move to San Francisco, where Jones had had his last church before fleeing to South America.

In 1979 the unit manager or first assistant director had the responsibility of creating a shooting schedule that would be printed and passed out to all the actors and crew. It detailed the order in which the scenes in the film would be shot, day by day, week after week. With a shooting schedule in hand everyone concerned would know what was happening. The unit manager or first assistant would first read the script and then break it down, scene by scene. He would use special strips of cardboard marked for movie production. On each strip he would write the name of the scene, whether it was an interior or exterior scene, day or night, what actors would be needed for each scene, indicating them by their assigned number, the stars being 1, 2, 3 as needed, and also specify on the strip any special requirements pertinent to that scene when it would be shot.

Let's say the script had 100 scenes. Each scene would be represented by one of those strips and numbered from 1 to 100. When completed, each strip would be fitted into a shooting board especially made to hold the strips, a board that could be folded for easy carrying. Once the 100 strips were in view, they would then be rearranged to discover how much time would be needed to film each scene. In rearranging the strips the aim was to make the shooting easier: strips with similar locations were grouped together; actor's length of their employment per their contract; night scenes; and as many other special conditions were noted. Some scenes might only take half a page as written, but when the director filmed it he would need a week. That had to be accounted for in the shooting schedule.

In the *Guyana Tragedy* shooting schedule the last two days were set aside for traveling to San Francisco and shooting two very brief scenes written for the streets of San Francisco. There were no major stars in those scenes. The producers looked at the schedule and reconsidered. Why spend all that money moving the crew and equipment to the city by the bay? The producers instructed the location manager to find sites in Atlanta that could double for San Francisco. That was easily accomplished.

The two San Francisco scenes required one speaking actor who was a member of Jones' Temple and one extra in each scene representing San Francisco citizens. Easy, thought the producers. In Atlanta there were several Hollywood actors, male and female, who were already playing Temple members. We'll just have one of them do the scenes. They were easy scenes, each was just one line. But that was not kosher with the Screen Actors Guild.

When an actor was hired, his contract specifically named the character he was playing. After the contract was approved and signed, that actor could not be assigned the role of another character that was already described and written in the original script. A different actor would have to be hired for that role. With so many SAG members seeking work, this was probably SAG's way of making sure acting opportunities and fees were spread around. SAG would not allow any of the actors on location play the parts.

The two San Francisco scenes were scheduled for one afternoon. The location manager found two streets in Atlanta that could pass for San Francisco. Then Billy Graham, the director, turned to me.

"Steve, I want you to play the Temple member when we shoot it tomorrow. Go to wardrobe and get fitted."

As I've said before, my main duty as a first assistant director is to assist and please the director. So to please Billy I reported to wardrobe and signed a contract to play the role. The two scenes were similar. In the first the Temple member was a businessman. I wore a suit, carried a briefcase and was talking to another suited gentleman. Saying we have to make sure we get our man elected, I urged the other man to vote for George Moscone, who at that time was running for mayor of San Francisco. In the second scene I was the same Temple member, now dressed very casually in blue jeans, talking with a similarly casually dressed street person, urging him to vote for George Moscone, saying we gays have to stick together to make sure we get our man elected. The scenes showed Jones' duplicity. Instead of using my real name in the credits I tacked my mom's maiden surname onto my first name and was billed as "Steve Grand." Billy Graham was pleased with my performance, but if I had had

On location, three members of the DGA. (L. to R.) Myself, the first assistant, Mitch Factor, my second assistant who was a grandson of Max Factor, the famous cosmetic manufacturer who created the first make-up movie stars used on film in the 1920s and Billy Graham, my friend and favorite director who directed *Guyana Tragedy*. AUTHOR'S COLLECTION

any illusions about being an actor, they vanished after that. Acting for me was hard work, not my cup of tea. I preferred working behind the scenes not in front of the camera!

Powers Boothe, who was cast as Jim Jones, not only looked like him but turned in an excellent performance. In September 1980, when the Emmy Awards were held and televised nationally, the Screen Actors Guild was in the midst of a strike. Powers, in defiance of his Guild, was one of the few nominees to attend the ceremonies. When his name was called as Best Actor in a Drama, he was the only winner and member of his union to go on stage that year to accept his Emmy, saying, "This is either the most courageous moment of

Powers Boothe as Jim Jones pressures his people to take the poisoned Flavor-Aid. In the lower left corner is Veronica Cartwright, who played his wife, Marceline. *Photofest*

my career or the stupidest." He continued, "I thought long and hard whether or not I would attend, but I came here because this is America and one must do what one believes. I believe in the Academy. I also believe in my fellow actors in their stand." Suffice to say, my performance in *Guyana Tragedy* was not nominated for an Emmy, but I did get residuals.

What determines an actor's pay? The quality of the part, his or her prominence, previous salary, and how many days of acting the part requires or simply what the actor's agent demands. Earlier, I mentioned Cloris Leachman being hired on *Butch Cassidy and The Sundance Kid* for one day at a thousand dollars a day which grew into five thousand when she was held over for five days. Colleen Dewhurst also had a one-day contract for her role in *Guyana Tragedy*. She and I knew adding another day or two to her schedule would not be appreciated by the producers of the film.

Colleen was hired to play Mrs. Myrtle Kennedy, who was Jim Jones' mentor when he was just a boy growing up. She was deeply religious and was the major reason why Jones became a preacher. Also working that day was another very gifted actress, Diane Ladd, playing Lynette Jones the young boy's mother. Both women had much in common besides being actresses. They had each married highly praised actors: Colleen's husband was George C. Scott, famous for refusing his Oscar for the movie *Patton* (1970); Diane's equally successful husband was Bruce Dern, an actor whose talent many believed far exceeded the roles he was offered. Both families had also produced second-generation actors, the Scotts' son, Campbell Scott, the Derns' daughter, Laura Dern.

When both couples were just beginning their careers in New York, they had been good friends. Diane was thrilled to see Colleen in Atlanta when they were both cast in *Guyana Tragedy*. The two actresses had not been in touch with each other for several years. Diane knew that Colleen was working only on a one-day contract. Tomorrow she'd be gone and Diane wanted more catch-up time with her old friend. The three of us were in a production van being chauffeured from one set to another. With a twinkle in her eye, Diane suggested if the director, for whatever reason, wink, wink, didn't get Colleen's last scene to his satisfaction, he might have to call her back for another day.

Colleen was noted for her resonant voice and hearty laugh—and she burst out in a roar of laughter! No, she didn't think they would want her back, "would they, Steve?" she said to me. Smiling, I shook my head "No."

Unknown to Diane, Colleen's pay for one day on *Guyana Tragedy* was a whopping twenty-five thousand dollars. Not many working actors could command that rich a paycheck for one day's work. In spite of it being only one day of work, the producers and director deemed the casting of the role so important because of the character's early influence on a young, impressionable Jones. It demanded casting a very strong actress. Colleen was a strong actress. Twenty-five thousand was her fee. For one day, okay. Double twenty-five thousand for two? That was another story.

FROM THE FRYING PAN
Into the Video Fire

Usually if I said to people that I created the *Video Fireplace* most people would have a blank look on their faces, not knowing what I was talking about. But if I said I was the guy who created a VHS cassette that when you put it into your VCR up came one hour of a roaring, crackling fire that turned your TV into a fireplace, well that might ring a bell for them. Yes, that was me, the first person in America to create and market the *Video Fireplace* as well as the *Video Aquarium*, which turned your TV into a water-filled fish tank teeming with beautiful fish. When these cassettes hit the market in 1982, there were scores of people I met who said they had had the very same idea. And I'd answer, "I guess I was the only one crazy enough to produce and market them!"

Indeed, there were those who thought it was crazy for me to think that I'd make any money selling those videos. Others said I was nuts to give up the security of the great job I had as an assistant director, nuts to risk being self-employed, even if I owned the firm which I had named The Video Naturals Company. Behind my back I knew friends were twirling a finger, pointing it at my head, mouthing the word "loco." My mother, puzzled, fearing I was off my rocker, kept asking me if I was sure. Wouldn't I rather have a regular job?

In a couple of years I would be 50-years-old. The old fires weren't burning within me as strongly. I was no longer striving to find a winning movie property that I could produce. Though I didn't have deep pockets loaded with cash to see me through the trials and tribulations of setting up a new business, that didn't faze me. For God sakes, I didn't even know I should have a business plan. I was simply unaware of how the do's and don'ts worked in setting up a business! All I had was guts! Just guts! And a strong belief in myself. What would be the worst that could happen? Lose my shirt and have to slink back to the DGA and beg to work again as an assistant director? One thing I didn't do when I produced and marketed my videos was to give up my membership in the Directors Guild. In fact, on March 1, 2011 I celebrated fifty years as a DGA member, retired!

What I secretly hoped when my business began was that my *Video Fireplace* would turn out to be another pet rock. Back in 1975 a man named Gary Dahl heard his friends talking about their pets and thought that's what he needed—a pet. But one you didn't have to feed, walk, bath or groom. He came up with the idea of a product he called a pet rock. It was just an ordinary gray stone. It came in a box that had some straw for the pet to rest on and holes for the pet to breathe. It also came with a 32-page booklet entitled "The Care and Training of Your Pet Rock," which was filled with gags, puns and fun and made that pet rock come to life and great fun to read! In a matter of six months Dahl sold enough to turn himself into a millionaire. That's what I hoped my *Video Fireplace* might do for me. Instead, it was the beginning of a 30-year business.

What set me on this wacky adventure that everyone else thought was crazy? One day I opened my mail to discover an invitation to a family wedding back east. I was in between film assignments so I had the time to attend. What I didn't know as I boarded the airplane that flew me back east was that a new chapter in my life would be opening for me.

My cousin Ruth's son Barry was being married. I always had a special place in my heart for Ruthie, her sister Gloria and their families. My mom and their mother, Mary, became bosom buddies working together when they were young girls during the First World War. They met when they were sewing machine operators in the sweatshops of Lower Manhattan. My mom thought her cousin Max, a handsome, eligible bachelor, might be attracted to Mary, so she introduced them. He was. She was. Soon they were married and having a family, their two daughters.

When I was four-years-old, my family moved from the West to the East Bronx into an apartment in the same building where Mary, Max and their daughters lived. It was from that small apartment

FROM THE FRYING PAN INTO THE VIDEO FIRE

building that I began enjoying my Saturday movie matinees at the Allerton Theatre.

While I was in New York, waiting to attend the wedding, the friends I was staying with took me along to a cocktail party on West 23rd Street between Eight and Ninth Avenues. It was a small one-room apartment. The host, who really didn't know me, kept introducing me to the other guests as a Hollywood producer, which impressed them no end. But, of course, I wasn't a producer. I was an assistant director. I should have corrected the host, but I rather enjoyed the promotion he had given me.

Feeling good, perhaps it was the cocktail, I looked over at his television set and video cassette recorder that were positioned in the center of three oak bookcases standing together on one wall. I've always wondered if subconsciously those bookcases and TV equipment as they were arranged suggested a fireplace to me and inspired me to say to my host out of the blue, "Gee, if you had a video of a fireplace with a fire burning, we could be having our drinks around a fireplace." His one-room apartment didn't have a real fireplace, an amenity usually only found in expensive New York City apartments.

To my surprise, the host said he did have a videotape of a fire burning that he had taped off-the-air previously. He pulled it out from his cache of VHS tapes and played it for me. It was a flame-filled fire burning brightly. As a Californian I didn't know that from 1966 to 1985, every Christmas Eve, WPIX-TV, Channel 11 in New York, ran a Christmas fire with holiday greetings and music from 6 p.m. till the first church service at 11 p.m. The TV station had taped this fireplace at Gracie Mansion, the official residence of the Mayor of New York. The first was in black and white. When color became a must, the WPIX producer went back to the city officials for permission to reshoot the Gracie Mansion fireplace in living color. Absolutely not, he was told. Apparently, when they filmed there the first time, they had burnt the Mayor's prized rug! The fire I was viewing had been taped elsewhere. Though spoken in jest, seeing my crazy idea come to actual life was a moment of epiphany for me.

I was as high as if I had taken an illegal drug! I stepped away from the people in the room, sat down on a chair by myself and thought, "I can do that!" I could do fire and I could also do water, a fish-filled aquarium. It was all very clear in my mind. What I would be creating is a new kind of furniture as well as a new use for one's television set. If a person didn't have a real fireplace, now he could. If the same person didn't have a fish tank, now he could. And both without any muss or fuss. All one needed for starters were a TV set and a VCR.

I was ecstatic! My mind was racing along at two hundred miles an hour. I was no longer interested in the party. I wanted to get out of there and back to California to begin turning my idea into a reality. A new product! A new business! A new life for me!

Once I was back in Hollywood I borrowed a friend's camcorder. I took it to another friend's house in Pasadena. I knew her home had two fireplaces, one in her family room that burned wood and one in her parlor that owed its flames to gas. I didn't tape the gas fireplace. It didn't sit well with me to tape a fake fire to create another fake fire. So I set my camcorder up in the family room and videotaped ten minutes of the blazing, wood burning fireplace as a test. No sound. I was only interested in seeing what the visual looked like.

I had read a book about how to market a new product. The author wrote that to test the waters, he advised running an advertisement that described the product. If you got any orders from the ad that meant the public wanted the product. Then go ahead and produce and package it. Looking back now at his advice, I question it. At that time, to inexperienced me, it seemed plausible. I wrote an ad to run in the *Z Channel Magazine*, the program guide for a unique cable channel that serviced Santa Monica, Beverly Hills, and Hollywood, California. I chose that magazine because I believed I was honing in on a specific audience living in those cities. Without a doubt more Z Channel subscribers would be visual, media-minded, television and movie professionals who I hoped would find my cassettes an interesting idea. Reading my ad in their issue of the *Z Channel Magazine,* I believed the concept of a fireplace on video would resonate positively with them. Not only might the ad produce some buyers, but, with luck, a financial backer!

Predominant in the ad was the fireplace. I'd named it *Romantic Fireplace*; a name which I hoped would create the aurora of two lovers sprawled passionately on a fur skin, their faces aglow in the light from the roaring fireplace behind them. The *Z Channel Magazine* was published every six weeks. The issue carrying my ad was scheduled to be delivered by mail on or before November 15. In my naiveté I thought I was hitting the Christmas gift-giving season and would have enough time to produce the product for Christmas. As an entrepreneur, boy, did I have a lot to learn. However, the Z Channel threw me a curve! Without telling me in advance, they switched their magazine to a monthly and it was mailed for December 1 delivery instead of November 15. I had lost two weeks of reading time that I thought I had paid for to reach my prospective buying audience.

I was outraged. I called the channel and spoke to the person in charge of the magazine. Two good things happened as a result of that telephone call. My money was refunded and the guy I was speaking to referred to my product not by the name I had given it, the *Romantic Fireplace*, but as a "video fireplace." My ears perked up. *Video Fireplace!* That had a certain ring to it. I immediately stored it in mind for future use! What I had forgotten was that in the copy I wrote for the Z Channel ad, I had written "turn your TV set into a video fireplace with our *Romantic Fireplace*." I guess I needed to hear the words "video fireplace" spoken out loud to grasp their value to me as the product's name.

Not one person called to buy the video. So much for that guy and his book. But on Monday morning, January 4, 1982, I got a phone call from a writer on the syndicated TV showbiz program *Entertainment Tonight*. The producer of the show had read my ad in the *Z Channel Magazine* and thought it would make a "hot item," he punned, for them. Did I have any video of it they could run? Yes, I did, I replied, but it had no sound. The writer said that didn't matter. They would use it silently in a box over the shoulder of the host Ron Hendron. That same evening it was the closing item of the show with Hendron quipping, "With the TV season as it is so far, this may be the hottest thing on TV."

In those pre-Mary Hart days, *Entertainment Tonight* also did a weekend show made up mostly from the stories that ran the previous week. The yet-unnamed *Video Fireplace* hit the airwaves a second time the following weekend. I was beside myself with joy. What great national publicity and it was free! I sensed momentum was building and I didn't even have a product. I remembered that a man I had met at a holiday dinner was said to own a videotape duplication house. His name was David Friedman and he would become a godsend, a good friend and my silent partner.

David was a fascinating guy. At one time he worked at Paramount Pictures doing publicity for Bing Crosby and Bob Hope. Under his own steam, he had produced a long list of soft-core pornography movies with titles like *Trader Hornee* and *The Erotic Adventures of Zorro*. Inexpensive to produce, they made a steady stream of money. With the sexual revolution of the 1960s mom and pop installed VCR's in their bedrooms to play arousing, erotic films. David invested in a video duplication business to keep those home VCR's loaded and playing! In 1963 he also co-produced with Herschell Gordon Lewis a gore-filled horror film called *Blood Feast*, which became a classic in its genre. It grossed four million dollars in the United States on an investment that David said to me privately was five thousand dollars, though officially the press was told twenty-five thousand.

I made an appointment with David Friedman, explained what I wanted to do and showed him the ten minutes of fire I had video-taped. David was an entertainment buff. Fortunately for me, he had seen both the weekday and weekend stories about the *Video Fireplace* on *Entertainment Tonight* and understood what I was up to. As a former public relations man, he liked my idea, thought it had legs and commercial possibilities. David was also a risk taker. He told me to film the videos, both the fireplace and aquarium, and then come back to him and he'd work with me.

Things were going well. I rented a professional video camera and a state-of-the-art recording machine. Since I knew absolutely nothing about cameras, I hired Monte Swann to operate the camera. Monte was a technician on the staff of the rental company. By hiring him, the owner of the company didn't require me to buy insurance on the equipment. He felt that with his man on hand all the equipment would indeed be in good hands, and it was! With Monte on board as cameraman I not only saved money, but had his technical know-how and expertise to fall back on. Next came the actual taping. Two friends had agreed to let me in their homes to tape what I needed. First, the fireplace on a Friday night in my friend Jay's home off Lake Hollywood Drive just up the hill from Burbank and Warner Bros. The aquarium would be taped the next morning in Jack's basement in the Silverlake section of Los Angeles.

When I got home Friday night, I looked at the fireplace we had just videotaped. I was devastated. The fire looked okay, but there was a strange image in the wood. One log had fallen down below the main log. It was red hot. That was all right, but on the big log above it there seemed to be a curved burn in the log that made it look like the upper lip of a woman. Taken together with the red hot log which had fallen below, the logs appeared to form a mouth. Oh no! Someone might think I was sending a subliminal message through that mouth, subliminal messages being a great fear and taboo in those beginning days of the home video business. I couldn't use this tape. I immediately called Jay, explained my problem and asked if I could come back the following afternoon to reshoot the fire. No problem. Come back.

The next morning we videotaped the aquarium without any problems. Then we packed up our equipment and returned to Jay's home to reshoot his fireplace. Coming back turned out to be a plus. Jay, knowing I was coming back to reshoot, had not bothered to clean out the ashes in the hearth left by the fire we had taped the night before. As soon as the new fire was lit, the ashes from the previous night began glowing red hot and beautiful! For me the glowing embers were a most welcome additional look, adding beauty and color to the video. It was an unexpected production value that greatly enhanced the look of the *Video Fireplace.*

Having worked as an assistant director for so many years, my experience in the crazy movie business now came to my aid. I had seen many scenes filmed with a burning fireplace. I knew that to enhance the look of the fire many movie cinematographers' often added spot lights to the fireplace. Usually they were rigged inside the chimney above the fire. I wasn't equipped to do that, So I used two table lamps from the room. I moved them as close to the fireplace as I could and still have them out of camera range. Then I removed their lamp shades and lit them so their light would fall on the fire. When the fire began to burn down and was no longer giving off enough of its own light to illuminate the fireplace, the additional light thrown from the lamps cast off just enough illumination so that the brick background of the fireplace didn't go pitch black. We could still see the texture of the bricks and the burn marks on the walls behind the blazing, crackling flames. For me that was a vital production value. When competitors began videotaping their own fires they didn't add extra light as I did. Consequently, most of those videos grew dim as their fires burned down and they lacked light, luster and beauty.

My concept in filming the fire or the aquarium was that the only movement would be what the viewer saw on his TV screen. The flames of the fire flickering as they sought air to consume in order to burn or the continuous darting to and fro as the fish swam inside their water-filled, glass home. The video camera would never pan or zoom. Just as an actual fireplace or fish tank in one's home never moved, it just sat there in its assigned place in your room, neither would the picture of the fire or the aquarium ever move but just sit there on the TV screen assigned to visualize it. I called my concept "non-directive" filming. There was no film editor to cut the action from one angle to another. There was no director framing his shots so that you saw what he wanted you to see. When my phrase "non-directive" saw the light of day on the printed page of *The Los Angeles Times*, I feared there would be a backlash from my fellow Guild brothers and sisters in the Directors Guild, that I'd be stripped of my membership and cashiered out of the DGA. That never happened. I think those who knew me were just glad I was working at something as crazy as it was!

I now had a fireplace with real fire sounds and an aquarium that needed a natural water sound or music in the background. I showed them both to David. He was pleased. By then I had names for the tapes. The fire was the *Video Fireplace*, the aquarium the *Video Aquarium*. Years later when I tried to get those names copyrighted, the U.S. copyright office wouldn't copyright them. The names were too generic. To overcome that, I began calling the fire *The Original Video Fireplace*, which seemed to draw in customers.

We were ready to package the tapes. With my art background I laid out suggested art work and wrote the copy for the boxes. Down the street from David's office was a talented commercial artist David often hired. I took my ideas over to him. He executed them beautifully. When David and I approved his work, it was sent to a printing house to be turned into packaging. David paid for it all.

It turned out David no longer had a financial interest in a duplication house. But he had friends who did. We ran off our first 100, one-hour VHS tapes, boxed them in the new boxes, had them shrink-wrapped and we were ready for our first sales.

By now it was October 1982. All the time I was preparing the videos I kept my day job and worked on any TV show I was offered. But my head and heart were in the videos. On my own I had placed the packaged videos in the Tower Records store on Sunset Blvd. in West Hollywood that was noted for selling a vast array of recorded music. They had opened a small section at the front of their store devoted to videos. I was delighted to have my videos available there because that store drew customers in record numbers! I also found an adventurous buyer at The Broadway, a department store in the new Century City Mall in Beverly Hills, built on what was once the movie backlot of 20th Century-Fox. But how, I wondered, were Los Angelinos to know that my videos were available for purchase as well as where they could be purchased?

We needed publicity and needed it fast to get sales rolling. I had no money for advertising and didn't feel I could ask David to take cash out of his pocket to buy advertising. So, thinking "free publicity," I contacted Lee Margulies, a staff writer at *The Los Angeles Times* who wrote a column called "Inside TV." With my videos in hand, I went to the Times-Mirror building in downtown Los Angeles, across from the City Hall, and played the videos for him. He laughed out loud. He found them amusing. Yes, Margulies said, he'd write them up in his column. Thrilled, I asked when. Not in next week's column, but in the column the week after. When I read the column two weeks later, it was terrific. He had devoted the entire column to my videos. He wrote, "Who said the video revolution doesn't have a sense of humor?" He hit all the buttons. Called them "atmosphere on videocassette" and that the *Video Fireplace* box boasted "No Logs to Haul. No Ashes to Clean" and the *Video Aquarium* enticed buyers with the promise "No Fish to Feed. No Tank to Clean." Both were slogans I had written. For years to come, those slogans would bring smiles, laughs, and giggles to people reading them whether they were on the box, in print advertising or on display where the videos were sold!

I was excited that Margulies planned to write about the videos in his column, but I was impatient! Very impatient! Two weeks! I couldn't wait that long until his column about my videos was in print and read by potential customers. The videos were already in stores waiting to be purchased.

That weekend I sat down and wrote a news release about the *Video Fireplace*. The following Monday morning, with copies of what I wrote, I went to the United Press Wire Service and the Associated Press Wire Service, both in downtown Los Angeles. To this day I haven't heard from the United Press, probably because shortly after I delivered the press release they went out of business. But that same night I had a call from the Associated Press. They had rewritten my news release in their style and were planning to run it on their wire to hundreds of newspapers, radio and TV stations across North America and the world. Did I have a picture of the *Video Fireplace* playing on a TV set? No, I didn't. The next day they sent one of their staff photographers out to my home and photographed me sitting alongside my TV playing my fireplace video. That afternoon the AP story with my picture went out over their wire and we had a million dollars' worth of free publicity. Their opening paragraph read: "Tired of the same old television programming? Exhausted by the bleeps, squawks and crunches of video games? Just want to relax? Steve Siporin thinks he has the answer for television viewers burned out by the video explosion of the past few years."

The story went on to describe my videos and how they worked and where they could be bought. Friends across the nation sent me clippings of the AP article as printed in their hometown newspapers. I was ten feet tall bursting with excitement. After that I realized there was something about the concept of my videos that caught the imagination of journalists. I didn't have to go to them. They would come to me. And they did. Not counting the massive publicity blast from the initial Associated Press wire story, over the years there were hundreds of free, unsolicited by me, newspaper and magazine stories about my videos not only in the United States but in Europe, Canada and South America. On top of that I gladly did radio and television interviews when asked.

A producer at CBS News read that very first AP wire story. He had an assistant call me and arranged for their reporter, Terry Drinkwater, to come to my home to interview and film me. His interview with me ran Thursday evening of that week on *The CBS Evening News with Dan Rather*. In promoting the story, Rather said it was "a fireplace to warm dreams by…and you don't have to throw another log on the fire." More great publicity, but we still didn't have many stores selling the products. Through David's connections in the video business individual stores began buying the videos for sale to their customers. But to my disappointment I soon discovered to my great surprise that video stores really weren't my market, unless they were like Tower Records and Video whose owners prided themselves on carrying everything possible that fit within their business parameters, no matter how crazy or unconventional it might be. Looking for more outlets I crashed a video distributors' breakfast meeting in San Diego hosted by Paramount Pictures Home Video. As the waiters were setting up the tables, I snuck into the room and placed my brochure on every attendee's chair.

Only one distributor took time to speak with me. He explained that video stores were in the rental business. They made their money every time they rented a cassette. The more times a cassette was rented the more money ended up in the video store's bank account. The industry looked at my videos as novelties, not as moneymakers. Because they weren't positioned for rental, most video stores wouldn't stock them. I'd have to find other outlets for selling my products.

At first the major movie studios were dead-set against the rental of videocassettes featuring their movies. They had gone to court to try and stop that practice. The movie studios had argued, as the original owners of the films on the cassettes, they should share in the profits from the rentals. But the courts ruled against them. The courts said that after the first sale by the studio of each cassette, the buyer owned that property and it was his to do with as he pleased. The courts ruled out buyers such as video stores setting up a screening room for those movie videos in the back of their stores and charging admission to viewers. That, the courts said, would infringe on the movie studios and their theater business. But video stores could rent each cassette as often as they could. The ruling angered the studios. They retaliated by setting higher purchase prices for each cassette the video store bought. Years later, when a movie became popular and home viewers were beginning to set up video libraries, then the movie studios finally lowered the first sale price anticipating mass consumer interest and mass sales. Money talks!

Shortly after our videos came on the market, we found ourselves written up by *The Los Angeles Times*. It was the lead story at the beginning of their "Television Weekly Listings" for the week of December 5, 1982. The article was headlined: "Updating the Video Explosion." The opening paragraph read: "There's no question about it . . . Steve Siporin is a man of vision! When the history of video technology is written—or, in keeping with the subject, programmed onto a micro-chip—it will be Siporin who'll go down in the annals as the pioneer of atmosphere television."

Heady words for me! The writer, James Brown, continued his article describing the *Video Fireplace* and *Video Aquarium* and fantasizing about a future with a Video Dog, Video Cat, Video Spouse and Video Kids. He would have been amazed that a few years later there were videos with several of his imagined concepts, but they didn't seem to catch on. More often than not over the years those aspiring video producers would contact me for advice. I was their guru. I had succeeded and made a million bucks they all thought. Just like the guy who marketed the Pet Rock! Far from it!

Just before Christmas of 1982 I was contacted by a programmer at an Anchorage, Alaska, cable channel. They were interested in licensing my fireplace and aquarium for what they called a *Mood Channel*. What a terrific idea, I thought! Thinking quickly, I told a little white lie. Coincidentally, I said, I had a project like that available that I also called *The Mood Channel*. It included the fireplace and aquarium and I would be filming two new mood pieces, ocean waves and a kinetic light sculpture, abstract shapes in rich colors moving gracefully across a velvet-black background. Since Anchorage hadn't videotaped any other segments for their *Mood Channel*, they agreed to license all four of my titles with a delivery date of February 1, 1983. Vunderbar! My business was really rolling and once again in a direction I had not anticipated or even dreamed of in my wildest, craziest dreams!

As soon as I could I rehired Monte Swann and arranged to videotape the two new titles. First on the schedule were the ocean waves. The day we went out to the Pacific Ocean at Marina Del Rey, just below Venice, California, we were in luck. There had been an El Niño storm a month or so before. Beautiful, non-threatening ocean waves caused by the El Niño were rolling in constantly. When they crested, they weren't too high as they rolled into the sandy shore that lay before them. Nine waves a minute! Without a break! For the entire hour we taped, the waves never stopped. Wave after wave after wave! What more could I have asked for on a videocassette I was to label and sell as *Ocean Waves!*

As to the *Light Sculpture* that video was the result of videotaping the artistic creations of my friend, the late John Beard. "Lumia" is the specific term used in the art world to describe kinetic light sculptures. Beard worked with the distortion factors of optics using lens, prisms, mirrors and electric light to create his works of art. The sculptures are mechanically driven by a series of motors. Each of Beard's Lumias are programmed by him to have an individual personality to repeat various themes, just as a musician might create recurring themes in a piece of music. All the moving parts were hidden from the viewer's sight, intricately enclosed in a black box. The sculpture came to life when you flipped a switch and turned on the electricity. Then everything inside was set in motion. Across a pitch-black background abstract shapes in rainbow colors were projected flowing leisurely across the front of the box which acted as the viewer's screen, much like the front of a TV set. The Museum of Modern Art (MOMA) in New York City owns kinetic light sculptures by a Danish artist. John Beard was pleased to let me film his sculptures because he considered viewing them as a way to relax and release stress, which was my intention for all the videos I offered. Although I filmed three of John's sculptures, I only released one on a videocassette. I named it *Light Sculpture.*

I sent my four mood channel videos on ¾-inch professional videotape to the Alaska cable station. The first four weeks they ran each of the four videos separately 24/7 each week. In retrospect, I am sure that would have set a Guinness Book of Records for broadcasting one television program 24/7, but we never submitted them for consideration. *The Mood Channel* ran in Anchorage, Alaska, for about two years until the cable station dropped it for something more profitable. It also ran in Opa Locka, Florida, for a year. I thought I was on to something, but interest in the concept waned as more and more cable channels were created and cable stations opted for programming product that would bring more revenue into their coffers.

Naturally, I packaged and marketed the *Ocean Waves* with real ocean sounds and the *Light Sculpture* with relaxing music. I now had four videos that I owned and could sell to the public. In 1985 I was visiting friends in Grosse Pointe, Michigan, who took me to a mansion on a private street where the automobile Fords lived. I was impressed with the house. I thought the library fireplace would be perfect for the Christmas-themed fireplace I was planning to produce. I asked the owners if I could come back at Christmastime to film their library fireplace, secretly thinking that the very imaginative and creative owners, Michigan's foremost team of interior decorators, would have amazing and beautiful Christmas decorations. Their decorations would be an added production value visually when I taped their fireplace. To my chagrin, the owners said they'd be traveling at Christmas, but I could come back any other time. So I did the following February. I brought my own logs, my own Christmas trimmings and my nephew Steve to play Santa Claus asleep in front of the burning fire. In post-production I was fortunate to discover wonderful holiday music to mingle with the fire sounds on the video. The orchestral music was originally recorded in Belgium with a full classical orchestra specifically for a Christmas LP, a long-playing vinyl record that was a promotional giveaway. The chorus singing Christmas carols was English, recorded in England but never before published. Once again, as I had done for *Ocean Waves* and *Light Sculpture* with the aid of my computer, I designed the box and wrote the copy for this video, *The Original Christmas Yule Log Fireplace*. I now had five videos that I owned and copyrighted and could sell.

Frequently, my customers would ask me if I had any more relaxing videos like the five I had created. One of my distributors, Alan Kessler of Ark Media Group in San Francisco, also distributed a host of nature tapes from producers around the country. Most of them had no narration, only music or natural sounds, perfect for my customers. I added many to my line and created my own catalog called *Very Nice Videos* and began mailing the catalog to my customers. The response to the new nature tapes was very gratifying. My business increased tenfold. When the Internet became a vital part of everyone's daily life, I created two websites, **www.videofireplaces.com** and **www.verynicevideos.com**. I was able to reach new customers thanks to Google and other Internet search engines. Much of my business was referral. People would see one of my videos at a friend's home or at a party and they had to have one for themselves. They wrote down the 800 number that they found on the box cover, then phoned me and ordered.

When dentists began using video cameras and monitors in their examining rooms to show patients the dental problems lurking inside their mouths, I began advertising my video line in dental magazines and once again expanded my business. Most people thought the dentists were just buying my *Video Aquarium* to replace the traditional fish tank that gurgled in dentist's waiting rooms. Not at all. Dentists were buying and playing our nature videos on the TV monitors in their examining rooms as an aid in calming patients as they sat full of fear in the dentist's chair awaiting the dentist's dreaded drill.

When a friend pointed out that recreational vehicles rarely if ever came equipped with a fireplace or an aquarium, another market was opened up for my videos. Nine out of ten motor homes did have a TV set and VCR. So I advertised in motor home magazines and also exhibited at conventions convened for owners of motor homes. Again, my business increased thanks to those folks with wanderlust who traveled our nation's highways in their homes with five wheels.

One area in which I spent considerable amounts of money trying to expand my business but failed was the promotional product industry. That's where a company buys your product, you put their name and information on the product, and then they distribute them free of charge as a goodwill gesture from their company. You've probably had a ballpoint pen in your possession at one time or another with some vender's name and phone number spelled out on it to remind you to buy from them. I gave out more free samples than I made sales. In truth as I looked around those convention floors there were no vendors selling videos as promotions. Perhaps

Our three original videos, first sold as VHS video cassettes then repackaged as DVDs above. AUTHOR'S COLLECTION

I persisted longer than I should have thinking my unique videos would be the ones to break through the barrier and attract customers. I was wrong!

When DVDs virtually wiped out the old VHS tape cassettes, I converted my own videos into DVDs. Today, my entire catalog, in print and on the Internet, only sells DVDs, either standard or in High Definition or in Blu-Ray. Though there were difficulties at first, eventually I had a thriving business. I found national catalogs that were happy to include my videos in their pages. *Movies Unlimited*, which today is the official catalog for the Turner Classics Movies channel, has sold my tapes from day one. With the Johnson Smith catalog, "Things You Never Knew Existed," I set a record. For over 20 years one or more of my videos, first on VHS and then on DVD, were sold in that or another one of their catalogs. All the while, my little secret was that the visual content of my DVDs was the same as the visual content on the original VHS cassettes I first created many years before. I never reshot them or felt I had to give them a new twist. To me, the quality was just as beautiful as when they first came on the market! And new customers still loved them!

One day in 1983 when my business was still in its infancy, something unexpected happened that thrilled me! Because of my crazy videos I was back in the crazy movie business...sort of!

CRAZY, CRAZY VIDEOS

In the early 1980s on the southeast corner of Broadway and 49th Street in Manhattan there stood an independent video store called Video Shack. It was owned by business acquaintances of my silent partner, David Friedman. As a favor to David they bought a couple dozen of our *Video Fireplace* and *Video Aquarium* and put them on display in the store window that faced Broadway. Great! Not only was the rent high on Broadway, but so was the foot traffic! Thousands of people, primarily tourists from around the country and even the world, would see our videos in the store's window.

Walking by one day was one of the screenwriters of a Universal Studios movie *The Lonely Guy* (1983) about to begin shooting. The movie was based on a humorous book by Bruce Jay Friedman titled *The Lonely Guys Book of Life*. The credit for the screenplay was shared by three writers, Neil Simon, Stan Daniels and Ed Weinberger. I was told by a producer that the writer who saw my videos in the Video Shack store window on Broadway thought if he wrote the videos into a scene or two in the movie they would make for some funny sequences. Which writer that was I never found out, but I'm thankful to whoever he was.

One morning a producer on *The Lonely Guy* phoned me asking to license both the Video Fireplace and Video Aquarium for the film. It starred Steve Martin and Charles Grodin, the very same actor/writer that Elaine May recommended to me when I was seeking a writer for *The Peter Principle* but I thought she had said "Charles Gordone." I was so excited, so flattered that my videos were being used in a movie, that I was quite naïve (read: foolish).

Here's one of the publicity photos I took with Steve Martin and a disinterested Charles Grodin, the stars of *The Lonely Guy*. Because Grodin was seated to my right I couldn't see what he was up to, which was trying to distance himself from me so that if we used the photo, we'd probably cut him out. Which we did! But not this time, Charles! AUTHOR'S COLLECTION

Instead of setting a fair price for their use, an amount that movie people could respect, I practically gave them away. I asked one dollar as the fee for each. The producer was kind. He said ten dollars each would read better. In addition, I asked to have a photograph taken with the stars that I could use in my business. That was written into the agreement.

Also, I asked for a credit at the end of the movie which read *Thanks to Video Naturals Co. for the Video Fireplace and Video Aquarium.* As a movie professional I always sat through the end credits as a courtesy to all my fellow professionals who I knew had worked so hard on their film. I forgot that the majority of everyday moviegoers usually don't sit through the credits; they get up and walk out of theater as soon as the words "The End" flash on the screen. And most moviegoers, seeing something unusual in a film like a *Video Fireplace*, don't think it's a product you can buy, but assume it's a special effect created by those clever movie people.

I was allowed to witness the filming of my videos. It was on a familiar Universal stage, one I had worked on just a few years before. The first scene had "lonely guy" Charles Grodin playing a mechanical board game by himself. Grodin loses the game and the mechanical board calls him stupid. During the game he gets a phone call from Steve Martin asking Grodin to go on the town with him that night. Grodin says he can't because he's playing a board game and then he's going to watch his *Video Fireplace*. He hangs up, loses the game and the voice of the mechanical board game mocks him as a loser. Then Grodin does stick a VHS into his VCR and the *Video Fireplace* burns brightly.

Towards the end of the movie, as Steve Martin's character is sinking deeper and deeper into his own lonely guy depression, Grodin is visiting Steve's apartment. Steve says, "I have something to show you," and plays the *Video Aquarium* on his TV. "Nice, very nice," says Grodin and they are off to other issues, like the girl Steve is in love with is about to marry another guy. More loneliness and depression!

Though I didn't make much money for the use of my videos in that movie, I was delighted to be back in the movie biz. And I learned my lesson. From then on I set five hundred dollars as the fee for using any one of my videos. There were many TV shows over the years that paid the price, mostly for the fireplace. Among those shows were NBC's *St. Elsewhere*, ABC's *The Drew Carey Show* twice, ABC's *The Middle*, CBS's *Northern Exposure* and HBO cable's prison show OZ.

Perhaps the best use of the *Video Fireplace* was in 1996 in a Columbia Pictures movie, *The Cable Guy,* starring Jim Carrey and Matthew Broderick, directed by Ben Stiller. When Jim Carrey was signed for the film, the big publicity story was that Carey was being paid twenty million dollars to star in the film. For him it was a dream come true. Many years before Carrey said he had written a check out to himself for twenty million dollars. He carried it with him in his wallet for years as a good luck talisman. And, now, he was actually going to receive that vast sum for playing the lead in *The Cable Guy*. Ain't life wonderful!

As it usually happens, one day I received a phone call from a production assistant on *The Cable Guy*. They wanted to license my

Video Fireplace for use in the movie. No problem, I said. And when I was asked what the fee would be, I remembered the exorbitant amount Carrey was being paid for the film, so I upped my price. Rather than the five hundred dollars I usually charged, I said one thousand greenbacks. The assistant said he'd have to check that out with the producer. The next day he called back and said it was okay. They sent me out a letter of agreement; I signed it and returned it with a DVD of the fire for their use.

A few months later a different production assistant called me. The movie was still in production. It seems the person I originally made the deal with was no longer working on the film. The new guy wanted to revise our agreement. I would only be paid the one thousand dollars if the *Video Fireplace* was actually used in the movie.

Now he didn't know that I had been an assistant director and knew my way around movie contracts. I reminded him that I had a letter of agreement which was binding. Nowhere in that letter was there anything written that the fee wouldn't be paid if the video didn't appear in the movie. In fact, once they signed the agreement it was a done deal. There were many possibilities I agreed why the *Video Fireplace* might not appear in the movie. No matter what the circumstances were, I had submitted the DVD and signed the agreement in good faith and payment was required. Period. Case closed.

The new production assistant kept trying to persuade me otherwise. To cut him short I asked him to have the film's lawyer call me to discuss the issue. The next day the lawyer, a woman, phoned me. I let her know I was movie savvy. I had worked on many a film where an actor was hired, did his day's work, but then his scene was cut when the movie was edited. The actor still received his pay for his day's work. The reason his part was cut may have had nothing to do with his performance. He had acted, literally, in good faith and per his contract had to be paid. The lawyer and I quickly came to an agreement. For me it was a compromise of a sort.

I would be paid five hundred dollars now. If the *Video Fireplace* was used in the film, upon completion of shooting, I would receive a second check of five hundred dollars per our agreement. My compromise was that the movie company would not have to pay me the second five hundred if the *Video Fireplace* did not appear in the final cut. I felt I was ahead because at least I was getting five hundred dollars now. The new production assistant had been negotiating to pay me nothing.

When the movie hit the big screens, I raced to check it out. Of course, they had used my *Video Fireplace*. It was part of a major story point in the film. A story point in a script is something that is vital to the plot or to the development of a character or a relationship. Without that story point there would be a gap in the story and make the plot confusing.

For those who haven't seen *The Cable Guy*, here's the story. Jim Carrey plays the cable guy who installs cable equipment in people's home. Unfortunately, he is seriously demented. Just casually call him "buddy" in conversation with him and Carrey thinks it means you are his best friend for life. That's how Matthew Broderick suddenly finds himself with a new best friend. No matter how Matthew tries to shake Carrey, he won't go. One night after being out together on the town, they come back to Matthew's apartment. This is the scene in which my *Video Fireplace* was to be used. We have seen Matthew's apartment before and know he only has a tiny TV set in his living room. To Matthew's surprise there is now a wall of stereo and TV equipment where the tiny TV once stood. Playing on the large TV set is my *Video Fireplace*. Matthew is dumbfounded. He realizes Carrey must have installed it all. Matthew feels violated because Carrey got into his apartment without his permission. Carrey admits he did it, thinking his "buddy" would be most appreciative. Matthew is not. He orders Carrey to remove it all. Reluctantly, Carrey agrees.

Later, in the movie, as Carrey's cable guy becomes vengeful because Matthew won't be his buddy, we learn that the wall of equipment is stolen property. Because the police know it was in Matthew's apartment, they arrest him for having stolen merchandise in his apartment and send him to jail.

The wall of equipment is the story point. If the wall of equipment had not been in the apartment, then there would be no reason to arrest Matthew later on in the film. My *Video Fireplace* was merely dressing for the television set. Expensive dressing for the story point! It could have been another video, not mine. But it was mine and therefore, per the letter of agreement, I had to be paid!

I don't think the second production assistant or the lawyer had read the script or knew what a story point was or about its importance to the plot. Just some more crazy misunderstandings in Hollywood. Oh, yes! I got the check for the second five hundred dollars in the mail!

What I find astonishing today is that the pivotal scene that I describe in *The Cable Guy* movie with our *Video Fireplace* playing in Matthew Broderick's living room can be accessed and viewed by anyone with a computer via YouTube. Thanks to YouTube everything can be saved for posterity and viewed ad infinitum. Probably every film or television show that I've ever worked on as well as performances by every actor or actress I've noted on these pages can be seen ad infinitum on our computer screens thanks to YouTube and whatever amazing new technologies are yet to be discovered traveling along the information highway.

Apparently, there seems to be no limitation to the length of a download. Complete movies, single performances or just a snippet that some enthusiast thinks the world can't live without; all can be downloaded for viewing. The size of the viewing screen is no longer a matter of concern, only the content. Manufacturers rush new devices to the market boasting how small the screen is! As the screens diminish in size from desktop monitors to laptop flip-up screens, to still smaller portable DVD players with seven-inch screens, to even smaller iPad screens to by far the smallest on a cell phone, there is no need to worry. They'll all play back the biggest movie that ten bucks will buy for you at your nearest widescreen movie theater! In this instance at least, movie lovers are advised size doesn't matter! For years movie studios and theater owners lured patrons into their theaters by proclaiming how big the screens were in Cinerama, in VistaVision, in Todd-AO in comparison to the small TV screen then at home in one's living room. Now in the information age, the reverse is the gospel! Small is good! View it alone, by one's self in the privacy of one's own home. No need to dress up and leave the nest!

Size does matter to me! There is something special about viewing a full-length movie on a big theater screen especially when I'm surrounded by other sentient people. Before sound came to the movies, it was said the common language of body movement and facial expression in silent movies united moviegoers the world over, no matter what language they spoke. Today, when we all laugh or cry or react to a movie together at the same time that sense of community still prevails. In that moment there is a bonding that reaffirms our communal existence without destroying our individuality and it seems to me we are at our happiest! Was that why I cherished my movie-going experience those Saturday matinees so long ago when I was a kid? I always thought it was solely for the entertainment that flickered up there on the silver screen. Now I think it could have been what was ignited within my soul and those who sat nearby me.

LOOKING BACK

Today people who love movies can access them in ways the pioneers of the movie industry, the D.W. Griffiths, the Irving Thalberg's, the Warner Bros., even the Charlie Chaplin's never imagined. Movie buffs need not go to their neighborhood movie theaters to catch the latest Hollywood release. New films as well as films that have lain dormant in studio vaults for many years are now finding new audiences and bringing in new profits via cable channels like *Turner Classic Movies*. Amazing technology now allows us to stream movies to our big screen TV sets, even to our small screen iPads and cell phones. We can enjoy international films from countries around the world that we never would have seen because they never would have been booked into our local movie palaces. Now they are welcome additions to movie cable channels always hungry for new product.

There are stand-alone websites like *Netflix* that charge a reasonable monthly fee to their customers for downloading or streaming a vast array of old and new movies as well as popular TV shows. There are pay-per-view channels you can access at home on your cable channel to view Hollywood's newest films after they've completed a specified run in movie theaters. Fees for pay-per-view films are a one-time charge and the cost varies depending on the movie itself. As this is written, movies released on DVD's seem to have lost their appeal to consumers and are no longer bringing in the revenue they did in previous years. The reason given by movie insiders is that today there are too many free films available on cable or for a minimal charge. Also, as this is being written, many of the major studios are arranging to be part of the cable channel YouTube, to have another outlet for films their company has produced in the past and will produce in the future that will be streamed to TV sets. iPads, cell phones, and whatever other new delivery systems technology will bestow on a waiting public! The direct involvement of these movie studios will result in a stronger selection of programming for the viewer and a new stream of revenue for the studios. The driving force behind Hollywood has always been making money, showing a profit. As new technologies are discovered for offering films and entertainment to a receptive public, the need for more product will be a challenge to movie producers the world over. More production will mean more jobs for industry professionals. If I were of the right age and stamina, without a question, I'd be putting my name on the availability list.

Certainly, I had an exciting wonderful time as an assistant director, meeting and working with a host of very talented actors, actresses, directors and dozens of exceptional technical people who enriched my life with their knowledge and expertise. Unquestionably, traveling and working in Mexico several times ranks high in my movie career. Ditto Wichita, Kansas, or California cities such as Stockton, Sacramento, San Francisco, and Los Angeles, my hometown from 1965 to 1993. In my years as an assistant director I saw amazing places and traveled to locations I surely would never have had access to if I hadn't been working in the movies.

Though I was content earning my living as an assistant director and believed I would do so until age or my legs forced me to retire, I wasn't an assistant in demand all the time with directors fighting over who would get my services. Sure, I did have certain colleagues, like my friend Tom McCrory, who always asked for me to assist him until I was promoted to his level as a first assistant. Or directors, like Billy Graham, who appreciated my style and was kind enough to ask for me when he was starting a new project. But there were many work weeks when I sat at home, my name on the DGA Availability List, just waiting for a call.

Then I went to New York, made that jest about a fire on video that turned a television set into a fireplace and my world changed. Something inside me clicked. Maybe it was just the thought of promoting my own creativity rather than always being a helping hand to others that set me on the road to discovering a new course in my life. Perhaps doing my own thing was something my psyche needed, that had up till that moment been missing in my scheme of life. Perhaps that was why I so often went into a dark place within myself and didn't always build goodwill for myself in the movie industry.

When Video Naturals and the videos I created turned into a reality, I was on top of the world. I was over the moon with expectations. Success seemed within reach! One thing I knew was in my favor. The concept of my videos resonated with the media and we would and did receive tons of free publicity. At first the buying public thought they were a novelty that wouldn't last long. But they did. And as the VHS and DVD business grew so did my business. For the past 30 years it has paid my bills.

VHS or DVD. It didn't matter. It was a hot business. Eager to make a buck, in the 1980s entrepreneurs created new catalogs devoted exclusively to special interest videos like mine. Thousands were mailed across the country. In every video catalog that offered my fireplace and aquarium videos they outsold the other videos in that catalog. The word in the business was that since brick and mortar video stores didn't stock special interest titles like mine, they would be surefire money makers via catalogs and direct mail. Unfortunately, that didn't happen. There weren't enough consumers intrigued by these non-movie videos or enough advertising money to create an awareness of them that would translate into sales. In a few short years those catalogs devoted solely to special interest videos folded.

Many people in the entertainment business who read *Billboard– The International News Weekly of Music, Video and Home Entertainment* were positive my company was pulling in the big bucks. Why? *Billboard* is noted for running charts that rank various entertainment industries such as movies, recording artists, music albums and so forth based on their sales. Just being listed on the chart was a big accomplishment. Rising to the top, to the Number One spot was the dream position for every item listed on a chart. It was in the mid-1980s that *Billboard* created the "Top Special Interest Videocassette Sales" chart compiled from a national sample of retail sales reports. It ran every two weeks. To my amazement three of my videos, the *Video Fireplace, Video Aquarium* and *Christmas Yule Log Fireplace* began appearing with regularity on that chart and like proverbial bullets, began shooting up the chart! For the week ending January 9, 1988, my *Video Aquarium* was in the Number One spot having been on the charts for 31 weeks in a row. Directly beneath it in the second position was our *Video Fireplace* with 19 weeks on the charts. We had knocked *Chef Paul Prudhomme's Louisiana Kitchen Vol. 1* into third place after 53 weeks on the charts. Great news! Top of the charts! But where were these figures coming from? They certainly weren't from me or reflective of cash in my bank account. They weren't my reality, but outsiders thought they were.

There's an old English proverb that says "money begets money." Unfortunately, we had no extra money we could put into advertising to sell our videos. Perhaps if we had an advertising budget our actual sales would really have shot up to match the sales figures the *Billboard* charts seemed to indicate. Or if I was able to find someone with deep pockets who wanted to back my business. The biggest sale Video Naturals ever scored was due not to paid advertising but to a free plug on a national television show. That was the Barbara Walters' ABC-TV talk show *The View* directed at a female audience.

On Friday, November 8, 2003, a production assistant on *The View* phoned our office. Starr Jones, one of the five women panelists on the show, occasionally did a segment where she recommended products. Starr was asking to feature our *Video Aquarium* in a show they were taping the following Tuesday. Was that okay with me and could I ship them the DVD for Tuesday? Within an hour it was in an overnight Federal Express packet on its way to NYC. It turned out the show they were taping on Tuesday wasn't for that week, but an extra show to be used later in the month. Because the cast and crew would be taking the Thanksgiving weekend off, they were taping two extra shows ahead of time to be shown during the holidays. My *Video Aquarium* was scheduled for Friday, November 29, 2003.

The day after Thanksgiving is a big football day on TV. In Southern California where I lived, *The View*, which was normally broadcast in the morning at 10 a.m., was rescheduled for 4 p.m. The football game that preceded it that afternoon ran long. The beginning of *The View* was up cut 25 minutes, only the last 35 minutes were shown in my town. Fortunately for me that included the Starr Jones product segment. And Starr did it beautifully. She even showed the aquarium playing on a flat-screen TV hanging on a wall in her home. *The View's* audience was told they could buy the DVD on Amazon or by calling my 800 number. Many viewers did call us directly thinking they would get their DVD faster through us in time for Christmas gift giving. But the majority of viewers bought their *Video Aquariums* through Amazon on the Internet. My check from Amazon for those sales totaled almost $25,000. In the month following the broadcast Amazon had sold over 2,700 *Video Aquarium* DVDs. I've always considered that as one sale due to the plug on TV, the biggest sale my company ever had, thanks to the ladies on *The View*. Imagine what our sales might have been throughout the years if we had had enough money to advertise properly, especially on TV.

As the years went by, more and more of my video business resulted from the Internet and new customers finding my websites online. Customers from years back would telephone or e-mail me, surprised that I was still in business and hoping that we were now selling their favorite VHS videos in DVD. They were ecstatic when they discovered we were still in business and had converted our products to DVD. With each phone call there was a lovely story of how much fun they had had with our fireplace or aquarium videos or how they enjoyed playing them for friends or giving them as gifts. I glowed with pride! When I first went into business, so many of my friends and relatives thought I was crazy and would never succeed. The feedback I was now getting reenergized me as I realized the fun and pleasure my videos had brought into so many lives for so many years.

Then, very unexpectedly, the video and DVD business began heading south and not only did my sales diminish but so did the sales of major studio movies on DVD. Why? The answer some gave was that the public was no longer building DVD libraries. Others said with the advent of TiVo recording machines and DVR (direct video recording) provided by cable companies, viewers no longer needed to buy. They could electronically save movies for a later screening. Again DVD sales dropped. When the ability to stream films for viewing directly to our TVs, iPads or cell phones was made available that was the final straw. Many small video companies went out of business.

I didn't! I simply couldn't! These weren't just anyone's DVDs. They were mine! They were my babies! If all I was able to sell were my *Video Fireplace, Video Aquarium* and *Christmas Yule Log Fireplace* and no other DVD, I'd make do! I strongly believe there are potential, new customers out there who, if they only knew about our DVDs would want to purchase them.

Perhaps because my video work was truly original with me, I think it gave me more satisfaction than my movie work. In the long run it didn't pay as well as my movie work or offer a pension as valuable as the one the Directors Guild of America did! But it gave me more satisfaction since I was creating something new! If imitation is the best form of flattery, then I was truly flattered by all the folks who followed my lead and produced their own fireplaces on video. Just Google "fireplaces on video" and be prepared for the deluge!

Do I have any misgivings about my career in crazy, crazy Hollywood? Once in a while my actions caused me to question what motivated and influenced me when I performed my duties. Had the results of my actions gone beyond the pale?

I was on location with the weekly, one-hour action series entitled *Movin' On* about truckers and the loads they hauled in their trucks. It was when we were filming in Mobile, Alabama, that I had second thoughts about my job. We were shooting a scene with our *Movin' On* heroes, Claude Akins and Frank Converse. With the aid of movie police they were capturing some villains. The script called for a helicopter in which the arresting officers were tracking the bad guys. We also needed background extras for the scene. A local agency provided extras. Among the group of extras I ordered was a farmer with his own pick-up truck. For using his truck he would get an extra fee beyond his payment for his day's work. The man cast actually was a farmer in his sixties, perfectly outfitted in overalls and a straw cowboy hat, the real thing. I explained to him what we wanted him to do and where to drive his truck.

Action was called and the actors began the scene, but the farmer didn't drive in on his cue. We needed to reshoot the scene. Once again, I explained to the farmer what was required of him. This time I said I would signal him with a wave of my hand when he was to drive in. We rolled the camera. The scene began. I signaled the farmer. He drove in as planned. I went over to the farmer to congratulate him, to tell him he had been perfect, that we would continue with additional shots to cover the scene. The farmer was slumped over the steering wheel. Unconscious! I quickly called over the medic-nurse on the set. Maybe a heart attack, she said.

Fortunately, there was a helicopter on the set. We immediately enlisted it to fly him to the nearest hospital. As we loaded him onto the helicopter, I snatched the straw cowboy hat from what might be a dying or dead man's head. I remember someone on the crew looking at me, disapproving of what I was doing. The cameraman had already filmed the wide establishing shot for the sequence. We certainly had seen the farmer in his truck in that opening shot. As we continued to shoot the additional coverage, we'd surely be seeing the farmer and his truck again and everything would have to match. Chances were we hadn't been close enough to see the farmer's face, but we might recognize his silhouette. And that silhouette included that straw cowboy hat. That's why I snatched the hat from his head. With the hat in my hand I selected another male extra to replace the hospitalized farmer. On the extra's head I placed the straw cowboy hat and sat him in the pick-up truck, ready for the coverage.

I felt queasy inside. Disturbed. Why was I thinking more about the next shot than about the farmer's mortality? Would he live or die? That was still unknown to me as he was being flown away in the helicopter. But that was my job, as crass as it might seem. It was my responsibility to be sure the director got the support he needed and that meant everything matched in continuity in the scenes we filmed. I didn't feel good about what I did, but I had to do it. Everyone was happy when we learned the farmer had not had a fatal attack. The entire cast and crew signed a get-well card that went along with a bouquet of flowers to the farmer in his hospital room.

Though the movies I worked on were terrific experiences for me, they weren't the result of my creativity. Movie making is a collaborative effort. Just look at those long, long credits that seem to run on forever at the end of today's movies. When I began working in the industry, second assistant directors didn't even get on-screen credit on feature films. Today they do as the result of contract negotiations. And today it seems that everyone in any shape or form connected with a movie in almost any capacity gets his name credited on screen. And rightly so! All those names, all those people, all those different jobs! All have contributed their part to make the movie whole.

Except for awards given out for accomplishment in skills in individual categories, the bulk of movie workers go unrecognized. It's the movie itself that gets the kudos and hopefully good reviews. I'm not ashamed to admit that I take great pleasure when the kudos for my videos mentions me. A bigger thrill was when customers wrote or phoned to tell me how much they loved the video or DVD they had bought. Not only did they find the products relaxing, but they were good for a smile and a laugh when they and their friends first saw them. I loved that! To my delight, people across the nation found uses for my videos that I would never have imagined.

One new mother said the water sounds on the aquarium soothed her crying baby suffering with the colic. She thought maybe the sounds of water on the video reminded the newborn of the gurgling the infant heard when still in mommy's tummy and that put an end to her infant's crying. That's what she believed! Then there was the community center in Atlanta that used the *Video Fireplace* in their Halloween haunted house. Or the Bullocks department store in downtown Los Angeles showing our *Ocean Waves* on TV sets in the department selling bathing suits.

As a new video entrepreneur in a niche business, I was asked to speak before 200 people at an industry video conference when special interest videos looked like they had a big future. I beamed for days. At long last a big payoff for the public-speaking classes I had taken in college. Outside of the many TV shows and several movies that incorporated one of my videos into their stories, I was pleasantly surprised by the professionals in other creative fields who were inspired by my creativity. One thrill was when a respected author had characters in her novel reference both my fireplace and aquarium videos.

When it was just a one-hour VHS cassette, my *Video Fireplace* was inspiration for novelist Nancy Williard's fertile imagination. In late 1992 I received a letter from Alfred A. Knopf, publisher, New York, asking my permission to allow Ms. Williard in her novel *Sister Water* to quote from the slipcase of the *Video Fireplace*. She was quoting from copy I had written for the box back in 1982, which included "No Logs To Haul! No Ashes to Clean!" The letter gave me a sampling of what she had written and it was good reading. The fact that the novel was set in Ann Arbor, Michigan, where I had gone to college may have also swayed me.

In my letter of permission I asked for no money, just a copy of the book when published and an acknowledgement at the end of the book that I had given permission. When I received my copy, I read it with delight. It was beautifully written.

Nancy Williard is noted for seamlessly mixing the magical and the mundane in her fictional worlds and for creating with words pictures of daily life so precisely observed that they leave after-images in her readers' minds. How mind blowing for me that in *Sister Water*, only her second novel, my creativity had ignited her creativity. I was thrilled! Her novel received high praise when published. The passages where the *Video Fireplace* appeared were warm and very real for me. On pages 243 through 245 in the hardback edition, one of her characters discussed the *Video Fireplace* as follows:

> "They drank coffee together in the kitchen like an old married couple, she telling him of her triumph: because she bought the last *Video Fireplace* in the store, she got two dollars off the reduced price of nine ninety-nine.
>
> "'The man said it's better than a real one,' she said. 'Listen. '*Video Fireplace*. Sixty flame-filled minutes. A fire for all seasons: loving, dining, reading, entertaining, quiet moments, meditation. No logs to haul. No ashes to clean! Relax in the flickering glow of a crackling fire. I offered to get one for Jessie, but Ellen said her mom would never give up her real fire. And they don't have a VCR. I don't have a VCR, but I might someday.'
>
> "'You should check it out right away,' said Harvey. 'If it's defective, you should return it.'
>
> "Mrs. Trimble rose from the table.

"'I told Ellen you have one VCR for upstairs and another for downstairs, and she was amazed.'

"'What did she say?'

"'She said, 'How amazing,' Can you reach me the can of filberts on that high shelf?'

"Now Mrs. Trimble was standing in front of him the *Video Fireplace* in her outstretched hand. He slipped it into the VCR and she sat down beside him on the sofa. Gray glowed rose, like a dawn breaking. Suddenly a fireplace, in which a modest fire filled the screen.

"'Nice fireplace,' said Mrs. Trimble. 'It's got andirons and all.'

"The fire burned.

"And burned.

"And burned.

"'Doesn't this kind of thing usually have music?' asked Harvey.

"From the left side of the screen a hand clutching a poker reached in and adjusted the logs, turning the flames a faint lime green.

"'I don't know,' said Mrs. Trimble. 'Do you want to borrow it?'

"Suddenly there flashed across his heart a longing for the pleasant heaviness that came over him as a child when he sat in front of his grandparents' fireplace, watching the flames and listening to the grownups chatter. 'Yes,' he said.

"He was glad to see her go. He trudged upstairs, kicked off

his shoes and slid the Video Fireplace into the VCR at the foot of his bed. The room felt chilly. He could not bear the thought of slipping off his clothes. He stretched out and turned on the machine and fell asleep.

"Even with the overhead light on in his bedroom—for he could never fall asleep in a dark room—the *Video Fireplace* flickered and glowed."

In August, 2007 I received a letter directly from Nancy Williard asking again for my permission to quote from the slipcase of the *Video Fireplace*. Her book was being reprinted in paperback by Wayne State University Press in Detroit, Michigan, less than a mile from where I went to high school at Cass Tech in Detroit. Permission granted.

I was equally pleased when I discovered that a world-famous choreographer had made our *Christmas Yule Log Fireplace* an integral part of the stage setting of his *The Hard Nut* ballet, his modern adaptation of Tchaikovsky's classic *The Nutcracker Suite*. The choreographer was Seattle-born Mark Morris, famed for his Mark Morris Dance Group in Manhattan. When the lights went up on the opening scene of the ballet, there was our *Christmas Yule Log Fireplace* burning brightly on a big screen TV set positioned stage left with a gaily decorated Christmas tree opposite it, stage right, and dancers poised to begin the ballet. Morris had choreographed *The Hard Nut* in Belgium. It was performed there first and then again on the dance stages of Europe. Finally, it was videotaped in Europe and was seen on several European television stations. The videotaped performance was purchased for showing in the United States over America's PBS broadcasting television stations. I discovered it was my video when I happened to see a promotional spot announcing the date and time the ballet would be seen on my Los Angeles PBS station. Since they were using my *Christmas Yule Log Fireplace* without my permission I immediately had my lawyer fire off a letter to the Mark Morris Dance Group indicating dire consequences unless I was reasonably recompensed. Morris settled to my satisfaction. But how exciting it was for me to discover another of my videos had found a place in someone else's imagination.

It seems to me that no other special interest line of videos has received as much positive publicity and attention or inspired as much creativity in other people as mine have. I would suggest that no other videos have entered the consciousness of the American people as deeply as mine have. For example, in the July 24, 1989, issue of *The New Yorker* magazine there was a cartoon without a caption. It pictured a man seated at home in an easy chair in his living room watching his TV set. He was wearing only sunglasses, his swimsuit and a hat with scuba gear at his feet. What was he watching on TV? A picture of ocean waves rolling in! Were those virtual ocean waves inspired by our VHS *Ocean Waves*? Perhaps! I never asked the cartoonist! There were other cartoonists over the years that drew cartoons of people enjoying a Video Pet, be it a cat, a dog, a bird or whatever! In 1993 "the boss" himself, Bruce Springsteen, performed in a video singing the song "57 Channels (and nothing to watch)," the lyrics decrying the sorry state of affairs television was in. Included in the visuals was our *Video Fireplace*. I didn't agree with the song's premise, but was thrilled to have my work in a Springsteen music video.

Nine years earlier in 1984 the British Broadcasting company (BBC-TV) had contacted me. One of their famous hosts, Clive James, was a doing a seven-part series called *Panorama* "The Television Revolution." His topic was the sudden proliferation of videos in the entertainment market. The opening set designed for the program was a wall of television sets. On each TV set a different video played. They licensed three of mine, the fireplace, the aquarium and the ocean waves. Shortly after, I received a check in payment from the BBC-TV office in America. A year later I was contacted again by the producers of the same Clive James show, *Panorama*. They had sold the series to several English-speaking countries. British television, unlike American, doesn't license your property forever, including all reruns and foreign possibilities. English television is more genteel. Their original license was just for that original, first run. Now that it was going into a foreign run, they were negotiating a separate fee. I was inexperienced in such matters, but knew what the term "favored nations" meant when it was mentioned. I agreed to be paid in accordance with what everyone else was being paid in this situation. After all, this money was unexpected manna from heaven. I was delighted that the English were honorable enough to contact me. Otherwise, I would never have known it was playing again. It was a princely sum, and instead of paying me by check as they had before, I requested they hold the money in cash at the BBC-TV offices in London. I was going to be in London at Christmastime and I would collect it at their offices. The pounds sterling would definitely cover some of my holiday expenses.

In 2002 I made a similar request to hold a license fee in Austria. I had licensed my *Video Fireplace* to the Technisches Museum Wien (Vienna Technical Museum), which opened in 1918 and specialized in the fields of engineering, technology and industry. They contacted me about including the *Video Fireplace* in an exhibit tracing the history of man-made products using non-fire heat resulting from electricity. The exhibit would be a retrospective from the early 1900s to the year 2000 of mechanical appliances incorporating metal wires or ribbons, straight or coiled, that when charged with electricity act as resistors to the electricity. This resistance materializes as heat which man has harnessed for a variety of heating purposes. The process is called Joule Heating, named after James Prescott Joule who discovered it.

The exhibit in Vienna showed the evolution of many appliances from very early rudimentary products to the more streamlined ones used today. Exhibited were steam irons for pressing clothes, toasters that darkened and toasted bread, electric blankets with ribbon heaters, even curling irons for milady's hair and assorted more sophisticated elements that provide heat for a myriad of industrial uses. Though my *Video Fireplace* didn't give off heat like the various appliances on exhibit (although some viewers over the years have sworn looking at it made them feel warm), it gave the Vienna museum patrons the visual of a fire without building a real fire in the museum. The appliances gave off heat. The Video Fireplace didn't! What they had in common was that they both owed their energy to electricity.

I flew to Vienna, saw the exhibition, saw my *Video Fireplace* burning brightly and collected my money which I spent in part at the Hotel Sacher enjoying the famous Sacher Torte, a fluffy Austrian chocolate cake with apricot filling under the glaze. Yum!

As I've written earlier, several network TV shows wrote my *Video Fireplace* into their plots as did such movies as Universal's *The Lonely Guy* and Columbia's *The Cable Guy*. Imagine my surprise when at Christmas time in 2011 on viewing the English-made Columbia Pictures 3-D animated feature *Arthur Christmas* I discovered a quick scene in Arthur's room that included an animated TV set hanging on the wall. Playing on its animated screen was a colorful burning fire, animated of course. There seems to be no end to the creative minds that have been inspired by my concept and have incorporated it in their creations.

When friends suggested I reshoot my *Video Fireplace* and bring it up-to-date, perhaps Blu-ray, I said no chance. After all, it had been on exhibition in an important museum in Vienna. It was now a classic. A work of art! I was only half jesting when I called it "art." To me it always was originally a work of conceptual art!

The late Elliott Zeldes, my lifelong friend, echoed what the curator in the Vienna museum had said about my videos. I met Elliott when we were both high school art students at Cass Technical High School in downtown Detroit.

Elliott always referred to my videos as conceptual art. If I hadn't packaged and marketed them as products for home VCR's, but kept what I had recorded on videotape as a marriage between art and technology, it was in its essence, he said, conceptual art. Elliott argued I might justifiably have labeled myself as a "video artist" and exhibited my various tapings on television sets in an art museum or art gallery, programmed to constantly repeat 24/7. Instead, I had gone commercial.

In my heart I agreed with Elliott. As an art student attending two art high schools, first the High School of Music and Art in New York City and then the art department in all-city Cass Technical High School, I was always a creative artist, but often uncertain in which direction I should go with my art and where best to display my talents. Instead, I used my visual acumen in the world of film and television.

Often when men of prominence are asked what they are most proud of aside from their business or professional accomplishments, many men will say that they are proud of their children: the way the man and his wife raised their children and how the children turned out. I've had no children. For me ever since I started Video Naturals, my original videos have been my offspring. They aren't babies anymore. The first two will be 30-years-old in 2012. The last one 26-years-old in 2012. And they are still for sale. To me they are just as wonderful as when they first entered my consciousness and sprang from my mind.

In 1982, James Brown, a columnist in *The Los Angeles Times* wrote, "It'll be Siporin who'll go down in the annals as the pioneer of atmosphere television."

Certainly I was flattered by his prophetic words. It seems to me that he could just as easily have written "as the father of atmosphere television," rather than "as the pioneer of atmosphere television." To my way of thinking the two words "father" and "pioneer" are interchangeable in that sentence.

Which do I prefer? Am I their father?

Well, I do think of my videos as my mental offspring!

Even now they are playable for enjoyment and relaxation, even now they are available to anyone seeking them out, and even now they can support their old papa!

And still they burn. And burn. And burn!

And still burning within me is my love of movie magic and those stories and images that flicker on silver screens around the world. Who knows? If I hadn't had those wonderful years in crazy, crazy Hollywood would I have understood my own potential and been ready when lightning struck me with the idea for the *Video Fireplace?* It seems my destiny was not to create images for the silver screen but for the cathode tube and its descendants.

THE END

DEAR READER:

To thank you for buying this book
The Video Naturals Company has created a DVD
especially for you. It's called *FISH & FIRE*.

On this DVD are two of our best selling videos:
The New Video Aquarium
and
The Original Video Fireplace!

Each program runs one hour and will repeat automatically
so you can play it for hours. Choose either one on the menu.
Play each separately with its own natural sound,
water bubbles or crackling fire
or with easy-listen music.

Your cost is only **$6.00** which includes shipping.
We will pay California State Tax, where necessary.
Just call toll free **1-800-950-5545** to place your order.
The CODE to purchase?
Just say you're our **DEAR READER!**

THANK YOU!

INDEX

Academy Awards (Oscars) 58-59
Adams, India 70-71
Adler, David 156-159
Adler, Warren 155-160
Akins, Claude 176-177, 220
Albright, Lola 28
Allen, Woody 46-50, 102, 149-150, 243, 245
Allerton Theater 1, 2, 5
A Man for all Seasons 51
Ann Arbor Theater Festival 77
AP News Wire Service 198
Arc Light Cinema 74
Arnaz, Desi 140
Arness, James 3
Arnett, James 117
Arthur Christmas (movie) 228
Astin, John 78, 80, 118, 122-123

Ball, Lucille 140, 165
Bachrach, Burt 240
Barrios, Richard 64-65
Barrymore, Drew 9
Barrymore, Jr., John 9
Baxter, Anne 40-43
Beaumont, Harry 65, 67-68
Bernhardt, Curtis 106
Bernhardt, Steven 106
Bewitched (TV series) 10, 87-89

Billboard Charts 217-219
Blake, Amanda 172-173
Bogart, Humphrey 46-48, 58, 151
Bogdanovich, Peter 74
Boothe, Powers 186-187
Borack, Phil 125, 127-129
Borgnine, Ernest 18, 240
Boy Wonder, The 3, 62, 65
British Broadcasting Company (BBC) 226
Broadway Melody, The (movie) 3, 4, 58-65, 69, 239
Broderick, Matthew 209-211
Brown, James 18
Butch Cassidy and the Sundance Kid 23, 105-108, 113-116

Cable Guy, The (movie) 209, 228
Call Sheets 109-110
Carradine, David 93-95
Carrey, Jim 209-211
Carroll, Diahann 18
Casablanca (movie) 46-47
Cassidy, David 174-175
CBS Evening News 198-199
Christmas Yule Log Fireplace 202, 204, 217, 220, 225
Colbert, Claudette 59-60, 98
Columbia Pictures 8, 13, 58-59, 69

Computer Generated Image (CGI) 90-92
Cowsills, The 173
Crawford, Joan 27, 70-71, 240

Daniels, William 31-33, 240
David, Saul 129-131
Davis, Bette 14-16, 29, 58-59, 106
Day of the Evil Gun (movie) 13-18
de Mille, Agnes 40
DeMille, Cecil B. 39-43
de Mille, Richard 39-40, 43
de Mille, William 39-40, 43
DePalma, Brian 118-120
Dern, Dixon 152
Desilu Productions 140-141
Devin, Marilyn 142-143
Dewhurst, Coleen 187-188
DGA Availability List 8
Dickinson, Angie 18, 177, 181-182
Directors Guild of America (DGA) 4, 7, 53, 145, 190
Doc (TV series) 139-142
Douglas, Kirk 28, 97-102
Dubbing 82, 84
Dunaway, Faye 132-135, 243

Eden, Barbara 3, 125-129
Entertainment Tonight 193-194
Extras, Movie 177-181

Fabray, Nanette 125-126
Field, Sally 91-92, 243
First Sale Rights 199
First To Fight (movie) 143
Fisher, Carrie 167-168
Fisher, Eddie 167
Flemyng, Gordon 18-20
Flying Nun, The (TV series) 91
Frankel, Ernie 176-177
Ford, Glenn 3, 13-17, 94, 169

Friedman, David 194, 196, 207

Gable, Clark 5, 59, 98
Gabor, Zsa Zsa 80-82
Garfield, Allen 123-124
Garland, Judy 1, 35, 62
Get to Know Your Rabbit (movie) 106, 117-123
Golden, Alfred 150
Goldman, William 111, 113, 242
Gordon, Michael 22-26, 151
Gordon-Levitt, Joseph 26
Gordone, Charles 148
Graham, William A. (Billy) 160, 82, 184-186, 216
Green Screen Process 91-92
Grodin, Charles 148, 207-209
Guber Peter 159-161
Guffey, Burnett 19-20, 241
Gunsmoke (TV series) 141, 172-173
Guyana Tragedy (TV movie) 182, 184

Hackford, Taylor 181
Hackman, Gene 18, 241-244
Hall, Conrad 111-113, 242
Hamilton, Margaret 175
Hard Nut Ballet 225
Harper Valley P.T.A. (movie) 125-129
Heaven with a Gun (movie) 94-95
Heffner Archives 30-31
Hershey, Barbara 93-95
Hill, George Roy 106, 112, 115-116, 243
Holzer, Baby Jane 148-150
Hunt, Helen 160, 244

Impossible Years, The (movie) 2, 22, 24 26, 31-33

Janssen, David 177-178

INDEX

Jazz Singer, The (movie) 57, 75
Jolson, Al 57, 74-75
Jones, James 33
Jones, Shirley 173-176, 241
Jonestown 183

Kearns, Marty 64
Keaton, Diane 46, 48, 243
Kellerman, Sally 171
Kelly, Gene 3, 62
Kessler, Allen 220
King Brothers, The 13, 100
Kleiser, Randall 181

Lacy, Jerry 46
Ladd, Alan 102
Ladd, Diane 188
Lazar Irving (Swifty) 151-152
Leachman, Cloris 107-108, 187, 242
Leigh, Vivien 5
Lemmon, Jack 3, 9-12, 243
Life Masks 28-31
Lip-Synching 3, 60, 68-69, 73
Lonely Guy, The (movie) 207, 228
Location Scouting 35-37
Looping 76, 79-82
Loren, Sophia 71-72
Lorne, Marion 87-89
Los Angeles Times 196-198, 200, 229
Louis, Herschell Gordon 194
Luv (movie) 8-10

Madonna 75-76
Maltese Bippy, The (movie) 31
Mannix (TV series) 141, 171
Mark Morris Dance Group 225
Martin, Ross 169-170
Martin, Steve 207-209
May, Elaine 9-12, 147-148, 207
Mayer, Louis B. 58, 59, 62, 66 135-137

McCrory, Tom 33-34, 38, 63, 174 216
Melies, Georges 89-90
Metro-Goldwyn-Mayer (MGM) 1, 30, 62-63, 102-103
Midnight Cowboy (movie) 129-130
Milli Vanilli 73
Minnelli, Liza 35, 74
Minnelli, Vincente 33-38, 241
Mirisch, Walter 100
Mood Channel, The 200-201
Moon, Lorna 39-40
Moon, Reverend Sun Myung 156-158
Moonies 155-158
Moonjean, Hank 14-15
Moorehead, Agnes 87-89, 245
Montgomery, Elizabeth 87-89, 102
Montgomery, Robert 102-104
Movin' On (TV series) 176-177, 220
Movies Unlimited Catalog 204
Mulligan, Carey 74-75

National Enquirer, The 105, 108
Nelson, Harriet 27
Nelson, Ozzie 26-27
Newman, Paul 3, 23, 31, 105-108, 110-116, 244
Niven, David 3, 22-25, 32, 240

Oscar Winners 239-245
Oppenheimer, Jesse 165-167

Parker, Eleanor 29-30
Parsons Jr., Lindsley 4
Partridge Family, The (TV series) 34, 63, 173-178
Pavarotti, Luciano 73
Peckinpah, Sam 111
Pet Rock 190
Peter, Laurence J. 146-147, 149

Peter Principle, The 146-149, 151-153, 207
Pettyjohn, Angelique 95-96
Pioneer of Atmosphere TV 229
Pillow Talk (movie) 23
Playback 3, 60, 67-73
Play It Again, Sam (movie) 46-48
Plowright, Joan 83
Poitier, Sidney 18
Presley, Elvis 27
Puttnam, David 159-163, 244
Pye, Merrill 61-68, 136, 245

Quick, Eldon 139-142

Rage in Heaven (movie) 102-104
Rains, Claude 48
Redford, Robert 111, 114, 116, 243-244
Reiner, Carl 152-153
Reinhardt, Gottfried 102-104
Rescuing David (story) 155-156
Reynolds, Debbie 7, 14, 63, 165-169, 245
Rich, Robert 100
Richlin, Maurice 151-152, 239
Rise of the Planet of the Apes (movie) 91-92
Rod Serling's Night Gallery (TV series) 76, 78, 80
Ross, Herb 49-50
Ross, Katherine 113-114, 118
Rush, Richard 93
Russell, Rosalind 72

Sarrazin, Michael 130-131
Schlesinger, John 129-130, 242
Scofield, Paul 51-53
Scorsese, Martin 90
Screen Actors Guild (SAG) 171, 185
Screen Extras Guild (SEG) 178

Serkis, Andrew 92
Shearer, Douglas 64-65, 68
Shearer, Norma 66
Shooting Schedule 184
Sinatra, Frank 19, 33, 36, 51
Sister Water (novel) 222-225
Smothers, Dick 7
Smothers, Tommy 7, 117-124
Some Came Running (movie) 33
Spartacus (movie) 83, 97
Split, The (move) 18
Springsteen, Bruce 226
Stand-Ins 180
Stanley, Kim 77-80
Stone, Peter 149, 139
Structural Visualization 34
Stunt Man, The (movie) 93-95
Sutherland, Donald 18, 20
Sutherland, Keifer 20

Thalberg, Irving 62, 65-68
Third Party Marketing 151
Thorpe, Jerry 13
Thorpe, Richard 13
Trumbo, Dalton 100-101, 240
Turner, Ted 62
Tuttle, William J. (Bill) 28-30, 241

Veidt, Conrad 48
Vienna Technical Museum 227
View, The (TV series) 218-219
Video Aquarium 189, 196, 200, 204, 207 218-220
Video Fireplace 189, 193-198, 200, 204, 209-210, 220, 222, 227, 229
Video Naturals Company 189
Voight, Jon 3, 129-131, 241

WABC-TV (NYC) 4, 8, 10
Washington Dossier 156
Wayne, Nina 9-10

INDEX

Wedding of the Painted Doll 60-68
Welles, Orson 3, 117-120, 239, 242
Wild, Wild West, The (TV series) 169
Williams. Michelle 72
Wrap Party 16-17, 31-32
Wyatt, Rupert 91

York, Dick 87

Z Channel Magazine 192-193
Zinneman, Fred 19, 51-55, 240
Zinneman, Tim 55

OSCAR WINNERS

As I prepared this book I was amazed at how many movie industry people I had worked with who had received the acclaim of their peers by winning the coveted Oscar Statuette presented to them by The Academy of Motion Pictures Arts and Sciences. Listed below by year are those who actually won the golden Oscar. Many of those listed have had other nominations for which someone else took home the gold. There are performers mentioned in this book who won Oscars, but because I didn't have the pleasure of working with them, they aren't listed.

Then there are the talented people I did have the pleasure of working with who were nominated but didn't win. I've listed them separately at the very end. Why? Because I think they should have won and this is my book!

YEAR	WINNER	FILM	FOR
1928/29	*The Broadway Melody*		Best Picture

(Merrill Pye worked on this film, the first musical and second movie to win Best Picture.)

| 1941 | Orson Welles | *Citizen Kane* | Best Writing/ Original Script |

(Worked with him on *Get to Know Your Rabbit*.)

YEAR	WINNER	FILM	FOR
1945	Joan Crawford	*Mildred Pierce*	Actress in a Leading Role

(Saw her looking unglamorous at Universal Studios but still an icon.)

1948	William Daniels	*The Naked City*	Cinematography (black & white)

(Worked with him on *The Maltese Bippy* and *The Impossible Years*.)

1951	Fred Zinneman	*Benjy*	Best Documentary (short subject)
1953	Fred Zinneman	*From Here to Eternity*	Best Director

(Heard him speak at the DGA.)

1953	Burnett Guffey	*From Here to Eternity*	Cinematography (black & white)

(Enjoyed working with him on *The Split*.)

1955	Jack Lemmon	*Mister Roberts*	Actor in a Supporting Role

(Worked with Jack in my first feature *Luv*.)

1955	Ernest Borgnine	*Marty*	Actor in a Leading Role

(Worked with him in *The Split*.)

1956	Dalton Trumbo	*The Brave One*	Best story and screenplay for film

(I knew Robert Rich, who picked up the Oscar fronting for blacklisted Trumbo.)

1958	David Niven	*Separate Tables*	Actor in a Leading Role

(Worked with David on *The Impossible Years*.)

OSCAR WINNERS

YEAR	WINNER	FILM	FOR

1958   **Vincente Minnelli** *Gigi*   Director
(My friend Tom McCrory worked with him on *Some Came Running*.)

1959   **Maurice Richlin** *Pillow Talk*   Best screenplay with S. Shapiro
(Hired him to write script for *The Peter Principle*.)

1960   **Burt Lancaster** *Elmer Gantry*   Actor in a Leading Role
(Worked with Burt in *The Gypsy Moths*.)

1960   **Shirley Jones** *Elmer Gantry*   Actress in a Supporting Role
(Worked with Shirley in *The Partridge Family*.)

1964   **Peter Stone** *Father Goose*   Story/Screenplay Written for Screen
(Met with him about doing script for *The Peter Principle*.)

1964   **William J. Tuttle** Honorary Award   Outstanding Make-Up Achievement
(Worked with him early mornings in MGM's Make-Up Dept.)

1966   **Fred Zinnemann** *A Man For All Seasons*   Director and Best Picture
(Heard him speak at DGA.)

1967   **Burnett Guffey** *Bonnie and Clyde*   Cinematography (color)
(Worked with him on *The Split*.)

1969   **Jon Voight** *Coming Home*   Actor in a Leading Role
(Worked with Jon in *The All American Boy*.)

YEAR	WINNER	FILM	FOR
1969	John Schlesinger	*Midnight Cowboy*	Director

(Spoke with him at Palm Springs VillageFest, gave him my videos, no charge)

1969	Conrad Hall	*Butch Cassidy & Sundance Kid*	Cinematography

(Worked with him on Butch Cassidy, my first one day upgrade to 1st. Assistant.)

1969	William Goldman	*Butch Cassidy & Sundance Kid*	Story & Screenplay
1969	Burt Bacharach	*Butch Cassidy & Sundance Kid*	Original Score Non-musical
1969	Burt Bacharach & Hal David	*Butch Cassidy & Sundance Kid*	Original Song "Raindrops Keep falling On My Head"

(Met them when I worked on *Butch Cassidy*.)

1970	Orson Welles	Honorary Award	For Superlative Artistry and Versatility Creating Films

(Worked with Orson on *Get To Know Your Rabbit*.)

1970	Arthur Hiller	*Love Story*	Director

(Met him when he used my *Video Fireplace* and *Video Aquarium* in *The Lonely Guy*.)

1971	Cloris Leachman	*The Last Picture Show*	Actress in a Supporting Role

(She worked in *Butch Cassidy & Sundance Kid*.)

OSCAR WINNERS

YEAR	WINNER	FILM	FOR
1971	**Gene Hackman**	*The French Connection*	Actor in a Leading Role

(Worked with Gene in *The Split* and *The Gypsy Moths*.)

1973	**George Roy Hill**	*The Sting*	Director

(His Second Assistant Director on *Butch Cassidy*.)

1973	**Jack Lemmon**	*Save the Tiger*	Actor in a Leading Role

(He starred in my first feature film *Luv*.)

1976	**Faye Dunaway**	*Network*	Actress in a Leading Role

(Second Assistant on TV movie *The Woman I Love*.)

1977	**Woody Allen**	*Annie Hall*	Director & Screenplay Written for the Screen

(Retakes on *Play It Again, Sam*.)

1977	**Dianne Keaton**	*Annie Hall*	Actress in Leading Role

(Worked with her in a *Rod Serling's Night Gallery* show before she was a star.)

1978	**Taylor Hackford**	*Teenage Failure*	Short Film (documentary)

(An extra on *Banacek*, now President of the DGA.)

1979	**Sally Field**	*Norma Rae*	Actress in a Leading Role

(Was her Second Assistant Director on *The Flying Nun*.)

1980	**Robert Redford**	*Ordinary People*	Director

(Was his Second Assistant Director on *Butch Cassidy*.)

YEAR	WINNER	FILM	FOR
1981	David Puttnam	*Chariots of Fire*	Best Picture

(I would have been working with him as a producer on a Moonie film.)

1985	Paul Newman	Honorary Award	Compelling Screen Performances, Integrity & Dedication to Craft

1986	Paul Newman	*The Color of Money*	Actor in a Leading Role

(Worked with Paul in *Butch Cassidy*.)

1992	Gene Hackman	*Unforgiving*	Actor in a Leading Role

(Worked with Gene in *The Split* and *The Gypsy Moths*.)

1993	Paul Newman	Jean Hersholt Humanitarian Award	

(Worked with Paul in *Butch Cassidy*.)

1997	Helen Hunt	*As Good As It Gets*	Actress in a Leading Role

(She was a teenager on the TV movie *Transplant*; I was the First Assistant.)

2001	Robert Redford	Honorary Award as an Actor, Director, Producer, & Sundance Festival Founder	

(Second Assistant Director on *Butch Cassidy*.)

YEAR	WINNER	FILM	FOR
2001	Arthur Hiller		Jean Hersholt Humanitarian Award

(He used my videos in his *The Lonely Guy*.)

2012	Woody Allen	*Midnight in Paris*	Screenplay Written for Screen

(Retakes for *Play It Again, Sam*.)

AND THESE TALENTED PEOPLE
Who Were Nominated and Should Have Won!

YEAR	WINNER	FILM	FOR
1942	Agnes Moorehead	*The Magnificent Ambersons*	Actress in a Supporting Role
1944	Agnes Moorehead	*Mrs. Parkington*	Actress in a Supporting Role
1948	Agnes Moorehead	*Johnny Belinda*	Actress in a Supporting Role

(Worked as the Second Assistant Director on TV's *Bewitched*.)

1959	Merrill Pye	*North By Northwest*	Art Direction (with others)

(A lunch buddy, worked with him on *The Partridge Family*.)

1964	Debbie Reynolds	*The Unsinkable Molly Brown*	Actress in a Leading Role

(First Assistant Director on *The Debbie Reynolds Show* TV sit-com.)

1964	Agnes Moorehead	*Hush, Hush Sweet Charlotte*	Actress in a Supporting Role

(Enjoyed working with her on TV's *Bewitched*.)

www.ingramcontent.com/pod-product-compliance
Lightning Source LLC
Chambersburg PA
CBHW062015220426
43662CB00010B/1334